THE CHANGING LAW OF FAIR REPRESENTATION

Jean T. McKelvey, editor

ILR Press
New York State School of
Industrial and Labor Relations
Cornell University

Cover design by Kathleen Dalton

Library of Congress Cataloging in Publication Data
Main entry under title:
The Changing law of fair representation.

    Papers presented at a national conference sponsored
by the Extension Division of the New York State School
of Industrial and Labor Relations, Cornell University,
October 20 and 21, 1983.
    Includes index.
    1. Arbitration, Industrial—United States—Congresses.
2. Trade-unions—Law and legislation—United States—
Congresses. I. McKelvey, Jean T. (Jean Trepp),
1908-   . II. New York State School of Industrial and
Labor Relations. Extension and Public Service Division.
KF3424.A2C45   1985   344.73'0188   84-27831
ISBN 0-87546-110-7   347.304188
ISBN 0-87546-111-5 (pbk.)

Copies may be ordered from
ILR Press
New York State School of
Industrial and Labor Relations
Cornell University
Ithaca, NY 14853

 ③

Printed in the United States of America by Rose Printing Company.
54321

Contents

Introduction

Jean T. McKelvey

On October 20 and 21, 1983, the Extension Division of the New York State School of Industrial and Labor Relations, Cornell University, sponsored a national conference in New York City on the duty of fair representation (DFR). It was attended by attorneys, personnel and labor relations specialists, union officers and grievance committeemen, and others engaged in collective bargaining, contract administration, and arbitration in both the public and private sectors. This was the second national conference on the subject. The first was held in the spring of 1977 and resulted in a book entitled *The Duty of Fair Representation*, which contained the papers delivered at that conference.[1] Because of the enthusiastic response accorded that publication and because of important new developments in the case law, the Extension Division decided to hold a successor conference in 1983 to deal with recent decisions in the areas of safety and health, negligence, exhaustion of internal union remedies, assessment of damages against employers and unions, time limits, and related procedural and substantive problems in grievance handling and arbitration.

For this second conference the sponsors were fortunate in securing as speakers all except one of the distinguished scholars and practitioners who had participated in the 1977 conference. In addition, the program included an eminent judge of the U.S. Court

---

1. J. T. McKelvey, ed., The Duty of Fair Representation (New York State School of Industrial and Labor Relations, Cornell University, 1977).

1

of Appeals for the District of Columbia Circuit, the current executive director and former member of the National Labor Relations Board, the chairman of the New York State Public Employment Relations Board, and three prominent attorneys who spoke as advocates for unions, management, and the plaintiffs in DFR suits.

Readers of this volume will note some repetition of the facts of each of the major recent cases comprising the changing law of fair representation. The most comprehensive analysis of this case law will be found in Benjamin Aaron's "Overview," which lays the foundation for all the chapters that follow. Because each author selects different aspects of the case law for emphasis, I have chosen not to excise the inevitable duplication of descriptive material. Readers who are interested in the various points of view expressed by the authors toward particular decisions will be aided by the case index.

Several areas of agreement and disagreement emerge from a reading of this volume. There is a shared consensus and concern about the growing volume of litigation of DFR suits, which, although rarely successful from the plaintiffs's point of view, are nevertheless costly to the defendant companies and unions in terms of time, energy, and legal fees.[2] All accept the premise that a union owes a duty of fair representation and a measure of due process to its members. The central thesis of this volume, however, is the failure of the judiciary to agree upon the standards for measuring the dimensions of this duty. This was expressed memorably by Aaron in the first volume. Referring to the problem of how to determine exactly what types of conduct constitute a violation of the union's duty of fair representation, he said,

> On this point the Supreme Court has spoken with such impenetrable ambiguity that the federal courts, which bear the burden of construing the nature and scope of the duty, are understandably in disagreement as to what the law is.[3]

Nothing has changed to resolve these ambiguities in the intervening years. If anything, the fog created by conflicts between state and federal courts, among the various federal courts of appeals, and in more recent decisions of the Supreme Court has become thicker and even more impenetrable, leading Aaron to comment here, with

---

2. Different attempts to measure this increase in litigation are made by Edwards, Jones, Newman, and Rabin.

3. B. Aaron, *The Duty of Fair Representation: An Overview*, in The Duty of Fair Representation, *supra* note 1, p. 18.

a change of metaphor, that "the Supreme Court's pronouncements in this area can most charitably be likened to a trumpet that gives an uncertain sound."

The mischief created by the judiciary is noted by all the participants. Former NLRB member John Truesdale observes, "The ambiguity in the case law in this area leaves both unions and employers in a quandary and exposes both to potential liabilities," and Clyde Summers notes that "the mirage of appealing adjectives has led courts far into an uncharted wasteland."

A divergence in points of view emerges more sharply, however, as the various authors address other more recent decisions of the Supreme Court in the areas of the exhaustion of contractual and internal union remedies (*Clayton*), the apportionment of damages for violation of the DFR (*Bowen* and *Foust*), and appropriate statutes of limitations for the filing of DFR actions (*United Parcel, DelCostello,* and *Flowers*).

The state of the case law is helpfully mapped by Aaron in his "Overview," which opens the volume. Richard Lipsitz then covers some of the important new procedural and substantive areas such as the statutes of limitations, apportionment of damages, exhaustion of internal union appeals procedures, competing employee interests, and union liability for unsafe or hazardous conditions in the workplace. He notes many of the paradoxes lurking in these decisions and discusses their implications for union activities and responses, both in contract negotiations and grievance processing.

Another important development in the case law concerns the grievant's exhaustion of internal union remedies. These developments are monitored in a fascinating case study of the UAW and its Public Review Board by David Y. Klein. The Supreme Court's decision in *Clayton* v. *UAW* limited the use of nonexhaustion of internal remedies as a defense in DFR litigation. Noting the irony in the fact that the defendant union has one of the more democratic systems of internal remedies, Klein examines the fourteen reported court decisions since *Clayton,* of which eight involved the UAW. He notes that in all the UAW cases, the motions of the defendants for summary judgment were granted, whereas in the other six, three such motions were granted and three denied. From this analysis, Klein concludes that the UAW has fared much better than most other unions in defending itself against DFR suits. That few unions to date have done little, if anything, however, to formulate a response to the challenge of *Clayton* is revealed in Klein's survey of the legal departments of all labor organizations listed in the 1982-1983 *Directory of U.S. Labor Organizations*, published by the Bureau of National Affairs. Of the thirty-seven international unions that responded to Klein's questionnaire, only seven reported that they were in the process of formulating a policy to meet the requirements of *Clayton*. From his experience as executive director of the UAW's Public Review Board and from his research findings, Klein concludes that unions that have viable systems of internal review and those of their employers who have contractual provisions for the reinstatement of grievances in the procedure, following internal review, will be the most successful in section 301 suits in relying upon the defense of the individual's failure to exhaust his or her internal union remedies.

Litigation in the public sector is reviewed by Harold Newman, chairman of the New York State Public Employment Relations Board. In spite of the tendency of the state public employment agencies to follow the narrower standards of union misconduct employed by the NLRB Newman finds a "staggering growth" of DFR litigation in the public sector, paralleling that in the private sector. DFR charges alone now account for 20 percent of his agency's annual caseload. According to Newman, two problems unique to the public sector are responsible for this explosion in DFR litigation. One is the effect of union security provisions in the form of the statutory authorization for agency fees, which was first enacted in New York State in 1977 and made provision for refunds of union fees expended on matters unrelated to collective bargaining. While conventional wisdom anticipated that this statute would obviate the unions' argument that they could not afford to represent "free riders," Newman reports that the opposite has occurred. These provisions seemed to stimulate DFR litigation. He offers an intriguing explanation for this paradoxical development, namely, that individuals who earlier had refrained from union membership or dues payments have experienced a rising expectation of services and fair representation from the union to whose support they must now contribute. This expectation attaches mainly to issues of grievance processing and contract administration, as is true in the private sector. In addition, the public sector has also experienced an increase in DFR litigation related not to contractual terms but to extracontractual obligations. Some of these novel and expanded areas include the union's duty to represent all unit members fairly in noncontractual performance review procedures established under civil service laws and regulations, as well as making the provision of internal union benefits such as pensions and medical insurance plans subject to the test of fair representation. Thus unions that deny such benefits financed in part by agency fees to nonmembers have been found to be in violation of their duty of fair representation. The test applied is that of substantial effect, so that *de minimis* benefits such as the distribution of union publications to members only have not been included as part of the duty of fair representation. Whether the private sector will follow these innovations in the public sector remains to be seen. Certainly Newman's thought-provoking analysis and defense of this expansion of the concept of fair representation adds a new and challenging dimension to the subject.

Harry Edwards's chapter concludes the section on litigation. Although agreeing with a number of the authors that the Supreme Court's decision, especially its dicta, in *Vaca* opened the door for judicial intrusion into the collective bargaining system, he argues that arbitration should be the forum to which the courts should remand these cases, since it provides an alternative method of dispute resolution superior to that offered by the judicial system. What Edwards deplores in particular is the fact that the circuit courts of appeals have been deciding the merits of underlying breach of contract claims by imposing sanctions in situations where no arbitral determination of liability has first been made (citing *Dutrisac*). Such judicial intrusion into the arbitral process he finds to be at odds with the Steelworkers Trilogy and with national labor policy as set forth in our labor relations statutes, thereby threatening the vitality of our private system of collective bargaining and grievance settlement.

The chapters of the section titled The Parties present the views of the advocates involved in the process for unions, management, and the plaintiffs, respectively. Speaking for the unions, Seymour Waldman, like the other authors before him, notes the "astonishing" number of DFR claims and the rapid expansion of litigation in this field. He observes that the doctrine has placed the duty of fair representation in "the forefront of union concerns" and has adversely affected the heart of the grievance-arbitration system. This adverse effect on grievance handling can be seen in the fact that unions are now processing frivolous and meritless claims through all the steps of the grievance procedure, eschewing settlements at the lower steps. They have found it necessary to rely upon more professional advocates instead of democratically elected lay representatives:

> The specter of fair representation lawsuits has resulted in more, but less conclusive, arbitrations, lengthier and more contentious hearings, greater formality and procedural niceties, and a tendency to advance every conceivable argument, however flimsy it may appear, for fear that failure to do so will later result in liability to the union.

Ironically, he notes, these constraints imperil the union's ability to act responsibly in negotiating contracts or settling grievances, as well as jeopardizing the rights of the entire bargaining unit when important contractual issues such as transfer, promotion, or seniority are brought to arbitration in the context of weak or damaging facts involved in individual grievances. Like Edwards, he deplores the substitution of litigation for the collective bargaining and grievance-arbitration model formerly espoused as our national labor policy.

Other conflicts with national labor policy are astutely analyzed by Waldman. For example, he notes that the judicial stress on the need for qualified and competent representatives to assure the union's provision of fair representation is at odds with Title IV of the Labor-Management Reporting and Disclosure Act (LMRDA) which limits a union's right to place qualifications of experience or competency on a member's right to run for office in the interest of maximizing democratic elections. Similarly, the union's ability to protect experienced shop stewards with superseniority has been severely limited by the NLRB and the courts. A final example is found in the limitation placed by the LMRDA on a union's ability to raise dues without membership approval. Yet if a union lacks the financial resources to process even meritorious grievances, it is not thereby relieved of its duty of fair representation. Thus, as a result of the expansion of the law governing the duty of fair representation, unions have been placed in a "no-win situation."

Like Waldman, Andrea Christensen, a management advocate, recognizes and assumes that unions will continue to process non-meritorious as well as meritorious grievances to arbitration. Since unions, employers, and arbitrators share a common interest in insulating the grievance and arbitration procedure from subsequent DFR challenges by individuals, Christensen provides a comprehensive review of the practical steps employers can take to ensure the finality of arbitration awards and to avoid the risk of underwriting a portion of potential back pay awards under the criteria set forth in *Bowen*. Although an employer's role in grievance processing is somewhat limited, she suggests that in prudent self-interest employers consider the possibility of calling the union's attention to contractual time limits, of persuading a union to take borderline just-cause cases to arbitration, and, in appropriate instances, of waiving the contractual time limits by executing a nonprecedential agreement to submit the dispute to arbitration. In addition, she suggests that the employer voluntarily disclose all pertinent information to the union to assist its preparation for arbitration, including the disclosure of the identity of the witnesses upon whose testimony the employer intends to rely.

Noting that it is in the arbitration forum, however, that the employer can function most effectively to ensure that the process is not procedurally defective, Christensen makes a number of practical and even startling proposals for diminishing the adversarial nature of the proceeding. She suggests that the employer should object, if the arbitrator does not, to the absence of the grievant, should not object to the grievant's retention of private counsel, should ensure that competing employee interests are represented at the hearing, and above all, should not insist on procedural or technical objections to thwart the introduction of relevant or even arguably relevant evidence at the hearing. Her comments on the responsibility of arbitrators in ensuring due process parallel in most respects those of Robert Rabin. What distinguishes her presentation, however, is her elucidation of what the employer can and should do in the absence of arbitral attention to and concern for due process considerations.

In his chapter on the plaintiff's view of DFR litigation, Paul Tobias takes issue not only with the union and employer advocates, but also with the representatives of administrative agencies, arbitrators, and legal scholars. His comments reflect the bitterness felt by the victims of unfair representation who lose most of their lawsuits and their disappointment, anger, and frustration with a legal system that has "abysmally failed" to protect the rights of individuals in the grievance-arbitration process. In particular, he deplores the short time limits for instituting lawsuits under the Supreme Court's decisions in *Mitchell* and *DelCostello*, the failure of existing law to provide adequate remedies for the victims of unfair representation, and the lack of competent counsel to represent plaintiffs because of the unwillingness of most labor attorneys to represent other than institutional interests. Unlike the other program participants, he advocates the award of punitive damages in DFR suits, contrary to *Foust,* deplores the exceptions to the requirement of exhaustion of internal union remedies carved out by *Clayton,* and criticizes *Bowen* both for making it impossible for plaintiffs with large damage claims to obtain a reasonable settlement and for discouraging lawyers from representing plaintiffs on a contingency fee basis. As a final stroke in this dismal portrait, he notes that because of "monstrous delays" in DFR litigation, many of the plaintiffs literally do not survive the decade or so it often takes to bring protracted litigation to a close.

On the other hand, Tobias notes a few bright spots in the picture. One is the fact that "the law is now more settled, well-known, and available to the labor relations community"—an assessment with which many of the participants do not agree. More important in his view, however, is that as a result of DFR litigation and the *Bowen* decision, unions are now affording individuals better representation in grievance and arbitration proceedings.

Tobias sets forth specific proposals for judicial expansion of the standards of fair representation and for increasing union liability for violation thereof. These stand in marked contrast to the remedies espoused by the other authors.

In the last chapter of the section, Clyde Summers attempts to get beyond the amorphous adjectives used by the courts and define individual rights in the grievance-arbitration process. He develops a brilliant and original analytic framework that distinguishes various categories of cases in terms of the particular duty of fair representation that attaches to each. As a starting point, he sets forth three premises:

1. The union's duty of fair representation arises not from its statutory status as the exclusive representative but from a collective bargaining agreement that provides that the grievance procedure and arbitration shall be the exclusive method for remedying breaches of contract.

2. Despite the existence of such an exclusive contractual procedure, the union does not "own" the grievance. An individual continues to have rights under the agreement and can sue to enforce these rights. Such a suit is barred only if the union has accorded him or her fair representation.

3. The union's role in processing grievances is completely different from its role in negotiating the contract. In negotiations, the union's duty is not to discriminate unfairly among various groups of employees in creating contractual rights. In grievance processing and arbitration, however, the union's duty is to enforce the contractual rights of individuals.

In this last area of contract administration, Summers distinguishes three categories of cases: those of contract interpretation, those involving factual disputes, and those related to procedural fairness or default. For each category he sets forth the appropriate standards or measures of the union's duty and the actions a union can take to fulfill its responsibility under the law. The crucial point of this analytical approach, he observes, is "that there is not one duty of fair representation that can be described with a single string of adjectives, no matter how long and colorful. There is a collection of duties of fair representation, each with its own size and shape. The need is to determine the proper measure for each of the different categories or types of cases."

Readers who are interested in the practical applications of Summers's elucidating analysis will find "relatively clear answers" in his concluding summary. This deals with the various ways in which a union can fulfill its duty of fair representation, depending upon the particular function it is performing at the time.

The final section, The Duty in Other Forums, examines how arbitrators and the National Labor Relations Board deal with problems of unfair representation. In view of the emphasis placed by many of the authors on arbitration as an alternative to lawsuits, Robert Rabin's examination of the dimensions of the duty of fair representation in arbitration proceedings is especially pertinent. After noting that the Supreme Court's landmark decision in *Hines* was more limited in its holding than has been commonly assumed by legal scholars, Rabin reports the results of his own analysis of all the reported lower court decisions that have been based on the dicta in *Hines*. Among his findings, he notes that the courts demand a minimum level of integrity in the arbitration process, that a union's perfunctory handling of a grievance represents a serious or fundamental malfunctioning of the process, but that despite the increasing volume of DFR litigation, the individual plaintiff rarely prevails. In fact, in the reported cases litigated to a conclusion, Rabin found only two that ended in a complete victory for the individual employee. Another finding of his study was that an "astonishing percentage of cases involve joint committees" sitting as an arbitration panel without a neutral. Like Aaron, Rabin deplores the fact that these joint committees have been accorded by the Supreme Court the status of an arbitral tribunal, when they should more properly be viewed as the final step in the grievance procedure precedent to arbitration.

Under the rubric "recipes for trouble," Rabin illustrates the types of conduct that may expose a union to a charge of unfair representation of a grievant in an arbitration proceeding. These include ignorance of relevant contract provisions, failure to raise a pertinent legal argument, failure to call witnesses, failure to notify the grievant of the hearing, and espousing a partisan position between employees with competing interests. For each of these infirmities he then prescribes antidotes for unions wishing to avoid subsequent charges of perfunctory representation by providing "quality representation."

Rabin also offers advice to arbitrators concerning their responsibility for assuring a fair hearing and due process for the grievants, including a readiness to consider issues of law and public policy, especially in the public sector, in order to ensure the finality of the award.

It is interesting to note Rabin's criticism of the NLRB's policy of deferral to arbitration on the grounds that "the Board has paid little or no attention to the quality of the union's representation in arbitration."[4] The Board's own standards for measuring a union's duty of fair representation are clearly presented and cogently analyzed by John C. Truesdale, who demonstrates by a careful review of the case law that the Board's standards are considerably narrower than those of the courts. In determining whether a union's handling of a grievance has violated section 8(b)(1)(A) of the National Labor Relations Act, the Board uses a standard of intentional misconduct, fraud, or invidious or discriminatory treatment. Unlike some of the lower courts, it has not found that union conduct that is merely "inept, negligent, unwise, insensitive or ineffectual," standing alone, consti-

---

4. Had Rabin been writing a few months later, his apprehensions doubtless would have been increased by the Board's January 19, 1984 decisions in *United Technologies* and *Olin Corporation,* which have narrowed still further the Board's scrutiny of the quality of the arbitration proceeding under review.

tutes unfair representation, nor does it consider the merits of the dispute. The Board examines the facts in each case, rather than relying upon the word tests applied by the courts. The Board is concerned with assuring only a minimum level of due process. In the interest of preserving the collective bargaining relationship between unions and employers, it does not hold shop stewards and committeemen to professional standards of competence—again a notable departure from the standards applied by most courts.

On the other hand, the Board has reviewed a broader scope of substantive areas of union conduct than is found in the court decisions. As Truesdale notes, in addition to disputes over the presentation of grievances, the Board has examined the union's duty of fair representation in such areas as the operation of union hiring halls and referral systems, the representation of employees at management interviews, the informing of employees of their rights and obligations under the collective bargaining agreement, and the operation of seniority systems.

Those readers who wish to explore further James E. Jones's argument for vesting exclusive primary jurisdiction in the NLRB rather than the courts will find Truesdale's exposition of the Board's standards extremely helpful in reaching a decision on the merits of Jones's proposal, depending upon whether they are concerned with institutional or individual interests. Jones proffers a detailed condemnation of the sins of the judiciary. These stem from the confusion of the Supreme Court in its earlier decision in *Vaca* v. *Sipes* and are compounded by its subsequent indulgence in ambiguous decisions that have led to "utter chaos in the courts." Accordingly, he argues that the time has come for a mid-course correction. To accomplish this, he proposes that Congress amend the National Labor Relations Act to remove primary jurisdiction over DFR cases from the courts by mandating that the NLRB be given exclusive and preemptive jurisdiction—a modest proposal in the Swiftian sense, which many of the authors either ignore or reject or toward which they are neutral or skeptical.

Consensus as to the problems surrounding DFR litigation evaporates as to the remedy. In light of Tobias's eloquent plea for reshaping the law of the duty of fair representation in favor of protecting the assertion of individual rights in the process, it is appropriate to recall the emphasis many of these authors place upon competing institutional rights. As Justice Goldberg stated in

his concurrence in *Humphrey* v. *Moore,* quoted by Justice Brennan in
DelCostello and cited approvingly by Aaron and Jones in this volume:

> (I)n this Court's fashioning of a federal law of collective bargaining, it is
> of the utmost importance that the law reflect the realities of industrial life
> and the nature of the collective bargaining process. We should not as-
> sume that doctrines evolved in other contexts will be equally well adapted
> to the collective bargaining process.[5]

Given the existing tension between the assertion of individual rights
and the protection of the institution of collective bargaining, it remains to be seen whether the law will tilt in one direction or the
other, or whether an accommodation can be found, a balance struck,
between these competing interests and values.

----

5. 375 U.S. 335 at 358, 55 LRRM 2031 at 2041 (1964).

The State of the Law

An Overview

Benjamin Aaron

When we first examined the duty of fair representation (DFR) for a similar conference and volume six and one-half years ago, I identified some of the principal problems.[1] These included clarification of the types of conduct constituting a breach of the duty; the proper scope of judicial review in DFR cases; and the degree of deference, if any, that should be accorded decisions reached in cases with DFR implications by joint committees of union and management representatives without the participation of a neutral. Of these, the first was clearly the most complex and the most confused: it embraced such questions as, What kind of conduct constitutes arbitrariness? Is negligence or mere ineptitude tantamount to bad faith? Is there any reasonable basis for distinguishing, for DFR purposes, between failure or refusal to process a grievance to arbitration and processing it carelessly, ineptly, or in a perfunctory manner? These questions, I regret to say, remain unresolved. There are conflicts between state and federal courts, between the federal circuit courts of appeals, and sometimes between decisions of the same circuit; and the Supreme Court's pronouncements in this area can most charitably be likened to a trumpet that gives an uncertain sound.

To these issues we must now add at least three more: exhaustion of contractual and internal union remedies, the nature and ap-

---

1. B. Aaron, *The Duty of Fair Representation: An Overview*, in The Duty of Fair Representation 8 (J. T. McKelvey ed., New York State School of Industrial and Labor Relations, Cornell University, 1977).

portionment of damages for violation of DFR, and time limitations on the filing of DFR actions.

Although I shall address each of these issues, I must disclaim any pretense of presenting more than a partial survey of DFR judicial decisions. A recent article notes that a LEXIS search of cases citing *Vaca* v. *Sipes* turned up approximately 1,225 listings.[2] I can thus only hope to mention the most significant judicial decisions.

Conduct Constituting a Breach

On the question of what kinds of conduct constitute a breach of DFR, I commented in *The Duty of Fair Representation* that "the Supreme Court has spoken with such impenetrable ambiguity that the federal courts, which bear the brunt of construing the nature and scope of the duty, are understandably in disagreement as to what the law is."[3] Even without definitive guidance from the Court, however, most of the federal courts of appeals seem to agree that a union can be found to have breached its duty even in the absence of allegations of bad faith, discrimination, or other wrongful motivation.[4] Thus, the Second Circuit has apparently abandoned its earlier view that proof of a violation of DFR requires a showing of "arbitrariness . . . of the bad faith kind"[5] and "[s]omething akin to factual malice,"[6] and has adopted the position that "at least in negotiating and implementing a contract, a union may breach the statutory duty by arbitrary or irrational conduct, even in the absence of bad faith or hostility in the form of ill will or common law [malice]."[7]

The Fourth Circuit construes the *Vaca* formula—i.e., that a breach of DFR occurs only when a union's conduct toward a member of the bargaining unit is "arbitrary, discriminatory, or in bad

---

2. Vandervelde, *A Fair Process Model for the Union's Fair Representation Duty*, 67 Minn. L. Rev. 1079, 1082 n.8 (1983).

3. Aaron, *supra* note 1, at 18.

4. Vandervelde, *supra* note 2, at 1097. In her article Vandervelde has reviewed most of the more important relevant cases on DFR; I acknowledge with thanks my reliance on her research, even though I do not agree with all her conclusions.

5. Cunningham v. Erie R.R., 266 F.2d 411, 417, 44 LRRM 2093, 2098 (2d Cir. 1959).

6. Jackson v. Trans World Airlines, 457 F.2d 202, 204, 80 LRRM 2362, 2363 (2d Cir. 1972).

7. Ryan v. New York Newspaper Printing Pressmen's Union No. 2, 590 F.2d 451, 455, 100 LRRM 2428, 2430 (2d Cir. 1979).

faith"[8]—as establishing three distinct types of misconduct, so that "[w]ithout any hostile motive of discrimination and in complete good faith, a union may nevertheless pursue a course of action or inaction that is so unreasonable and arbitrary as to constitute a violation of the duty. . . ."[9] The Fifth Circuit also gives a disjunctive reading to the *Vaca* triad,[10] as do the Sixth Circuit,[11] the Seventh Circuit,[12] the Ninth Circuit,[13] and the Tenth Circuit.[14] That is about as far as the consensus goes, however, as a closer examination of the various characterizations used by the Supreme Court to describe conduct that breaches the DFR will reveal.

"Arbitrary" and "Perfunctory" Conduct

Despite the general agreement that arbitrary conduct by a union, for example, in the handling of a grievance, may violate the DFR even without a showing of bad faith, there is no such accord on what constitutes arbitrariness. Most of the confusion can be traced to dicta in Supreme Court opinions. In *Amalgamated Ass'n of Street, Elec. Ry. & Motor Coach Employees* v. *Lockridge,* a preemption case, the Court commented in passing that to make out a claim of violation of DFR, an employee must have proved "'arbitrary or bad-faith conduct on the part of the union,' and that there must be 'substantial evidence of fraud, deceitful action or dishonest conduct.'"[15] In *Hines* v. *Anchor Motor Freight, Inc.*[16] the Court repeated some of the *Vaca*

---

8. Vaca v. Sipes, 386 U.S. 171, 192, 64 LRRM 2369, 2376 (1967).

9. Griffin v. UAW, 469 F.2d 181, 183, 81 LRRM 2485, 2486 (4th Cir. 1972).

10. Sanderson v. Ford Motor Co., 483 F.2d 102, 110, 83 LRRM 2859, 2863, *reh'g and reh'g en banc denied,* 84 LRRM 2976 (5th Cir. 1973).

11. Ruzicka v. General Motors Corp., 523 F.2d 306, 90 LRRM 2497 (6th Cir. 1975) (Ruzicka I) ("Union action which is arbitrary or disciminatory need not be motivated by bad faith to amount to unfair representation").

12. Archie v. Chicago Truck Drivers Union, 585 F.2d 210, 219, 20 FEP Cases 473, 478 (7th Cir. 1978) (processing a grievance in a "perfunctory" manner, even if in good faith, violates the DFR).

13. Ness v. Safeway Stores, Inc., 598 F.2d 558, 568, 101 LRRM 2621, 2622 (9th Cir. 1979) ("A showing of bad faith is not required . . . ; and a finding of arbitrary or perfunctory handling of an employee's grievance will be sufficient to show a violation of the union's duty").

14. Foust v. IBEW, 572 F.2d 710, 715, 97 LRRM 3040, 3044 (10th Cir. 1978), *rev'd on other grounds,* IBEW v. Foust, 442 U.S. 42, 101 LRRM 2365 (1979) ("the evidence adduced as to the perfunctory manner of handling the claim was sufficient justification for the submission of the issue of breach of duty to the jury").

15. 403 U.S. 274, 299, 77 LRRM 2501, 2511 (1971).

16. 424 U.S. 554, 91 LRRM 2481 (1976).

language ("a union may not arbitrarily ignore a meritorious grievance or process it in a perfunctory fashion");[17] stated that Congress
could not have intended to foreclose the employee from his section
301 remedy "if the contractual processes have been seriously flawed
by the union's breach of its duty to represent employees honestly
and in good faith and without invidious discrimination or arbitrary
conduct";[18] and implied that erroneous arbitration decisions should
not stand where the employee's representation by the union has
been "dishonest, in bad faith or discriminatory."[19]

Is it any wonder, then, that similar confusion is reflected in decisions of the state and lower federal courts? Consider, for example,
the following decisions in the Seventh Circuit. In *Barton Brands, LTD
v. NLRB* the court declared that "seniority decisions . . . may not be
made solely for the benefit of a stronger, more politically favored
group over a minority group. To allow such arbitrary decision-making is contrary to the union's [DFR]."[20] In *Baldini* v. *Local 1095,
United Auto Workers* the court observed:

> If the union has made an honest, informed, and reasoned decision not to
> proceed, it has not breached its duty, even though the decision leaves the
> individual employee without recourse, other reasonable men might have
> decided differently, or the union appears in hindsight to have been sim-
> ply mistaken in the factual premises of its reasoning.[21]

In *Miller* v. *Gateway Transportation Co.*, the court held that union representation of an aggrieved employee that consisted solely of a
"perfunctory reading" of his grievances without prior investigation
raised a question of fact material to the question of fair representation.[22] In *Hoffman* v. *Lonza*,[23] however, a majority of the court declared that neither *Miller* nor *Baldini* held "that the 'arbitrary' conduct of *Vaca* may be anything less than intentional wrongdoing. . . ,
and that a DFR action

> cannot be based solely on some action or omission by the union that re-
> sults in an employee not receiving a "fair" hearing on the merits of a
> grievance. The legal action based on the union's duty to fairly represent
> might be more properly labeled as an action for the union intentionally
> causing harm to an employee involved in a grievance proceeding. The

---

17. *Supra* note 8, at 191, 64 LRRM at 2377.
18. 424 U.S. at 570, 91 LRRM at 2487.
19. *Id.* at 571, 91 LRRM at 2487.
20. 529 F.2d 793, 798, 91 LRRM 2241, 2245 (7th Cir. 1976).
21. 581 F.2d 145, 151, 99 LRRM 2535, 2538 (7th Cir. 1978).
22. 616 F.2d 272, 276, 103 LRRM 2591, 2595 (7th Cir. 1980).
23. 658 F.2d 519, 108 LRRM 2311 (7th Cir. 1981).

"duty" is not breached and the employee has no remedy without substantial evidence of fraud, deceitful action or dishonest conduct.[24]

Decisions by other courts of appeals reflect a similar lack of agreement on an appropriate standard. The Fifth Circuit has held that the careless but unintentional misnumbering of an employee's grievance, resulting in an untimely filing "neither constitutes nor is evidence of that 'arbitrary, discriminatory or . . . bad faith'" conduct required to satisfy the *Vaca* standards, and "does not furnish so much as a scintilla of evidence to support [a] claim of arbitrary conduct by the Union."[25]

The decisions of the Ninth Circuit exhibit an attempt to draw distinctions that are, to say the least, extremely nice. That court has said that "[a]cts of omission by union officials not intended to harm members may be so egregious, so far short of minimum standards of fairness to the employee and so unrelated to legitimate union interests as to be arbitrary," and that a union's failure to disclose to an employee that her grievance would not be submitted to arbitration, thus causing her to reject her employer's offer of settlement, could reasonably be found by a trier of fact to have been "without rational basis or . . . reckless and extremely prejudicial," and a violation of a union's DFR.[26] On the other hand, the court has followed the Sixth Circuit[27] in holding that "the failure to notify an employee of a meeting between the union and company concerning a grievance was perhaps negligent, but not enough to constitute a breach of the union's [DFR]."[28] But the court has also held that evidence that a union did not investigate a grievance and accorded the grievant only a sham interview might be sufficient to support a charge of arbitrary and perfunctory conduct in violation of DFR.[29]

The Sixth Circuit has also modified its test of perfunctory conduct that constitutes a breach of DFR. In *Ruzicka I*[30] the court held

---

24. *Id.* at 521, 522, 108 LRRM at 2313, 2314.

25. Coe v. United Rubber Workers, 571 F.2d 1349, 98 LRRM 2304 (5th Cir. 1978).

26. Robesky v. Qantas Empire Airways Ltd., 573 F.2d 1082, 1091, 98 LRRM 2090, 2095 (9th Cir. 1978); *id.* at 1091, 98 LRRM at 2097.

27. Whitten v. Anchor Motor Freight, Inc., 521 F.2d 1335, 1341, 90 LRRM 2161, 2164-65 (6th Cir. 1975), *cert. denied*, 425 U.S. 981, 94 LRRM 2201 (1976).

28. Singer v. Flying Tiger Line, Inc., 652 F.2d 1349, 108 LRRM 2392 (9th Cir. 1981).

29. Hughes v. IBT, Local 683, 554 F.2d 365, 368, 95 LRRM 2652, 2654 (9th Cir. 1977).

30. *Supra* note 11.

that the union's unexplained failure to file a grievance after being granted two extensions amounted to perfunctory handling in breach of its DFR. In *Ruzicka II*, however, in which, incidentally, the court referred to its decision in *Ruzicka I* as holding that "absent justification or excuse, a union's *negligent* failure to take a basic and required step unrelated to the merits of the grievance, is a clear example of arbitrary and perfunctory conduct"[italics added], it went on to say that the union might not be guilty of a breach of DFR if its "omission is based on a wholly relevant consideration, is not intended to harm its member, and is not the type of arbitrariness which reflects disregard for the rights of the individual employee."[31]

The Third Circuit, although suggesting in a dictum that a union's "perfunctory" handling of a grievance might breach its DFR,[32] has adhered to the view that "[p]roof of arbitrary or bad faith union conduct in deciding not to proceed with the grievance is necessary to establish lack of compliance with the [DFR]."[33]

The Eighth Circuit has held that an employee's claims that he had great difficulty in persuading his union to take up his grievance, that the union failed to process it in a timely manner, that it conducted no investigation and refused to discuss the grievance with him, and that it failed either to keep him informed of the status of the grievance or to tell him that the grievance had been dropped, if fully credited, would support "an inference of bad faith and arbitrary and capricious conduct."[34] In a subsequent case, however, the court held that the mere failure of a union steward to file a grievance within the time limit specified in the collective bargaining agreement did not establish that he had been "unconcerned, unsolicitous, or indifferent"—attitudes the court felt must be proved in order to support a charge of perfunctory handling of the grievance.[35]

---

31. Ruzicka v. General Motors Corp., 649 F.2d 1207, 107 LRRM 2726 (6th Cir. 1981); *id.* at 1211, 107 LRRM at 2729; *id.* at 1212, 107 LRRM at 2730.

32. Ely v. Hall's Motor Transit Co., 590 F.2d 62, 66 n.10, 100 LRRM 2206, 2208 n.10 (3d Cir. 1978).

33. Findley v. Jones Motor Freight, 639 F.2d 953, 106 LRRM 2420 (3d Cir. 1981).

34. Minnis v. UAW, 531 F.2d 850, 853 n.5, 91 LRRM 2081, 2083 n.5 (8th Cir. 1975).

35. Ethier v. United States Postal Service, 590 F.2d 733, 100 LRRM 2390 (8th Cir. 1979), *cert. denied*, 444 U.S. 826, 102 LRRM 2440 (1979).

Negligence

Although it is possible to draw a comprehensible distinction between arbitrary, capricious, and perfunctory conduct, on the one hand, and negligence, on the other, the courts have tended to use these terms interchangeably in what may fairly be termed a capricious, if not arbitrary, manner. Nevertheless, in a few cases the effect of negligence alone has been addressed.

In *Hoffman* v. *Lonza,* for example, the court flatly declared that "[m]ere negligence cannot rise to the level of misconduct necessary to support an action for breach of the Union's [DFR]."[36] And in *Ruzicka II* the court similarly stated that "we cannot hold a union liable for breach of [DFR] based upon simple negligence."[37]

The Supreme Court has thus far not decided squarely what degree of negligence, if any, will sustain a charge of violation of DFR. It has, however, skirted the problem. In *International Bhd. of Elec. Workers* v. *Foust* the issue before the Court was the propriety of awarding punitive damages for violation of a DFR. A jury had found that the union had violated its DFR by handling the plaintiff's grievance in a perfunctory manner, and the Court's opinion did not question that finding. The concurring opinion of four Justices declared, however, that the union's conduct "betrayed nothing more than negligence, and thus presented an inappropriate occasion for awarding punitive damages under any formula."[38] At least four members of the Supreme Court saw no difference between treating a grievance in a perfunctory manner and handling it negligently.

The issue of negligence is easier to deal with when it involves only lapses in observance of contract procedures, such as the failure by a union steward to file a grievance within the prescribed time limits. Depending upon the specific facts involved, one might plausibly distinguish a negligent failure to file in which the steward simply forgot from an arbitrary or capricious refusal to file, on the alleged ground that the grievance was a "bum beef" or was too trivial to warrant further action, or from a perfunctory dropping of the grievance without sufficient investigation, or from a bad faith refusal to

---

36. 658 F.2d 519, 523, 108 LRRM 2311, 2314 (7th Cir. 1981) (see text at note 23 *supra*).

37. Ruzicka v. General Motors Corp., 649 F.2d 1207, 1210, 107 LRRM 2726, 2730 (6th Cir. 1981) (see text at note 31 *supra*).

38. 442 U.S. 42, 101 LRRM 2365 (1979) (see note 14 *supra*); *id.* at 53, 101 LRRM 2365.

file because the grievant was not a member of the union or was a member actively in opposition against the current union administration. Putting aside the bad faith case, however, the lines between negligent, arbitrary, capricious, and perfunctory conduct tend to become hopelessly blurred. Indeed, in *Bowen* v. *United States Postal Service*, a federal district court found that the union's refusal to arbitrate an "apparently meritorious grievance . . . in an arbitrary and perfunctory manner . . . ." amounted to "reckless and callous disregard of the grievant's rights," thus virtually obliterating any distinction between arbitrary and perfunctory behavior and actual malice.[39]

Rational Basis

In cases such as *Bowen*, in which there has been no inadvertent failure to comply with procedural requirements but rather a conscious decision not to pursue an available remedy, courts may look, not for negligence or arbitrary, capricious, or perfunctory behavior but for an absence of rational judgment as a basis for a finding that the DFR has been violated. The constitution of the United Auto Workers (UAW) offers an interesting analogy. It provides in part that the UAW Public Review Board shall have no jurisdiction of any appeal relating to the handling of a grievance or other issue involving a collective bargaining agreement "unless the appellant has alleged before the International Executive Board [IEB] that the matter was improperly handled because of fraud, discrimination or collusion with management, or that the disposition or handling . . . was devoid of any rational basis."[40] The Public Review Board applied the rational basis standard in sustaining a member's appeal and remanding to the IEB, with directions that the union seek reinstatement of his grievance. The member, with twenty years seniority, had been discharged for overstaying his leave; and the grievance was withdrawn as unmeritorious after being in the procedure for more than two and one-half years.[41]

Vandervelde has pointed out that because the failure to follow the appeals process correctly can "terminate a grievance on a basis other than by a reasoned union decision. . . the rational decision-

---

39. 470 F. Supp. 1127, 1129, 103 LRRM 2366, 2367 (W.D. Va. 1979).
40. Constitution of the International Union, UAW, art. 33, § 4(i) (1980).
41. Resnick v. Local 906, UAW, Case No. 549 (Dec. 31, 1981).

making standard encompasses those union actions proscribed by the negligence standard as well."[42] By the same token, rational basis also encompasses arbitrary, capricious, or perfunctory behavior.

Scope of Judicial Review

One of the dangers created by the ambiguous terminology employed to describe violations of DFR is that it invites a broader scope of judicial review than is desirable; and this has resulted in some truly bizarre decisions that indicate the vast ignorance of many judges about how unions operate and how collective bargaining functions. Example number one in my chamber of DFR horrors continues to be the now hoary decision in *Clark* v. *Hein-Werner Corp.*, a case growing out of a seniority grievance, in which the Wisconsin Supreme Court declared:

> where the interests of two groups of employees are diametrically opposed to each other and the union espouses the one in . . . arbitration, it follows *as a matter of law* that there has been no fair representation of the other group. This is true even though, in choosing the cause . . . to espouse, the union acts completely objectively and with the best of motives. The old adage, that one cannot serve two masters, is particularly applicable to such a situation [italics added].[43]

The issue in that case was whether the union violated its DFR by failing to give one of the competing groups notice of the arbitration and by going ahead with the arbitration without any member of that group being present. The mischievous dictum I have just quoted was totally unnecessary to the decision, and it reflected the obviously incorrect belief that in cases in which one or more members of a bargaining unit submit conflicting claims under a seniority provision, the union must, as a matter of law, maintain an absolutely neutral stance, even though it believes in good faith that the position taken by one of the competing individuals or groups is wholly at odds with the meaning of the seniority provision in question.

In cases of this kind, of course, the union has a duty to investi-

---

42. Vandervelde, *supra* note 2, at 1101. She cites the following cases as lending support to both theories: Foust v. IBEW, 572 F.2d 710, 97 LRRM 3040 (10th Cir. 1978), *rev'd on other grounds*, 442 U.S. 42, 101 LRRM 2365 (1979); Minnis v. UAW, 531 F.2d 850, 91 LRRM 2081 (8th Cir. 1975); and Ruzicka v. General Motors Corp., 523 F.2d 912, 90 LRRM 2497 (6th Cir. 1975).

43. 8 Wis.2d 264, 272, 99 N.W.2d 132, 137 (1959), *reh'g denied*, 100 N.W.2d 317 (1960).

gate carefully the competing arguments; to give the respective sides an opportunity to present their points of view, although I would argue that the union may do this informally, without necessarily holding a hearing for that purpose; and, finally, to make an impartial decision as to which of the rival arguments to support. Courts faced with issues of this kind, however, are likely to fall into the same error as that committed by the Wisconsin Supreme Court. A recent example is *Smith* v. *Hussmann Refrigerator Co.*[44] In this case a seniority provision stated that when "skill and ability to perform are substantially equal, seniority shall govern." The company filled some vacancies in a skilled maintenance classification with junior employees, arguing that their skills and ability were superior to those of the senior applicants. In protest, some twenty-six unsuccessful applicants filed grievances; of these, the union elected to process four filed by employees whose seniority was greater than that of those selected by the company and who claimed to possess skill and ability substantially equal to theirs. The four grievances were processed to arbitration; the remaining grievants were given no notice of the arbitration and did not appear. Unaccountably, the arbitrator's award purported to establish job rights in the classification in question for six, rather than four, employees. His award also contained significant factual errors. Accordingly, representatives of the company and the union agreed between themselves on a "clarification" of the award that was, in fact, a modification, inasmuch as it materially changed the award. For reasons known only to themselves, they then met with the arbitrator, with no others present, and prevailed upon him to issue a new award based on their agreement. A subsequent action under section 301 of the Labor Management Relations Act (LMRA), 1947[45] was brought by several of the employees whose assignment to the skilled maintenance classification by the company had been

---

44. 619 F.2d 1229, 103 LRRM 2321 (8th Cir. 1980).

45. Section 301 of the LMRA, 29 U.S.C. § 185, among other things, authorizes suits for violations of collective bargaining agreements between employers and labor organizations representing employees in an industry affecting commerce. The Supreme Court has held that a union can be sued under section 301 for violation of its DFR that affects an employee's rights under a collective bargaining agreement. Humphrey v. Moore, 375 U.S. 335, 55 LRRM 2031 (1964). For a criticism of that decision, *see* the concurring opinion of Justice Goldberg, *id.* at 351–55, 55 LRRM at 2038–41, and Feller, *A General Theory of the Collective Bargaining Agreement*, 61 Calif. L. Rev. 663, 808 (1973).

upheld by the arbitrator's first award but overturned by the second. They charged that the union had violated its DFR and won a favorable verdict, which was sustained on appeal by the Court of Appeals for the Eighth Circuit.[46]

Now, it is certainly arguable that the union violated its DFR by not investigating more carefully the claims of those employees the company had assigned to the disputed jobs, before electing to process the four grievances filed by senior employees whose bids were rejected by mangement. But the court went unnecessarily and disastrously far afield in deciding the case. Like the Wisconsin Supreme Court, it advanced reasons in support of its decision that seem to me quite wrong.

The first point emphasized by the appellate court was that the company's selection of the plaintiffs in preference to more senior employees because of the formers' alleged superior skill and ability "vested them with rights as third party beneficiaries of the collective bargaining agreement," rights "which the union had a fiduciary duty to protect."[47] Whether or not the plaintiffs were third-party beneficiaries of "rights" created by the collective bargaining agreement,[48] how could those rights to the disputed jobs have inhered in the plaintiffs unless and until the union's challenge to the propriety of the company's assignment had been disposed of by mutual agreement or by an arbitrator's decision?

That question has a bearing on another finding by the court that the union had violated its DFR by failing to notify the plaintiffs of the initial arbitration hearing or to invite them to be present. Let us concede at once that the union would have been wise to have done so; the question, however, is whether, legally, it had no alternative. It is a truism that the union owns the grievance and that, subject to its DFR, it is not required to give a grievant notice of an arbitration hearing or to permit the grievant to attend. If we assume that the union had made the requisite impartial investigation of all competing grievances, as well as the claims of the employees assigned by the company to the classification involved, before deciding to pro-

---

46. The facts in Hussmann are more complicated than as stated in this paper; I have included only those bearing directly on that aspect of the case I want to discuss.

47. *Supra* note 44, at 1238 n.10, 103 LRRM at 2327 n.10; *id.* at 1238, 103 LRRM at 2327.

48. *See* Feller, *supra* note 45, at 774–92.

cess the four grievances it deemed meritorious, I can see no legal reason why the plaintiffs should have been invited to the hearing and called by the union as witnessess in their own behalf.

The appellate court in *Hussmann* also held that the jury could properly have found that the resubmission of the issue to the arbitrator constituted both a breach of the collective bargaining agreement and a violation of the union's DFR, because the arbitrator's first decision constituted a "final and binding resolution of the dispute," as provided in the collective bargaining agreement, and "the union and the company substantially altered the award by taking away plaintiffs' rights granted by arbitration."[49]

This, surely, cannot be true. As a prinicipal party to the collective bargaining agreement, a union, so long as it acts in good faith and not in a negligent, arbitrary, capricious, or perfunctory way, may legally agree with an employer to ignore or modify an arbitration award or, for that matter, to delete, modify, or add to the terms of the collective bargaining agreement itself. Of course, the appellate court in *Hussmann* accepted a finding that the union had *not* acted properly in respect of its DFR; but the language of its opinion seems entirely too broad.

Exhaustion of Contractual and Internal Union Remedies

Republic Steel Corp. v. *Maddox*[50] established the principle that an employee who claims he has been victimized by his employer's violation of a collective bargaining agreement must exhaust the grievance and arbitration procedures provided by that agreement before suing his employer for its breach under section 301 of the LMRA. In *Vaca,* the Supreme Court reaffirmed that principle, but noted that "because those contractual remedies have been devised and are often controlled by the union and the employer, they may well prove unsatisfactory or unworkable for the individual grievant."[51] Thus, it declared that a discharged employee is relieved of the exhaustion requirement if the employer's conduct "amounts to a repudiation of those contractual procedures," or if "the union has sole power under

49. *Supra* note 44, at 1242, 103 LRRM at 2330.
50. 379 U.S. 650, 58 LRRM 2193 (1965).
51. Vaca v. Sipes, *supra* note 8.

the contract to invoke the higher stages of the grievance procedure, *and* if . . . the employee-plaintiff has been prevented from exhausting his contractual remedies by the union's *wrongful* refusal to process the grievance [italics are the Court's]."[52]

The extent to which an employee is required to exhaust his internal union remedies for an alleged violation of DFR before seeking the aid of a court was considered by the Supreme Court in *Clayton* v. *ITT Gilfillan*.[53] In that case, the UAW processed the grievance of a discharged employee, Clayton, through the grievance procedure and requested arbitration, but then withdrew the request. At the time this case arose, the UAW constitution provided:

> It shall be the duty of any member or subordinate body who feels aggrieved by any action, decision, or penalty imposed upon him or it, to exhaust his or its remedy and all appeals therefrom under the rules of this International Union prior to appealing to a civil court or governmental agency for redress.[54]

The constitution provided for a series of appeals from the local union to the international union level and from there either to the Convention Appeals Committee or to the Public Review Board.[55]

Clayton did not appeal from the union's decision to withdraw his grievance from arbitration; instead, he filed a section 301 action against the union and the company. The district court sustained the defense relied upon by both the union and the company, namely, that Clayton had failed to exhaust the internal union appeals procedures. It held that those procedures were adequate as a matter of law and were not futile, and, accordingly, dismissed Clayton's suit against both defendants. The Court of Appeals for the Ninth Circuit affirmed the dismissal of the suit against the union, holding that by pursuing his internal remedies, Clayton would have obtained the same remedy, damages, that he sought in his section 301 action against the union.[56] Conversely, it reversed the dismissal of the ac-

---

52. *Id.*

53. 451 U.S. 679, 107 LRRM 2385 (1981).

54. Constitution of the International Union, UAW, art. 33, § 12 (1977). The constitution was amended in 1980. The substance of art. 33, § 12 now appears in art. 33, § 5.

55. 1977 UAW Constitution, art. 33, § § 1–11.

56. The only reference to damages in the UAW constitution is to allegations of violation of the union's ethical codes made in "bad faith or with malicious intent and in a willful effort to divide and disrupt the Union." The Public Review Board (PRB) has power to punish such offenses by imposing a fine of not less than $100 nor more than $500. *Id.* at art. 32, § 7. The PRB ruled in Appeal of Egres, et al., Case No. 19 (Apr.

tion against the company because the internal procedure could not have provided either Clayton's reinstatement or the reactivation of his grievance.[57]

The Supreme Court, speaking through Justice Brennan, held that "where an internal union appeals procedure cannot result in reactivation of the employee's grievance or an award of the complete relief sought in his § 301 suit, exhaustion will not be required with respect to either the suit against the employer or the suit against the union."[58] Justice Brennan distinguished *Maddox* on the ground that the exhaustion rule in that case was designed to protect the integrity of the collective bargaining process, not that of internal union procedures. In respect of the latter, he declared that the policy of deferring judicial interference until they have been exhausted "does not extend to issues 'in the public domain and beyond the internal affairs of the union.'"[59] An allegation that the union had violated its DFR, said Justice Brennan, "raises issues rooted in statutory policies extending far beyond internal union interests." Conceding that an exhaustion requirement might lead to nonjudicial resolution of some contractual grievances, Justice Brennan nevertheless declined to impose a universal exhaustion requirement "lest employees with meritorious § 301 claims be forced to exhaust themselves and their resources by submitting their claims to potentially lengthy internal union procedures that may not be adequate to redress their underlying grievances."[60] Citing the Court's earlier decision in *NLRB* v. *Marine Workers,* he declared that courts have discretion to decide whether to require exhaustion of internal union procedures.[61]

Because Clayton conceded that the union's internal appeals

22, 1959) that the power to reimburse a successful appellant for the expenses of his appeal "has not been bestowed upon this Board by the International Constitution." In Dawkins v. Local 3, UAW, Case No. 284 (May 9, 1973), however, the Board said: "There is nothing in the Constitution which states that a member cannot present [to the membership] a claim for back pay based upon the alleged negligence or refusal of his steward to file a grievance on his behalf . . . and, indeed, the Union has argued in numerous briefs that its membership has precisely this right under its system of internal remedies."

57. Clayton v. ITT Gilfillan, 623 F.2d 563, 104 LRRM 2118 (9th Cir. 1980).

58. *Supra* note 53, at 685, 107 LRRM at 2387.

59. *Id.* at 688, 107 LRRM at 2388 (citing NLRB v. Marine Workers, 391 U.S. 418, 426 n.8, 68 LRRM 2257, 2260 n.8 (1968)).

60. *Id.* at 688, 689, 107 LRRM at 2388, 2389.

61. *Id.* at 689, 107 LRRM at 2389 (citing 391 U.S. 418, 426 n.8, 68 LRRM 2257, 2260 n.8 (1968)). Justice Brennan suggested a three-prong test to guide courts in making that decision: (1) Are union officials so hostile to the employee that he could

procedures are fair and reasonable and that he could have received an impartial hearing of his claim, Justice Brennan turned next to the question whether the relief available was adequate. The parties had stipulated that the Public Review Board can award back pay in an appropriate case, but the union admittedly had no power to reinstate Clayton or to reactivate his grievance. Justice Brennan concluded, therefore, that the national labor policy favoring the relatively rapid disposition of labor disputes would be undermined by an exhaustion requirement "unless the internal procedures are capable of either reactivating the employee's grievance or of redressing it."[62]

There remained only the question whether exhaustion, even if not required in the suit against the employer, ought to be required in the suit against the union. Reversing the appellate court on that issue, the Supreme Court held that exhaustion could not be required in the suit against either defendant. As Justice Brennan explained,

> If [a trial court] stayed the action against the employer pending resolution of the internal appeals procedures, it would effectively be requiring exhaustion with respect to the suit against the employer, a result . . . [that] would violate national labor policy. Yet if it permitted the action against the employer to proceed, and tolled the running of the statute of limitations against the union until the internal procedures had been exhausted, it could very well find itself with two § 301 suits, based on the same facts, proceeding at different paces in its courtroom.[63]

Whether the Court would have been wiser, as urged by Justice Rehnquist in his dissenting opinion, to have required a delay in filing a section 301 action until Clayton had pursued his internal union

---

not obtain a fair hearing? (2) Are the available remedies unable to ensure either reactivation of the employee's grievance or its full monetary relief? and (3) Would the exhaustion of internal union procedures unreasonably delay the employee's opportunity to obtain a judicial hearing on the merits? If any of these conditions exist, he said, the court may properly excuse the employee's failure to exhaust. *Cf.* Detroy v. American Guild of Variety Artists, 286 F.2d 75 (2d Cir. 1961), *cert. denied*, 366 U.S. 929 (1961), holding that it is within the courts' discretion to decide whether to require a union member, pursuant to section 101(a)(4) of the Labor-Management Reporting and Disclosure Act of 1959 (LMDRA), 29 U.S.C. § 411(a)(4), "to exhaust reasonable hearing procedures . . . within such [labor] organization before instituting legal or administrative proceedings against such organization or any officer thereof."

62. 451 U.S. at 691 n.18, 693, 107 LRRM 2389 n.18, 2390. Justice Brennan noted that the Court had been informed by the UAW that "[s]ome employers and unions have, through collective bargaining, agreed to allow the reinstatement of withdrawn grievances where a union tribunal reverses the union's decision." In such cases, he conceded, "the relief available through the union's internal appeal procedures would presumably be adequate."

63. *Id.* at 695, 107 LRRM at 2391.

remedy for at least four months, is debatable. As previously indicated,[64] enforcement of that requirement, which Justice Rehnquist borrowed from section 101(a)(4) of the LMRDA, is a matter for the discretion of the court in any given case. The virtue of the rule announced in *Clayton* is that it is one of the very few in this area that is unambiguous and readily understood by the lower courts.

Review of Arbitration Awards

Allegations in a section 301 action that although a union has taken a grievance to arbitration, it has lost the case through negligent or inept handling, or has deliberately "thrown" it, present special difficulties. As I indicated in *The Duty of Fair Representation*, I think courts should be very wary about finding a violation of DFR on the basis of their own conclusions that the union's representative "overlooked obvious legal arguments and had not been sufficiently aggressive in protecting the grievant against improper questioning by the arbitrator," or "by taking an unsuccessful position in arbitration that was 'doomed to failure.'"[65] It still seems to me that once the grievant's claim of contract violation against the employer has been arbitrated, only in the most egregious cases in which there is clear evidence of bad faith on the part of the union should a court entertain a section 301 action against the union for breach of DFR.

On the other hand, I continue to be troubled by the willingness of courts to accept the submission of employee grievances to bipartite arbitration boards as evidence of a union's good faith. There has been a sufficient number of cases, of which *Hines* v. *Anchor Motor Freight, Inc.* is only one conspicuous example,[66] that suggest a strong possibility of collusion between the employer and union representatives who make up the board on joint committees. At the very least, courts should give much closer scrutiny to proceedings before such bodies than they give to those before a tripartite board or a single, neutral arbitrator.

---

64. *See* note 61 *supra.*

65. Aaron, *supra* note 1, at 20–22 (citing Holodnak v. Avco Corp. and UAW Local 10, 381 F. Supp. 191, 87 LRRM 2337 (D. Conn. 1974), *aff'd in part and rev'd in part,* 514 F.2d 285, 88 LRRM 2950 (2d Cir. 1975), *cert. denied,* 423 U.S. 892, 90 LRRM 2614 (1975); Thompson v. IAM Lodge 1049, 258 F. Supp. 235 (E.D. Va. 1966)).

66. *Supra* note 16.

Damages

Punitive Damages

International Bhd. of Elec. Workers v. *Foust*[67] remains the most authoritative word on the issue of whether punitive damages may be awarded in a successful action for violation of DFR. The Supreme Court, in an opinion by Justice Marshall, held in that case that "[b]ecause general labor policy disfavors punishment, and the adverse consequences of punitive damage awards could be substantial . . . such damages may not be assessed against a union that breaches its [DFR] by failing properly to pursue a grievance." Among the arguments relied upon by Justice Marshall to support that conclusion were "the possibility that punitive awards would impair the financial stability of unions and unsettle the careful balance of individual and collective interests which this Court has previously articulated in the unfair representation area"; and the likelihood that juries would impose heavy and unpredictable damages, thus compelling unions "to process frivolous claims or resist fair settlements."[68]

In a concurring opinion, joined by three other justices, Justice Blackmun rejected what he termed the Court's "per se rule" in favor of a more flexible one. He argued that in cases of "intentional racial discrimination, deliberate personal animus, or conscious infringement of speech and associational freedoms," a court should be free to award punitive damages. He made it clear, however, that he would restrict punitive damages to "those rare cases where the union's conduct can truly be described as outrageous."[69]

For the reasons advanced by Justice Marshall, I hope the majority's view will continue to prevail, but I have my doubts. Justice Stewart, who joined the Court's opinion in *Foust,* is no longer on the Court and has been replaced by Justice O'Connor. From my reading of her opinions to date, I think it likely that if the Court should consider the same issue again, she would take a position at least as favorable to the award of punitive damages as that advanced by Justice Blackmun.

Apportionment of Liability

Among the things Justice White discussed in *Vaca* was the apportionment of liability when the employer has violated the collective

---

67. *Supra* note 38.
68. *Id.* at 52, 48, 101 LRRM at 2369, 2368.
69. *Id.* at 60, 101 LRRM at 2372.

bargaining agreement and the union has breached its duty of fair representation. He declared that the "governing principle . . . is to apportion liability between the employer and the union according to the damage caused by the fault of each."[70] Thus the union should not be charged with damages attributable to the employer's misconduct, but should be liable for any increases in those damages resulting from the union's breach of its duty of fair representation.

A few years later, the Court dealt with a similar but not identical situation in *Czosek* v. *O'Mara*.[71] In that case, a group of railroad employees sued the carrier for wrongful discharge and the union for arbitrarily and capriciously refusing to process their claims, in breach of its duty of fair representation. The employees had failed, however, to pursue their administrative remedies under the Railway Labor Act (RLA),[72] and the claim against the carrier was therefore dismissed. The claim against the union was allowed to stand because the union's duty of fair representation was held not to be affected by the employees' failure to pursue their administrative remedy. The union, understandably, was concerned that because the carrier was not joined as a party defendant, it might be held liable for damages for which the carrier was wholly or partly responsible. The Supreme Court, again speaking through Justice White, offered the following assurance:

> [J]udgment against [the union] can in any event be had only for those damages that flowed from [its] own conduct. Assuming a wrongful discharge by the employee independent of any discriminatory conduct by the union and a subsequent discriminatory refusal by the union to process grievances based on the discharge, damages against the union for loss of employment are unreasonable except to the extent that its refusal to handle the grievances added to the difficulty and expense of collecting from the employer.[73]

The Court had no further occasion to rule on this particular issue until its recent decision in *Bowen* v. *United States Postal Service*.[74] That case arose out of Bowen's disciplinary discharge, which the national office of his bargaining representative, the American Postal

---

70. 386 U.S. at 197, 64 LRRM at 2379.

71. 397 U.S. 25, 73 LRRM 2481 (1970).

72. Section 3 First (i), (j) of the RLA, 45 U.S.C. 153, provides that an employee whose grievance remains unresolved may seek relief from the National Railroad Adjustment Board, which is authorized to provide remedies similar to those available in a court suit.

73. *Supra* note 71, at 29, 73 LRRM at 2482.

74. 103 S. Ct. 588, 112 LRRM 2281 (1983).

Worker Union (APWU), refused to take to arbitration, despite the recommendation of responsible union officers at each step of the grievance procedure that it do so. Bowen then brought suit in federal district court against the Postal Service and the APWU for damages and injunctive relief.[75] After a jury trial, the court instructed the jury that the apportionment of liability "was left primarily to its discretion"; that it could equitably "base apportionment on the date of a hypothetical arbitration decision—the date at which the Service would have reinstated Bowen if the Union had fulfilled its duty"; and that the Postal Service "could be liable for damages before that date and the Union for damages thereafter."[76]

The jury found in favor of Bowen, and the court entered judgment, holding that the Postal Service had discharged Bowen without just cause, that the union had handled his "apparently meritorious grievance . . . in an arbitrary and perfunctory manner . . . ," and that both the union and the Postal Service had acted "in reckless and callous disregard of [Bowen's] rights."[77] The jury found that between his discharge and the time of the trial, Bowen had sustained losses in wages and fringe benefits of $47,000. The trial judge added $5,954 to cover the period between the end of the trial and the filing of posttrial motions and assessed $30,000 of the total amount ($52,954) against APWU and the remainder against the Postal Service. The jury also found that the Postal Service and the union were both liable for punitive damages; but the court held that punitive damages could not be assessed against the Postal Service because of its sovereign immunity, and that it would be unfair to hold the union liable when the employer was immune. The court also made a finding of fact that if Bowen's grievance had been arbitrated, he would have been reinstated by August 1977 (he had been terminated in March 1976). Bowen did not appeal from the ruling on damages.

The Court of Appeals for the Fourth Circuit upheld the damage award against the Postal Service but vacated the portion assessed against the union.[78] It held as a matter of law that because Bowen's compensation was at all times payable only by the Postal Service, it remained the exclusive responsibility of the service; therefore, no

---

75. The action arose under the Postal Reorganization Act, 39 U.S.C. § 1208(b), which is identical to section 301 of the LMRA in all material respects.

76. *Supra* note 74, at 591, 112 LRRM at 2282.

77. *Supra* note 39.

78. 642 F.2d 79, 106 LRRM 2701 (4th Cir. 1981).

portion of that amount was chargeable to the union. The appellate court also refused to increase the damage award above $22,954, despite the undisputed fact that Bowen's actual damages amounted to $52,954.

The Supreme Court, in a five-to-four decision, reversed the court of appeals and ordered apportionment of damages against both the Postal Service and the union in the manner determined by the district court. Writing for the majority, Justice Powell, relying upon *Vaca,* reaffirmed that if an employer wrongfully discharges an employee, it remains liable for the employee's back pay and that when both employer and union have caused the damage suffered by the employee, the union is responsible for the increase in damages resulting from its wrong and must bear its portion of the damages. Justice Powell stressed the necessary reliance by the employer on the union's decision not to pursue an employee's grievance, declaring, "Just as a nonorganized employer may accept an employee's waiver of any challenge to his discharge as a final resolution of the matter, so should an organized employer be able to rely on a comparable waiver by the employee's exclusive representative." He thought that when the default of both employer and union contributes to the employee's injury, unless there is apportionment of damages, incentive to comply with the grievance procedure would be diminished and that imposing total liability on the employer "could well affect the willingness of employers to agree to arbitration clauses as they are customarily written."[79]

Justice White, joined by Justices Marshall, Blackmun, and Rehnquist, wrote an opinion concurring and dissenting in part. Emphasizing that the union's failure to represent Bowen fairly was completely independent of the Postal Service's wrongful discharge, Justice White declared that the employer should be primarily liable for all back pay. He conceded that the union cannot escape liability for the natural consequences of its wrongful conduct, but insisted that the employee's damages recoverable from the union in such a case "are simply of a different nature than those recoverable from the employer."[80] In support, he cited the same excerpt from the Court's decision in *Czosek* relied upon by Justice Powell, especially

---

79. *Supra* note 74, at 597, 112 LRRM at 2286–87.
80. *Id.* at 602, 112 LRRM at 2290.

the statement that unions would not be forced to pay damages for which the employer was even partly responsible.[81]

Justice White also pointed out that most of the cases of this nature reviewed by the Supreme Court have taken almost a decade to run their course and because an arbitration decision is normally reached within a year following the discharge, under the Court's rule "the union will be subject to large liability, far greater than that of the employer, the extent of which will not be in any way related to the union's comparative culpability." He observed, also, that the employer, unlike the union, "can stop backpay accretion at any moment it desires, simply by reinstating the discharged employee."[82]

Justice White was of the view that matters of this kind should be governed by the principle of contract law "that a breaching defendant must pay damages equivalent to the total harm suffered, 'even though there were contributing factors other than his own conduct.'"[83]

Neither the collective bargaining agreement nor the union's duty of fair representation, said Justice White, provides support for the Court's conclusion that the union had committed itself to protect the employer or that the employer could rightfully rely on the union to terminate its liability. He charged the majority with reading "an indemnification provision into the collective bargaining agreement, even though the employer can and . . . should be required to bargain for such a provision, if desired."[84]

In the final portion of his opinion, in which Justice Rehnquist refused to join, Justice White argued that the court of appeals should have assessed the Postal Service the $30,000 "that the District Court erroneously charged against the union."[85] Justice Rehnquist felt that Bowen should be denied recovery of that amount because his counsel had failed to file a conditional cross-appeal, seeking to increase the amount of the judgment against the Postal Service should the union be held not liable.

The most striking and, in my view, the most questionable aspect of the *Bowen* case, noted but not challenged in any of the Court's

---

81. *See* 397 U.S. at 29, 73 LRRM at 2482.
82. *Supra* note 74, at 603, 112 LRRM at 2291.
83. *Id.* (citing 5A Corbin on Contracts § 999 (1964)).
84. *Id.* at 605, 112 LRRM at 2293.
85. *Id.* at 607, 112 LRRM at 2294.

three opinions, was the district court's assumption that because the jury had found a breach by the union of its DFR, it followed automatically that had Bowen's grievance been arbitrated, he would have been reinstated with full back pay. I am unaware of any doctrine of the federal common law of arbitration developed under section 301 of the LMRA that justifies such a conclusion by a court or jury. Surely, the insistence of union officials at the various steps of the grievance procedure that Bowen's discharge should be appealed to a higher step, including arbitration, was more or less pro forma and did not constitute proof that the discharge was in breach of the collective bargaining agreement. The trial court accepted the jury's finding that the Postal Service had violated the collective bargaining agreement when it discharged Bowen; it assumed that an arbitrator would have reached the same conclusion. The danger of relying upon a jury's findings on such questions is suggested by the dissenting opinion of Judge Murnaghan in the Fourth Circuit decision, pointing out that the district court and jury were persuaded that Bowen would have won his grievance in arbitration by the testimony of an "expert" witness, whose expertise was based on twelve years as secretary and president of a local union unconnected with the APWU, during which she handled grievances and assisted in preparation of some arbitration cases on the local level, and on attendance at her union's labor relations school.[86] This experience hardly qualified her as an expert in predicting the outcome of arbitrators' awards, which are no easier to predict than are the decisions of the Supreme Court.

The discharge apparently was the result of an altercation between Bowen and another employee. Even if an arbitrator might have reinstated Bowen, he or she might also have denied back pay. Under these circumstances, therefore, the measure of damages determined by the jury seems highly speculative at best. The Court's failure to take these considerations into account is another indication of its ignorance of the practice of industrial relations.

As between the conflicting arguments advanced by Justice Powell and Justice White, those of the latter seem to me much more persuasive. Given their mutual, albeit unwarranted, assumption that the discharge was unlawful, as well as the undoubted fact that the union's breach of its duty of fair representation was wholly unre-

---

86. 642 F.2d at 84, 106 LRRM at 2704–5.

lated to the employer's misconduct, it is indeed "bizarre," as Justice White said, "to hold . . . that the . . . union is *exclusively* liable for the bulk of the back pay."[87] Justice Powell was correct, of course, in rejecting the union's argument that because its breach of duty was unrelated to the wrongful discharge, its default merely lifted the bar to Bowen's suit on the contract against the employer and did not subject the union to any monetary damages. He was wrong, however, in assuming that only by making the union responsible for a continuing back pay liability following its refusal to arbitrate could the integrity of the collective bargaining relationship be maintained. He overlooked or chose to ignore that, as Justice White pointed out, the *Vaca* rule provides for a credible deterrent against wrongful union conduct: "Attorney's fees and other litigation expenses have been assessed as damages against unions, because such damages measure the extent by which the union's breach of duty adds to the difficulty and expense of collecting from the employer."[88]

On the other hand, Justice White's opinion is not entirely satisfactory. My principal objection is to his suggestion that the Postal Service could have terminated its back pay liability simply by reinstating the discharged employee. If Justice White's comment was intended as one of general application, it betrays an ignorance of the real world of collective bargaining. To reinstate an employee believed to have been rightfully discharged simply to terminate back pay liability would be a sacrifice of principle to expediency that many, if not most, employers would find unacceptable.

Statute of Limitations

Given the large number of DFR cases, the determination of the appropriate statute of limitations in suits brought under section 301 of the LMRA against employers for breach of contract and against unions for breach of DFR is a matter of considerable importance.

The Supreme Court first confronted part of this issue in *Auto Workers* v. *Hoosier Cardinal Corp.*,[89] which involved a suit by a union under section 301 against the employer for breach of a collective bargaining agreement. The LMRA provides no federal statute of limitations applicable to such cases, so the Court had to choose be-

---

87. *Supra* note 74, 112 LRRM at 2292.
88. *Id.* at 602 n.6, 112 LRRM at 2291 n.6.
89. 383 U.S. 696, 61 LRRM 2545 (1966).

tween devising a uniform time limitation, as the union urged, and applying an existing federal or state statutory measure. The union's proposal was based on the alleged need for uniformity in rules applicable to section 301 actions generally, but the Court, speaking through Justice Stewart, rejected the argument, saying,

> The need for uniformity . . . is greatest where its absence would threaten the smooth functioning of those consensual processes that federal labor law is chiefly designed to promote—the formation of the collective agreement and the private settlement of disputes under it. For the most part, statutes of limitations come into play only when those processes have already broken down. Lack of uniformity in this area is therefore unlikely to frustrate in any important way the achievement of any significant goal of labor policy.[90]

Although he referred to the six-months limitation provision governing unfair labor practice proceedings under the NLRA, Justice Stewart did not discuss its possible application to this case.[91] Instead, he relied upon the well-established rule that "state statutes of limitations govern the timeliness of federal causes of action unless Congress has specifically provided otherwise."[92] Accordingly, the decision was that the timeliness of a section 301 suit is to be determined, as a matter of federal law, by reference to the appropriate state statute of limitations, in this case a six-year period applicable to suits for breach of contract cognizable at common law. In a footnote, however, Justice Stewart cautioned, "Whether other § 301 suits different from the present one might call for the application of other rules on timeliness, we are not required to decide. . . ."[93] Justices White, Douglas, and Brennan dissented, believing that because Congress had provided no specific statute of limitations, the Court was obligated to fashion a governing federal rule that would apply to all section 301 actions.

Fifteen years later, the Court dealt with another aspect of the problem in *United Parcel Service, Inc.* v. *Mitchell*,[94] a case involving a so-called hybrid action against the employer for breach of contract and the union for violation of its duty of fair representation. The plaintiff had been discharged for stealing. He denied the accusation

---

90. *Id.* at 702, 61 LRRM at 2548.

91. Section 10(b), 29 U.S.C. § 160(b), provides in part: "*Provided* . . . no complaint shall issue based upon any unfair labor practice occurring more than six months prior to the filing of the charge with the Board . . . ."

92. *Supra* note 89, at 703–4, 61 LRRM at 2548.

93. *Id.* at 705 n.7, 61 LRRM at 2549 n.7.

94. 451 U.S. 56, 107 LRRM 2001 (1981).

and filed a grievance that was processed by the union up to the final step of the grievance procedure: a hearing before a grievance committee composed of three union and three company representatives. Its decision upholding the discharge was, under the terms of the collective bargaining agreement, binding on all parties.

Seventeen months later, the plaintiff brought suit under section 301 against both the company and the union. A federal district court granted summary judgment in favor of both defendants on the assumption that the suit was barred by New York's ninety-day statute of limitations for actions to vacate arbitration awards. The Court of Appeals for the Second Circuit reversed, holding that the district court should have applied New York's six-year limitations period for actions alleging breach of contract.[95]

The Supreme Court reversed, holding that the proper limitations period was the ninety days for actions to vacate arbitration awards. Justice Stewart, who concurred in the result, urged that the appropriate statute of limitations was the six-month period prescribed in section 10(b) of the NLRA. He considered the decision in *Hoosier* inapplicable because in *Mitchell* the two elements of the "hybrid action"—the contract claim against the employer based on section 301 and the fair representation claim against the union derived from the NLRA—were "inextricably interdependent."[96] Arguing that when the six-month period provided in section 10(b) has passed the employee should no longer be able to challenge the alleged breach of its duty by the union, Justice Stewart concluded that inasmuch as such a suit is a precondition for suing the employer for breach of contract, an action against the latter should also be foreclosed. The majority refused to consider adopting section 10(b) as the appropriate statute of limitations, however, because none of the parties had presented that argument before either the Supreme Court or the courts below.

Justice Stevens concurred in part and dissented in part, arguing that the plaintiff's suit against the employer was properly barred by New York's ninety-day statute of limitations for actions to vacate arbitration awards, but that the suit against the union was conceptually different and more akin to a malpractice claim.

---

95. Mitchell v. United Parcel Service, Inc., 624 F.2d 394, 105 LRRM 2301 (2d Cir. 1980).

96. *Supra* note 94, at 66–67, 107 LRRM at 2005.

We come, at long last, to *DelCostello* v. *International Brotherhood of Teamsters*,[97] decided by the Supreme Court in 1983. This decision consolidated two cases: the first was an action brought by Del-Costello, who sued his employer, Anchor Motor Freight, for wrongful discharge and his union, the Teamsters, for representing him in the grievance and arbitration procedure, in which the discharge was sustained, in a discriminatory, arbitrary, and perfunctory manner; the second was an action brought by Flowers and another against their employer, Bethlehem Steel, for violating the collective bargaining provisions relating to job assignments and their union, the Steelworkers, for handling the grievance, which was lost in arbitration, in a manner so careless and inept as to be arbitrary and capricious.[98] In *DelCostello* the district court granted summary judgment for both defendants, concluding that the decision in *Mitchell* required application of Maryland's thirty-day statute of limitations for actions to vacate arbitration awards, rather than the state's three-year limitations period for actions on contracts.[99] The Court of Appeals for the Fourth Circuit affirmed.[100] In *Flowers*, a district court in New York also dismissed the complaint against both defendants, holding that the entire suit was governed by New York's ninety-day statute of limitations for actions to vacate arbitration awards. The Court of Appeals for the Second Circuit reversed, however, adhering to its prior holding in *Mitchell* that such actions are governed by New York's six-year limitations for actions on contracts.[101] The Supreme Court granted certiorari and vacated and remanded for consideration in the light of its reversal in *Mitchell*.[102] On remand, the Second Circuit applied the ninety-day arbitration statute and affirmed the dismissal as to the employer, but reversed it

---

97. 103 S. Ct. 2281, 113 LRRM 2737 (1983).

98. On various occasions, the Supreme Court has held union conduct violative of its duty of fair representation if it is "arbitrary, discriminatory or in bad faith," Vaca v. Sipes, *supra* note 8, or if it is shown by substantial evidence to have involved "fraud, deceitful action or dishonest conduct," Humphrey v. Moore, 375 U.S. 335, 348, 55 LRRM 2031, 2037 (1964). *See also* Lockridge, *supra* note 15, and Hines v. Anchor Motor Freight, Inc., *supra* note 16.

99. 524 F. Supp. 721, 111 LRRM 2761 (D. Md. 1981).

100. 679 F.2d 879, 111 LRRM 3062 (4th Cir. 1982) (mem.).

101. Flowers v. Local 2602, United Steelworkers, 622 F.2d 573, 105 LRRM 2304 (2d Cir. 1980) (mem.).

102. United Steelworkers v. Flowers, 451 U.S. 965, 107 LRRM 2144 (1981).

in respect of the union, concluding that the correct statute to apply was New York's three-year statute for malpractice actions.[103]

The Supreme Court decided that the six-month limitations period in the NLRA for filing unfair labor practice charges was the appropriate statute of limitations to apply in actions against both employers and unions for alleged breach of the collective bargaining agreement and of the duty of fair representation. Justice Brennan, for the majority, declared that there was no clear analogy to such actions in state law. Because state statutes of limitations can be unsatisfactory vehicles for enforcing federal law, he observed, in those instances "it may be inappropriate to conclude that Congress would choose to adopt state rules at odds with the purpose or operation of federal substantive law."[104] He distinguished *Hoosier* for the reasons set forth in Justice Stewart's concurrence in *Mitchell*.[105] Although agreeing with the majority position stated in *Mitchell* that the employee's claim against the employer was more analogous to an action to vacate a commercial arbitration award than to a suit for breach of contract, Justice Brennan argued that in a labor setting, the typical employee, unsophisticated in collective bargaining matters and usually represented only by the union, "is called upon, within the limitations period, to evaluate the adequacy of the union's representation, to retain counsel, to investigate substantial matters that were not at issue in the arbitration proceeding, and to frame his suit."[106] He concluded that state limitations statutes for vacating arbitration awards are, typically, too short to provide an employee with a fair opportunity to vindicate rights under section 301 and the fair representation doctrine.

By contrast, Justice Brennan found the limitations period in section 10(b) of the NLRA "actually designed to accommodate a balance of interests very similar to that at stake here—an analogy . . . more apt than any of the suggested state law parallels."[107] Noting that on two previous occasions the Court has refused to decide the correctness of the NLRB's contention that all breaches of the union's

---

103. Flowers v. Local 2602, United Steelworkers, 671 F.2d 87, 109 LRRM 2805 (2d Cir. 1982).

104. 103 S. Ct. at 2289, 113 LRRM at 2740.

105. 451 U.S. at 966-67, 107 LRRM at 2005.

106. 103 S. Ct. at 2291, 113 LRRM at 2742.

107. *Id.* at 2293, 113 LRRM at 2743–44.

duty of fair representation are in fact unfair labor practices,[108] and declining to rule on that question in this case, Justice Brennan argued, nevertheless, that "the family resemblance [between breaches of the duty and unfair labor practices] is undeniable, and indeed there is a substantial overlap."[109] He pointed out, moreover, that violations by an employer of a collective bargaining agreement may also be an unfair labor practice. The justice concluded by conceding, however, that even when there is no "obvious state-law choice for application to a given federal cause of action . . . resort to state law remains the norm for borrowing of limitations periods."[110]

Justices Stevens and O'Connor filed separate dissenting opinions, arguing that the Court should have applied the appropriate state statutes of limitations, namely, those applicable to malpractice suits against attorneys.

I wholeheartedly agree with the Court's decision in *DelCostello*. Justice Brennan chose to relegate to a footnote perhaps the most persuasive argument against the use of state arbitration statutes of limitation when a union's breach of duty consists of a wrongful failure to pursue a grievance to arbitration or a refusal to pursue it through even preliminary stages. In such circumstances, he pointed out,

> [t]he parallel to vacation of an arbitration award seems tenuous at best . . . ; it is doubtful that many state arbitration statutes would themselves cover such a case in a commercial setting. . . . Moreover, the difficulty of detecting and mustering evidence to show the union's breach of duty may be even greater in these situations, and it may not be an easy task to ascertain when the cause of action accrues—obviously a matter of great importance when the statute of limitations may be as short as 30 days.[111]

In addition, Justices Stevens's and O'Connor's argument that a suit for violation of the duty of fair representation is analogous to a suit for malpractice against an attorney seems to me mistaken. Malpractice suits are primarily based on charges of negligence, a standard that I believe is not suitable to apply in many cases to alleged breaches of the duty of fair representation. This is particularly true when a union has processed a grievance to arbitration but has presented it, as alleged in *Flowers*, in a "careless and inept" manner.

---

108. *See* Vaca v. Sipes, *supra* note 8, at 186, 64 LRRM at 2373–74 (1967); Humphrey v. Moore, *supra* note 98, at 344, 55 LRRM at 2035 (1964).

109. 103 S. Ct. at 2293, 113 LRRM at 2744.

110. *Id.* at 2294, 113 LRRM at 2744.

111. *Id.* at 2291 n.16, 113 LRRM at 2742 n.16.

Union representatives are usually not lawyers, and, as I argued in *The Duty of Fair Representation,* they should not be required to observe the same standards of professional competence.[112]

It seems to me, however, that the majority complicated matters unnecessarily by laboring to distinguish *Hoosier* from *DelCostello* on the ground that the latter involved a direct challenge to the private settlement of disputes under a collective bargaining agreement. Both cases, in fact, grew out of a collective bargaining relationship, in respect of which the state statutes of limitation were not really apposite. Whether a suit is for breach of a collective bargaining agreement or for violation of the duty of fair representation, or a combination of both, the application of a uniform federal law seems to me to outweigh the blind adherence to the rule of resorting to state law, which has only the virtue of age to recommend it. I find Justice Stewart's elaborate rationalization for applying that rule in *Hoosier* as unconvincing as his suggested departure from it in *Mitchell* is persuasive. The best statement on the matter, although uttered in another context, is to be found in Justice Goldberg's concurrence in *Humphrey* v. *Moore,* which was quoted by Justice Brennan in *DelCostello:*

> "[I]n this Court's fashioning of a federal law of collective bargaining, it is of the utmost importance that the law reflect the realities of industrial life and the nature of the collective bargaining process. We should not assume that doctrines evolved in other contexts will be equally well adapted to the collective bargaining process."[113]

Concluding Observations

I have refrained from commenting on NLRB decisions concerning DFR, because that is the specific topic of one of the other contributors.

So far as the role of the courts in DFR cases is concerned, I remain unconvinced that they are doing more good than harm. Although, in the absence of proof of a demonstrably better system, I support the principle that employees injured by a union's breach of its DFR should be able to seek redress in the courts, I have concluded, as previously indicated, that the courts, and especially the

---

112. *See* Aaron, *supra* note 1, at 18–24.
113. *Supra* note 98, at 358, 55 LRRM 2031, 2041 (1964).

Supreme Court, have provided no clear guidance as to what constitutes a violation of DFR and have made a real hash of determining the allocation of damages. It is my impression that many others share these views, so perhaps we should be looking for alternative methods to resolve these disputes.

Few, I suspect, would argue strongly against the proposition that unions must do a much better job in representing employees for whom they bargain, especially in those cases in which rival claims based on seniority and ability are advanced by two or more members of the same bargaining unit. The necessity for a union carefully to investigate each claim and weigh it against the others is obvious. If a union fulfills that obligation, however, its ultimate good-faith decision to support one or more claims against others should not be set aside by courts with little or no knowledge of the nature of collective agreements or collective bargaining practices.

Cases of negligence or incompetence fall into two broad categories. In the first category are those in which a union carries a case to arbitration but loses it because of incompetent handling, which some courts, at least, are likely to equate with negligence. It is often argued that union officers generally have no professional training and frequently have had minimal formal education, and that, therefore, they should not be held to professional standards in the presentation of cases in grievance and arbitration procedures. I support that position. The second category consists of those cases in which negligent handling forecloses the grievant's opportunity to obtain a hearing of his grievance on the merits. In such cases I think this argument should not prevail. When, for example, a shop steward loses a grievance or files it too late, it seems clear to me that the union, rather than the employee, must bear the consequential cost. The problem is to determine what that cost is, because it cannot be known whether or not the grievance was meritorious unless and until someone makes a finding to that effect. Thus, I am compelled to conclude that the proven negligent handling by the union of an employee's grievance is a breach of its DFR, even though the damages to the employee may prove to have been minor.

The growing number of so-called hybrid cases, in which an employee sues a union for violation of its DFR and an employer for breach of contract, lends urgency to a reconsideration of the question of damages. Cases such as *Bowen* give impetus to the quest for ways to avoid leaving this matter to the not-so-tender mercies of juries and trial judges.

One proposal, previously rejected by the Supreme Court in *Vaca*, is to vest exclusive jurisdiction of all DFR cases in the NLRB.[114] Presumably, this proposal is based on the not entirely irrebuttable presumption that the Board has greater expertise than the courts in these matters and would render decisions based upon a better understanding of collective bargaining and internal union affairs. To be effective, however, this proposal would require statutory changes, because at present the Board has no power in an unfair labor practice case against a union only and based on its alleged violations of DFR to order full relief that includes action by an employer, such as reinstatement of a discharged employee. Also, as pointed out in *Vaca*, the charging party would be subject to the NLRB general counsel's unreviewable discretion to refuse to institute a complaint.

Another, somewhat less radical proposal assumes no change in the present system that gives the union exclusive control of a grievance and allows the grievant to bring a court action against the union for violation of DFR and against the employer for breach of contract. The change would come if a jury found against the union on the DFR issue. The court would then have to remand the matter to the union with directions to arbitrate the grievance. The objection that in virtually every case the time limit for appealing to arbitration will have expired could be met by treating the time limit not as a jurisdictional barrier to arbitration but as analogous to a statute of limitations, which would be tolled if the grievant filed his lawsuit within a reasonable time after being officially advised by the union that it would not process his case to arbitration. If the arbitrator found that the employer had violated the collective bargaining agreement, he or she could, as usual, determine the appropriate remedy, including reinstatement with or without back pay. All back pay would be payable by the employer, as I think the Supreme Court should have held in *Bowen*. The employer would then have a cause of action against the union to recover costs fairly chargeable to the union because of its violation of DFR. These, as previously indicated, would consist of attorney's fees and other litigation expenses growing out of the plaintiff's suit against the employer.

---

114. *Supra* note 8, at 176–88, 64 LRRM at 2371–76.

Only someone of more sanguine temperament than I will entertain the hope that any improvement in the law of DFR is likely in the near future. Thus, unions will be able to avoid unenlightened treatment at the hands of the courts only by improving their own procedures and taking even more seriously than before their obligations to represent all employees in the bargaining unit as fairly and impartially as they can.

Finally, even if the Supreme Court's decisions in DFR cases have left most of the area in a state of hopeless confusion, the lawyers who argue these cases before the Court must, in fairness, share part of the blame; for it is their responsibility to explicate industrial relations practices, as well as technical points of labor law, and thereby enhance the possibility that the Court's decisions will make sense and seem fair to those who must live with the results.

New Substantive and Procedural Areas

Richard Lipsitz

This chapter is devoted to the more significant new procedural developments in duty of fair representation cases, and it reviews some of the interesting substantive issues expressed in a number of court decisions (not, however, NLRB decisions, except for a limited consideration of some circuit court enforcement proceedings). It also discusses a series of cases that reflect an effort to extend the doctrine to cover what might be described as common law negligence, a substantive development worthy of separate consideration.

Statute of Limitations

The various circuit courts had held that DFR cases are a hybrid of ·breach of contract (by the employer) and tortious conduct (e.g., malpractice, negligence by the union), and therefore are governed by a six-year, a three- or perhaps one-year statute of limitations. Then, in *United Parcel Service Inc.* v. *Mitchell,* the Supreme Court reviewed the Court of Appeals for the Second Circuit decision.[1] That court had decided the New York Civil Practice Law and Rules (CPLR) breach of contract six-year statute was applicable. The trial court had earlier dismissed the complaint, asserting the New York CPLR ninety-day statute to vacate arbitration awards applied.

In *Mitchell,* the Supreme Court decided where a plaintiff in a

---

1. 451 U.S. 56, 107 LRRM 2001 (1981).

DFR case sought relief after an adverse arbitration decision (actually a joint board panel with the same effect), the cause of action was governed by the New York State ninety-day statute of limitations. In arriving at its decision, the Court stated the discharged plaintiff's underlying claim against the employer was, of course, based upon a collective bargaining agreement (breach of contract), but that the "indispensible predicate" for such an action was allegation and proof that the labor union party to such collective bargaining agreement had breached its DFR at the arbitration proceeding. The Court found the lawsuit was analogous to a proceeding to vacate an arbitration award, rather than to a breach of contract action. It rationalized that the American industrial system of self-government, with its heavy emphasis on "grievance, arbitration and the law of the shop," would become quite unworkable if its results were called into question as late as six years afterward.

Thus, *United Parcel Service Inc.* v. *Mitchell* held that a DFR suit against the employer was governed by the applicable state statute governing the vacation of arbitration awards (the defendant union had not sought review of the court of appeals decision). In reversing the court of appeals, however, the Supreme Court majority stated, "we think the district court was correct when it chose the 90-day period imposed by New York for the bringing of an action to vacate an arbitration award."[2]

An amicus brief by the AFL-CIO urged the Court to apply a six-month statute of limitations, based upon section 10(b), National Labor Relations Act. While the majority did not consider this argument, Justice Stewart did in a separate concurring opinion, and he concluded, "[I]n order to safeguard the stability of collective bargaining agreements . . . ," he would have applied that six-month statute, "as the appropriate limitation period for lawsuits such as this."[3]

Then came the long and eagerly awaited decision by the Supreme Court, accepting Justice Stewart's conclusion, *DelCostello* v. *International Brotherhood of Teamsters* and *United Steelworkers of America* v. *Flowers and Jones.*[4] In those companion cases, the question considered by the Court was, What statute of limitations applies in an employee suit against an employer and a union, alleging of course the employer's breach of the collective bargaining agreement and the

---

2. *Id.* at 65, 107 LRRM at 2004.
3. *Id* at 70, 107 LRRM at 2005.
4. 103 S. Ct. 2281, 113 LRRM 2737 (1983; 7-2 decision).

union's breach of the DFR by mishandling an ensuing grievance or arbitration proceeding? In *DelCostello,* a joint committee dismissed the discharge grievance, and the union was powerless to proceed further. The committee's decision was final on December 20, 1977; DelCostello filed suit March 16, 1978, alleging against the union that it had represented him in a discriminatory, arbitrary, and perfunctory manner. The district court granted summary judgment applying a Maryland thirty-day statute of limitations to vacate arbitration awards; the Court of Appeals for the Fourth Circuit affirmed. In *Flowers,* arbitration was invoked by the union. The arbitrator denied the grievance on February 24, 1978, and on January 19, 1979, the lawsuit was filed alleging against the union that its "preparation, investigation and handling [of the grievances were] so inept and careless as to be arbitrary and capricious." The complaint was dismissed by the district court, which concluded the entire lawsuit (against both the employer and the union) was governed by New York State CPLR ninety-day statute of limitations to vacate arbitration awards. The Court of Appeals for the Second Circuit reversed the dismissal, and appeal was taken in Supreme Court. The latter vacated and remanded.[5] Upon the remand, the court of appeals affirmed the dismissal as to the employer because of the ninety-day statute, but reversed as to the union, asserting that the New York State three-year statute for malpractice governed. Certiorari was granted; the Supreme Court held the six-month statute under section 10(b) of the NLRA would be applied.

In arriving at that conclusion after a comprehensive review of the entire problem, the Court observed the obvious, that the suit against an employer is based upon section 301 and against the union for breach of the DFR, "implied under the scheme of the NLRA."[6] Referring to its *Mitchell* decision, the court then observed, "Yet the two claims are inextricably interdependent," and "[t]o prevail against either the company or the union [plaintiffs] must not only show that their discharge was contrary to the contract, but must also carry the burden of demonstrating a breach of duty by the Union"; observing further that a plaintiff may choose to sue one defendant and not the other, the Court, nevertheless concluded ". . . but the case he must prove is the same whether he sues one, the other, or

---

5. 451 U.S. 965.
6. 103 S.Ct. at 2290, 113 LRRM 2741.

both."[7] The Court then expressly rejected its *Mitchell* conclusion that the state statute of limitations to vacate an arbitration award should be applied, because it failed "to provide an aggrieved employee with a satisfactory opportunity to vindicate . . . his rights under §301 and the fair representation doctrine."[8]

It held the section 10(b) six-month statute was applicable, dismissed and reversed *Flowers,* but remanded *DelCostello* because of a factual question of whether or not the six-month statute had been tolled.

While in each case the facts involved postarbitration litigation, apparently under section 10(b) the six-month limitation also applies to prearbitration events, that is, where the union has declined or refused to arbitrate and the cause of action against the union is based upon arbitrary conduct, negligence, or perfunctory handling.[9]

Although the Court did not reach the question of retroactivity,[10] the fact is that the six-month statute was applied retroactively in both cases. We (and no doubt other practitioners) have recently moved for dismissal of a number of preexisting cases based upon *DelCostello* and *Flowers.* In one of them, federal judge John Curtin has directed the parties to brief the question of retroactivity.[11]

Also left undisturbed by the decisions is the Supreme Court's holding in *International Union of United Automobile Workers* v. *Hoosier,* in which the Court held where the union party to a collective bargaining agreement sued the employer party for breach of contract, a six-year Indiana state statute was applicable.[12] In that case, the lawsuit dealt with the alleged employer violation of certain employee va-

---

7. *Id.* at 2291, 113 LRRM at 2742.

8. *Id.*

9. My partners and colleagues unanimously agreed that the result of this decision would be a reduction in the quantum of DFR cases. But the business of predicting is hazardous. Since June 1983, our intake of those cases from labor union clients has accelerated. In spite of the welcome relief granted in DelCostello, the case may have encouraged the filing of lawsuits to accommodate the need to proceed within six months. Perhaps some of these cases would have been forgotten, been forgiven, or simply disappeared if a longer statute of limitation had been applied.

10. 103 S. Ct. at 2287 n.11, 113 LRRM at 2739 n.11 (1983).

11. Johnson v. International Union United Automobile Workers, Civil No. 79-443, U.S. D.C., W.D. N.Y., a pending and as yet, with respect to this issue, unreported decision. Also reported at 641 F.2d 1075, 106LRRM 2688 (2d Cir. 1981), reversing a dismissal against employer and union for failure to exhaust internal union remedies.

12. 383 U.S. 696, 61 LRRM 2545 (1966).

cation rights and damages to employees. Apparently, such suits will continue to be governed by state contract statutes of limitations.

Apportionment of Union and Employer Liability for Damages

In *Vaca* v. *Sipes,* the source of most wisdom in DFR cases, the Court held liability for damages to the wronged employee may be apportioned between the employer and the union.[13] In *Bowen* v. *United States Postal Service,* the Court has instructed us on how this problem will be resolved.[14]

In that case, a special jury verdict in a contract-DFR case, found that plaintiff employee had been wrongfully discharged by the employer and that the union had handled his "apparently meritorious grievance . . . in an arbitrary and perfunctory manner" (at each step of the procedure, the responsible union officer had recommended arbitration, but for no reason apparent on the record, the international office had declined to do so).[15] The Court also found both defendants had acted in "reckless and callous disregard of plaintiff's rights."

Instructing the jury on how to determine the amount of compensatory damages to be awarded and how to apportion liability between the defendants if each were found at fault, the district court judge told the jury it could consider the date of a hypothetical arbitration decision, had the case been taken and the award been positive, and that such date would be the hypothetical time when the employer would have reinstated the employee. Assuming the hypothesis, the court then instructed that the employer would be liable for damages before that date and the union thereafter. The jury found $52,954 damages for lost benefits and wages and apportioned the sum of $30,000 to the union and $22,954 to the employer.

Both defendants appealed. The Court of Appeals for the Fourth Circuit reversed as against the union. Although accepting

13. 386 U.S. 171, 64 LRRM 2369 (1967).
14. 103 S. Ct. 558, 112 LRRM 2281 (1983; 5-4 decision).
15. The jury sat as an advisory panel on the claim against the employer because of a provision at 28 U.S.C. § 2402 that actions of this kind against the United States were to be without a jury. The federal courts have not been uniform with respect to jury trial against unions and nongovernment employers in DFR cases.

the findings of fact, it held as a matter of law that because plaintiff's compensation at all times was payable by the employer, reimbursement of lost earnings continued to be its exclusive obligation, with no portion chargeable to the union. That court relied upon *Vaca* v. *Sipes*.

The Supreme Court reversed, thus reinstating the trial court verdict. It held if the plaintiff's damages were caused initially by the employer's unlawful discharge and were increased by the union's breach of its DFR, apportionment of damages was required by *Vaca* v. *Sipes*. Furthermore, it was not necessary, the Court held, to consider degrees of fault if the trial court found both parties acted in "callous and reckless disregard of plaintiff's rights."

The majority decision read *Vaca* to require apportionment of liability between defendants "according to the damage caused by the fault of each." During an exhaustive review of the relationships among employer, union, and bargaining unit employees, the Court asserted that the grievance procedure requires the union to discharge its duty and responsibility "faithfully" in determining "whether or not to press" grievances, that an employer has a right to rely upon the union's failure to proceed, and that if an employer cannot rely upon a union decision not to proceed, the grievance procedure would not provide the "uniform and exclusive method" for the orderly settlement of employee grievances which has been established as essential to a national labor policy. Requiring the union to pay its share, the court majority asserted, "would provide an additional incentive for unions to process its members' claims where warranted."[16]

Obviously, this decision has verified previously expressed alarm by the labor movement. Indeed, as in *Bowen*, in view of the normal timetable (a relatively short period between discharge and the hypothetical arbitration date but a relatively longer period between that date and a court's decision), the allegedly offending union is necessarily left with the greater obligation, notwithstanding the decision to discharge was exclusively by the employer.[17] The decision may also encourage taking many unmeritorious grievances to arbitration, as an alternative to potential exposure to back pay awards.[18]

---

16. 103 S. Ct. at 597–98, 112 LRRM at 2284–85 (1983).

17. *Id.* at 603 n.7, 112 LRRM at 2291.

18. Naturally, most employer counsel welcome this "sharing." But for the rare case of a union's collusion in a discharge case, however, only the employer controls

The Court, however, did offer one consoling comment: even though the union may primarily be liable for increasing damages resulting from its failure, that does not absolve the employer from liability. Thus, the court asserted if plaintiff could not collect damages from the union, the employer remained secondarily liable.[19]

Finally, the Court suggested a union might limit or minimize its liability "if it realized it had committed an arguable breach of duty," by bringing "its default to the employer's attention."[20] Presumably, once the lawsuit has been commenced and the union client concludes, with or without advice of counsel, that perhaps there is merit to it, it should demand arbitration, even though time limits have expired. In due time, judges and juries will no doubt consider whether that should have a positive effect, as to the union's apportionment. A number of international unions have so advised.

Effect of Internal Union Appeals Procedures

The traditional wisdom and widely accepted view, at least until *Clayton* v. *UAW* has been that precedent to a section 301 DFR suit the offended employee must attempt to exhaust any internal union procedures provided by the union constitution.[21]

In *Clayton*, the union pursued the discharged employee's grievance to the last step in the grievance procedure, requested arbitration, but then withdrew the request. The plaintiff was not notified until after the time for requesting arbitration had expired.

The UAW's constitution contains a comprehensive procedure for aggrieved members against union officers and representatives.[22] But plaintiff declined to use those procedures and instead

---

continued employment. The union may default, but nothing prevents the employer, at any time, from conceding its error and arranging with the union to reinstate the discharged employee, to promote the senior employee, and so forth. And what about the employees whose rights might then be prejudiced? The answer is simple—the parties may at any time properly adjust grievances.

19. 103 S. Ct. at 595 n.12, 112 LRRM at 2286 n.12 (1983).

20. *Id* at 597, 112 LRRM at 2287.

21. Clayton v. UAW, 451 U.S. 677, 107 LRRM 2385 (1981; 5-4 decision).

22. At least one circuit court decision, Johnson v. General Motors and United Auto Workers, has characterized those procedures, whether accurately or not, as being surrounded by confusion. For obvious reasons, I disagree. I represented the UAW in the case.

commenced his action against the union and the employer. Consistent with the traditional view, the district court dismissed the lawsuit for failure to exhaust internal union appeals procedures. The Court of Appeals for the Ninth Circuit affirmed against the union, but reversed against the employer, holding the failure to exhaust was fatal to the claim against the union, because the result might have been the receipt of money damages, the relief he sought against the union. In reversing as to the employer, however, that court held the suit against the employer was not barred because the union procedure could not result either in reinstatement to his job, which he sought, or in reactivating his grievance, which would have had the potential of providing reinstatement.

The Supreme Court reversed the circuit court decision as against the union and affirmed its decision reversing the dismissal against the employer, holding that where an internal union appeals procedure cannot result in reactivation of the employee's grievance or in an award of the complete relief sought, exhaustion of internal union remedies will not be required with respect to either the suit against the employer or against the union.

Notwithstanding the established line of cases to the contrary, the Court emphasized the impossibility of the procedures providing the relief sought (reinstatement) and established three tests: (1) whether the union officials are so hostile that plaintiff could not hope to obtain a fair hearing during the internal procedures, (2) whether those procedures would be inadequate either to reactivate the grievance or to afford plaintiff full relief, and (3) whether exhaustion of internal procedures would unreasonably delay plaintiff's ability to obtain a jurisdictional hearing.

If any one of these tests is met, a trial court may properly excuse an employee's failure to exhaust internal union remedies.[23]

---

23. The UAW has a contractual agreement with General Motors Corporation and other employers for reinstatement of grievances. It provides that in situations in which one of the appropriate bodies, including the Public Review Board, finds that as a result of one of the internal procedures a grievance has been disposed of improperly by the union, the union may inform the employer that the grievance is reinstated in the step at which it was abandoned. The agreement also provides certain monetary protection to the employer where that occurs and also limits the employee's ability to use court or administrative agency procedures to pursue the claim for damages against the employer.

Limitation of Monetary Awards

Perhaps the only unadulterated good news is found in *IBEW* v. *Foust*.[24] The Supreme Court reversed the Court of Appeals for the Tenth Circuit, which had affirmed a punitive damage award against a union found at trial to have breached its DFR by failing to file a grievance within the sixty-day time limitation and thereby finalizing the employee's discharge. The court of appeals noted that punitive damage is appropriate if the union had acted "wantonly, or in reckless disregard for the grievant's rights."[25]

The Supreme Court flatly held that punitive damages may not be assessed against a union which breached its DFR by failing properly to pursue a grievance.[26] Based upon a long line of decisions, including *Vaca*, and its view that the national labor policy was to compensate, not to punish in such cases, the Court found that the purpose of relief is to make the injured employee whole. Punitive damages, the Court correctly observed, might deter future misconduct, but the reasons for such policy are outweighed by the distinct possibility that, given the nature of the relationship and the presumed sympathy with the individual plaintiff, unpredictable and potentially substantial punitive awards would impair financial stability of unions, a result adverse to the national interest in collective bargaining. The prospect of punitive damages, the court stated, quite possibly would undermine the broad discretion that union's presently have in handling and disposing of grievances. For these and other similar reasons, the Court concluded that punitive damages may not be assessed against a union that breaches its DFR properly to pursue a grievance.[27]

---

24. 442 U.S. 42, 101 LRRM 2365 (1979; 5 join for majority, 4 concur on the result).

25. In my judgment, failure to file within time limits (especially if these are adequate) that results in an otherwise meritorious grievance being neither heard nor arbitrated is an objective standard for labor union misconduct. At risk of offending clients and fellow labor union practitioners, if the record can establish that this failure was purposeful and done with full awareness of the merits, an employee should be able to maintain an effective argument that some punishment other than simple reimbursement for damage would be warranted.

26. Although this case arose under the Railway Labor Act, the decision is clearly applicable to other DFR cases.

27. Ironically, in Bowen the Court recognized it was correctly protecting defendant unions in Foust, but nevertheless, came to the conclusion that compensatory

Standards of Conduct: Arbitrary, Neglectful and Perfunctory

Before trial in the Northern District of California, in *Dutrisac v. Caterpillar Tractor Co.*, the trial court granted summary judgment for one of the plaintiffs against the defendant union, but after trial, on the wrongful discharge claim against the employer, found there had been good cause for the discharge and dismissed that portion of the complaint.[28]

Notwithstanding, the defendant union was ordered to pay all legal costs and attorney's fees as damages resulting from the breach of the DFR.

The facts were simple and undisputed. Plaintiff was discharged February 10, 1978, and filed a grievance asserting it was racially motivated; defendant union processed his grievance at the appropriate step, and the union representative was notified the grievance was rejected, which notice began a thirty-day period within which to request arbitration. The union representative asked plaintiff several times to supply him with certain information with regard to the prospective arbitration, but he failed to. Nevertheless, a decision was made by union officers to submit the grievance to arbitration. In fact, it was submitted two weeks late. The arbitrator ruled the grievance was untimely and, therefore, not arbitrable. The trial court found and the record established that the union representative had no animus towards plaintiff and that the failure to request arbitration in a timely manner was an "inadvertent omission" (nor was the dischargee's failure to provide requested information relevant to the

---

damage awards "normally will be limited and finite [and] moreover the union's excuse of discretion is shielded by the standard necessary to prove a breach of the dfr." 103 S.Ct. at 597 n.16, 112 LRRM 2287 n.16. I suggest an inherent inconsistency between the rightful concern expressed in Foust, notwithstanding the facts in that case are as egregious as one might imagine (absent an outright concession that the failure to submit to arbitration was to punish the employee) and the court's rationalization in Bowen that compensatory damages "normally will be limited and finite." We are not enlightened by any explanation by any of the meaning of those terms as expressions of discharge damages. May not the finite and limited damages of a thirty-five- year-old plaintiff be based upon at least thirty years of expected employment? While finite, the limitations are rather broad instead of narrow.

28. 511 F. Supp. 719, 107 LRRM 2195 (N.D. Cal. 1981). Dutrisac was one of two plaintiffs. He did not participate after his portion of the complaint was dismissed by the trial court; but the case title continued with his name.

delay in filing). The union's representative simply had no explanation for going beyond time limits.

On its appeal, the union asserted the failure was mere negligence and, in any event, that it did not prejudice plaintiff employee, because his claim of an unjust discharge was found after trial to be nonmeritorious.

The Court of Appeals for the Ninth Circuit decision in *Dutrisac* of July 1983 appears, in that circuit at least, to be an expansion of the arbitrary standard previously prevailing: an unexplained and unexcused mistake or failure to act may constitute a breach of the DFR. Earlier, in *Robesky* v. *Qantas Empire Airways, Ltd.* that court held an unintentional mistake was arbitrary if it reflected "reckless disregard" for the rights of the individual employee, but not if it reflected simple negligence, violating the common law tort standard of due care.[29] In that case, the failure to tell the plaintiff the union was not willing to take the case to arbitration led plaintiff to reject a settlement offer she otherwise would have accepted.

In *Dutrisac*, however, after noting that the standard for determining when an unintentional mistake by a union official should be considered arbitrary was still evolving and that most decisions finding simple negligence insufficient involved alleged errors in the union's evaluation of the merits of a grievance, its presentation of the grievance at arbitration, or its interpretation of a collective bargaining agreement (all matters of judgment), the court concluded, "the union should be responsible for total failure to act that is unexplained and unexcused." Because of its concern that broadening the DFR duty regarding negligence might weaken unions financially and impair their ability to function effectively, the court limited its holding that union negligence may breach the DFR "to cases in which the individual interest at stake is strong and the union's failure to perform a ministerial act completely extinguishes the employee's right to pursue his claim." The court found the facts in *Dutrisac* to include such a case. It also observed that notwithstanding the employee's failure against the employer, it was not a frivolous claim, as indeed the union itself had determined to submit it to arbitration.

Thus, that court was unable to agree the employee was not prejudiced, for the arbitrator may have decided differently from the

---

29. 573 F.2d 1082, 98 LRRM 2098 (9th Cir. 1980).

court on the merits, or the grievance may have been settled, had the union's omission not completely extinguished the right to pursue the claim. The court indicated it probably would have reversed if the record had supported a conclusion the underlying claim was "so meritless as to be frivolous."

The award of damages against the union, essentially attorney's fees, was based upon the fact that the need for legal representation was in fact the harm done to the employee, a cost he would not have had to incur but for the union negligence.

This present view of the Ninth Circuit is a minority. But in attempting to delineate the confines of the arbitrary or perfunctory standards of *Vaca* v. *Sipes* (a union "may not arbitrarily ignore a meritorious grievance or process it in a perfunctory fashion"), some of the circuits have in effect held as the Ninth in *Dutrisac*; that is, a negligent failure to act which is unexplained and unexcused may be actionable. Thus, in *Journeymen Pipefitters Local 392* v. *NLRB,* the Sixth Circuit denied enforcement of an NLRB order that the union violated sections 8(b) (1) (A) and 8(b) (2) by breaching its DFR by an unexplained modification of hiring hall procedures, about which it failed to inform members or prospective applicants to the procedure.[30] Nevertheless, that same court has consistently reiterated that its governing standard of breach of the DFR was articulated in the three *Ruzicka* v. *General Motors Corporation* cases (*Ruzicka I, Ruzicka II,* and *Ruzicka III*).[31]

While Ruzicka was ultimately defeated in his claim, that court of appeals did assert that union action that is arbitrary or perfunctory need not be motivated by bad faith to be a violation of the DFR and that "when a union makes no decision as to the merits of a grievance, but merely allows it to expire by negligently failing to take the basic and required step towards resolving it, the union has acted arbitrarily and is liable for a breach of its duty of fair representation."[32]

The Tenth Circuit in *Foust* v. *IBEW,*[33] reversed by the Supreme Court only on the issue of punitive damages, held that a failure to file a discharged employee's grievance within the specified contrac-

---

30. 712 F.2d 225, 113 LRRM 3500 (6th Cir. 1983).
31. Respectively, 523 F.2d 306, 90 LRRM 2497 (6th Cir. 1975); 649 F.2d 1207, 107 LRRM 2726 (6th Cir. 1981); and 707 F.2d 259, 113 LRRM 2562 (6th Cir.1983). Limitations of time and space preclude a detailed discussion of these cases.
32. Ruzicka I, 523 F.2d at 310, 90 LRRM at 2500
33. 572 F.2d 710, 97 LRRM 3040 (10th Cir. 1978).

tual period was sufficient to find a breach of DFR, because such conduct is within the arbitrary or perfunctory standard of *Vaca* v. *Sipes*.

A district court in the Second Circuit, without, however, directly discussing the concept as one of negligence, has held that a negligent failure to process a grievance in a timely fashion is the kind of arbitrary and perfunctory conduct that amounts to a DFR violation.[34] In that case, the union had simply lost the record of the grievance, as a result of which it was not timely filed.

In *Harris* v. *Schwerman Trucking Company*, the Eleventh Circuit noted that neither negligence on the part of the union nor a mistake in judgment is sufficient to support a claim that the union acted in an arbitrary or perfunctory manner and that "nothing less than a demonstration that the union acted with reckless disregard for the employee's rights, or was grossly deficient in its conduct will suffice to establish such a claim."[35] It noted, however, a claim "the union acted perfunctorily requires a demonstration that the union ignored the grievance, inexplicably failed to take some required step or gave the grievance merely cursory attention." This is equivalent to the Ninth Circuit standard in *Dutrisac*. In *Harris*, the plaintiff complained about the quality of the union's advocacy during a grievance hearing, claiming the representation was inept and ineffective. The court stated those allegations do not constitute an appropriate standard by which to evaluate a claim of perfunctory conduct. When considering the quality of a union's representation at a grievance or arbitration hearing, the court observed, those procedures are not conducted in a judicial forum and "union representatives are not held to strict standards of trial advocacy . . . [and] that the union representative is not a lawyer and he cannot be expected to function as one."

Implicit in most of the related decisions is that even where the courts reject negligence as an appropriate standard, they nevertheless are willing to hold a union responsible for what may only be characterized as a negligent procedural default, without any explanation, or in the absence of a valid explanation, which in turn prejudices the grievant by leaving the employee without a remedy.[36]

---

34. Reid v. New York Metro Area Postal Union, 109 LRRM 3065 (S.D. N.Y. 1982).

35. 668 F.2d 1204, 109 LRRM 3135 (11th Cir. 1982).

36. *See* Connally v. Transcon Lines, 583 F.2d 199, 203, 99 LRRM 3102, 3104 (5th

Some circuit courts, however, have not been willing to go that far. Thus, the Seventh Circuit in *Hoffman* v. *Lonza, Inc.* refused to hold the union liable where it simply permitted the grievance to be terminated by failing to file a timely notice to arbitrate.[37] The court held there had to be a showing of intentional union misconduct causing harm, in other words, a bad faith standard.[38]

In *Wyatt* v. *Interstate & Ocean Transport Company*, the court held the DFR claim may not be predicated on simple negligence, but "a union representative could be so indifferent to the rights of members or so grossly deficient in its conduct purporting to protect the rights of members that the conduct could be equated with arbitrary action."[39]

Obviously, one of these days the differences, inconsistencies, and disparities pointed out here will be resolved by the Supreme Court. In the meantime, while simple negligence, not the result of any invidious motive, may normally not be actionable, if it involves an unexplained failure to comply with time limits, as a result of which all employee rights are extinguished, labor unions do face jeopardy.

This is indeed a perplexing aspect of the DFR problem; but certainly a reasonable argument may be made that unions have at least a minimum obligation to avoid such neglectful acts, a burden which is hardly a difficult one, and over which the innocent employee obviously has no influence. By contrast, bad or negligent advice, failure to act as capable advocate, failure fully to investigate and prepare, are layperson frailties for which, most of the courts have quite correctly observed, a union should not be held responsible, certainly not in the absence of proof the failures are motivated by animosity, or some other improper cause.

Cir. 1978); Findley v. Jones Motor Freight, 639 F.2d 953, 958–61, 106 LRRM 2420, 2422–23 (3d Cir. 1981); Curtis v. United Transportation Union, 700 F.2d 457, 112 LRRM 2864 (8th Cir. 1983); Freeman v. O'Neal Steel Inc., 609 F.2d 1123, 1127, 103 LRRM 2398, 2401 (5th Cir. 1980); and Grovner v. Georgia-Pacific Corp., 625 F.2d 1289, 105 LRRM 2706 (5th Cir.1980), *cert. denied,* 449 U.S. 833.

37. 658 F.2d 519, 108 LRRM 2311 (7th Cir. 1981).

38. To the same effect, *see* Dober v. Roadway Express, Inc., 707 F.2d 292, 113 LRRM 2595 (7th Cir. 1983) (negligence even when gross does not violate the DFR); Superczynski v. PTO Services, Inc., 706 F.2d 200, 113 LRRM 2402 (7th Cir. 1983) (a union member must prove the union deliberately failed properly to pursue his claim); and United Steelworkers of America v. NLRB, 692 F.2d 1052, 111 LRRM 3125 (7th Cir. 1982).

39. 623 F.2d 888, 104 LRRM 2408 (4th Cir. 1980).

Competing Employee Interests

Many courts have examined the DFR obligation in the context of conflicting or competing employee interests, during collective bargaining and also during grievance and arbitration. Those conflicts obviously exist within a bargaining unit, e.g., younger employees contend with older employees over whether to negotiate additional wage increases or to bargain for increased pension benefits. While the majority usually will be accomodated, that is not always so.

Some courts have dealt with the issue arising from the application of collective bargaining provisions for promotions that are based upon seniority and a number of other factors. Unions naturally place greater emphasis on seniority than on the others. Conflict arises, of course, where a junior employee is promoted and a senior employee grieves. What then is the obligation of the union to the senior, if in fact the junior may be the more qualified?

Several years ago, the Eighth Circuit considered this dilemma in *Smith* v. *Hussmann Refrigerator Co.*[40] In that decision, fairly widely criticized by writers and commentators, the court sitting en banc reviewed a U.S.D.C., E.D., Missouri, decision that set aside a jury's verdict in favor of three bargaining unit employees who had sued, alleging the usual hybrid and also alleging race discrimination. The court of appeals held the evidence was sufficient to support the jury's verdict that the union had breached its DFR with regard to grievances arising under a seniority provision, and also that the employer had. Accordingly, the court substantially vacated the lower court decision.

In the complaint, plaintiffs asked for money damages and also for affirmative injunction relief, to be awarded the several promotions to the various vacancies involved. The pertinent collective bargaining agreement typically provided, "Seniority, skill and ability to perform the work required shall be considered by the Company in making promotions, transfers, layoffs and call-backs. Where skill and ability to perform are substantially equal, seniority shall govern." During April 1975, the employer posted two openings in temporary positions for maintenance pipefitters. Sixty-four employees bid, and two of the plaintiffs were selected; however, they were not

---

40. 619 F.2d 1229, 103 LRRM 2321 (8th Cir. 1980), *cert. denied*, 449 U.S. 839, 105 LRRM 2657 (1980).

the senior employees. In May 1975, when an opening was posted for permanent maintenance pipefitter, forty-six employees bid and one of those two plaintiffs was again selected. Later in May, two more openings arose, and the third plaintiff was awarded a temporary position as maintenance pipefitter. Twenty-six of the unsuccessful bidders grieved alleging violation of their seniority rights; the union selected four grievances filed by employees with greater seniority than the successful bidders and presented these to the grievance procedure and thence to arbitration. At the arbitration hearing, each grievant was present and testified regarding skill and ability; the plaintiffs were not invited to attend, and their interests were advanced only by the employer, which defended the selections. The arbitrator denied two of the grievances, upheld two, and directed the employer to place the two successful grievants in pipefitter positions; but the arbitrator apparently added those to the four involved in the facts preceding the grievances, the three awarded to the three plaintiffs and one other not involved in the lawsuit. The union informed the employer it objected to the award because the arbitrator asserted authority to create two more maintenance pipefitter jobs. Thereafter, union and employer representatives met to discuss those problems arising from the award and subsequently, agreeing only four employees should be in the classification, removed two of the plaintiffs and retained one. "Then," as the court described it, "ostensibly to seek 'clarification' of the award they returned to the arbitrator," who scheduled another meeting. No additional testimony was taken, and no employees were present. The parties informed the arbitrator of their postaward agreement, and he issued a supplemental award incorporating that agreement.[41]

In its decision, the court of appeals held that the DFR is breached if a union represents senior employees against junior employees without also representing the interests of the successful junior employees, an obligation that required the union, the court said, to evaluate their comparative merits.

> The collective bargaining agreement clearly provided that employees promoted by the company on the basis of superior skill and ability are entitled to hold their promotions, even against challenges by employees with greater seniority. Thus, plaintiffs possessed rights under the collective bargaining agreement that the union had a fiduciary duty to protect.
>   . . . The nature of the union's duty in a dispute among employees is not

---

41. While other relevant facts were involved, this summary adequately describes in substance what occurred.

changed by the company's taking a position in the grievance procedure. Even though a company may take a position favorable to a particular group of employees, the union may not abandon that particular group to the representation as afforded by the company favoring them. . . . The union is the agent of all employees in the unit and owes a fiduciary duty to represent their interests and rights under the collective bargaining agreement. Here the union not only abandoned the plaintiffs but took an adversary attitude towards them regarding the positions they received by reason of the company's opinion of their skill and ability. . . . The union's choice to process all grievances based on seniority discriminated against employees receiving promotions on the basis of merit. This conduct may be viewed as a perfunctory dismissal of the interests and rights of plaintiff. The union simply failed to represent them in any way. . . . Disregard for the qualification of superior skill and ability could manifest an arbitrary and perfunctory approach to promotion interests, as could ignoring the qualification of seniority or selection by the company.[42]

The court also asserted the DFR is breached if an employee is prejudiced by not having notice of the hearing at which the union "inadequately prepared or presented such employee's interests." The fact that the employer may have represented the plaintiff's interests does not overcome the absence of the performance of the duty by the union."[43]

Three months later, the employer petitioned for a rehearing which was denied. The court, however, did modify and summarize its en banc decision by asserting, "the evidence failed to establish that the union breached its duty of fair representation to plaintiffs at the first arbitration hearing by advocating the promotion of employees senior to appellants."[44]

But on the rehearing denial, the court went on to say, "the subsequent collaboration between the employer . . . and the union for the purpose of obtaining a modification of the previous arbitration award, without notice or opportunity to junior employees [plaintiffs] to protect their rights operated to deprive appellants of valuable employment rights and constituted sufficient evidence in this case for a jury to decide that the union had breached its duty of fair representation to appellants and that the company had breached its collective bargaining agreement."[45] Thus, while seeming to back away from

---

42. 619 F.2d at 1238–39, 103 LRRM at 2327–28.

43. *Id.* at 1241–42, 103 LRRM at 2329.

44. *Id.* at 1253, 103 LRRM at 2976. This statement is clearly in direct contradiction to the very strong views stated by the court in the en banc decision.

45. *Id.* These words succinctly explain why most union attorneys in these cases seek to avoid jury trials.

the original concept regarding the union's duty to the successful junior employees, the court, nevertheless, asserted a union obligation to notify and provide an opportunity to the junior employees to protect their rights, the absence of which constituted breach of the DFR.

Earlier in *Buchholtz* v. *Swift & Co.*, the same court held a union did not breach its DFR, when, after a plant closing, grievances were filed by certain employees for vacation pay and the union then negotiated certain pension benefits for active, longer seniority employees, but in return gave up the vacation pay claims.[46] The employees claiming vacation pay did not participate in the settlement agreement. They commenced an action against both parties asserting that the trade of their claim for benefits to the older active employees was a breach of the DFR and also that the employer had breached the agreement by failing to pay their vacations. Obviously, this decision more completely comports with the accepted union view that the DFR obligation is to do what is in the best interests of the bargaining unit, even though some employees may be hurt in the process.

Union Liability for Unsafe Workplace

In the last fifteen years or so, several courts have considered a developing theory that a provision in a collective bargaining agreement regarding the union function in workplace safety creates some kind of obligation by the union to the bargaining unit employees to perform whatever is expected of it under such a provision. In instances in which the union fails its obligation, the cases are pleaded in terms of a common law negligence action against the union.[47] But in adjudicating some of these claims, some courts have more accurately dealt with them in terms of the DFR obligation; fortunately, from

---

46. 609 F.2d 317, 102 LRRM 2219 (8th Cir. 1979), *cert. denied,* 444 U.S. 1018, 103 LRRM 2143 (1980).

47. Because in some jurisdictions workers' compensation statutes act to prohibit negligence suits against employers by providing workers' compensation as the exclusive remedy, lawsuits have been brought against unions whose collective bargaining agreement contains some safety or responsibility language and have alleged a negligence tort or failure of the DFR. Some of the defendent unions have then moved to bring the employer into the lawsuit as a third-party defendant, on the theory that if the union is held responsible, then the union has a claim against the employer, which has the primary obligation to provide a safe workplace. This explains why employers that might otherwise not be sued have sometimes been involved in these lawsuits.

the union view, the cases have been substantially more unsuccessful than the contrary.

In one of the earlier cases, *Brough* v. *United Steelworkers,* when the plaintiff was injured at the workplace, he sued the employer and the union in a New Hampshire state court, claiming failures by the employer safety advisers subjected the employer to negligence liability, and by the union, which by contract was entitled to a safety committee.[48] The union removed the case to federal district court, claiming any duty to plaintiff was a DFR obligation. The lawsuit against the union was dismissed upon summary judgment motion. The court of appeals asserted that any duty by the union was based upon a DFR obligation, "not a general duty of due care."[49]

Shortly thereafter, the Court of Appeals for the Sixth Circuit, decided *Bryant* v. *United Mine Workers.*[50] In that case, the collective bargaining agreement provided for a mine safety committee that included union members and that

> may inspect any mine development or equipment used in producing coal. If the committee believes conditions found endanger the life and bodies of the mine workers, it shall report its finding and recommendations to the management. In those special instances where the committee believes an immediate danger exists and the committee recommends that the management remove all mine workers from the unsafe area, the operator is required to follow the recommendation of the committee.

The survivors of a number of miners killed by an explosion commenced litigation against both the employer and the union. The plaintiffs asserted that the union undertook a duty to enforce compliance with safety standards and that, having failed to do so, the failure led to a "foreseeable result" that the deceased might then become injured or killed.[51] The district court granted summary judgment in favor of the employer and union; the plaintiffs appealed only from the denial of relief against the union. In analyzing the complaint, the court stated that the plaintiffs in part had advanced the breach of the DFR duty as a theory in the complaint. "Of course the union is not without responsibility toward its members with re-

---

48. 437 F.2d 748, 76 LRRM 2430 (1st Cir. 1971).

49. *Id.* at 750, 76 LRRM at 2431.

50. 467 F.2d 1, 81 LRRM 2401 (6th Cir. 1972), *cert. denied,* 410 U.S. 930, 82 LRRM 2597 (1973).

51. For those not acquainted with tort law, these are words usually used to connect acts (or nonacts) with the consequent injury, a relationship required to prove negligence.

gard to the safety program. . . . This duty includes the obligation to enforce fairly the provisions of any collective bargaining agreement." But the court also asserted, "It would be a mistake of vast proportion to read every power granted the union by management as creating a corollary contract right in the employee as against the union. Such interpretation of collective bargaining agreements would simply deter unions from engaging in the unfettered give and take negotiation which lies at the heart of the collective bargaining agreement." Referring to the precise language creating the mine safety committee, however, the court commented that plaintiffs "contended that this language places a duty to inspect upon the local and International Unions. We do not accept this contention. The use of the permissive 'may' rather than obligatory language in the clause clearly negates the possibility that any duty was to be created." It concluded that "[T]o saddle labor unions with standards introduced into the contract at the union's bidding would simply be to discourage the inclusion of similar or more effective standards in later contracts. Such result would not serve the interest of miners. . . ."[52] It affirmed dismissal against the union.

In a lower court case, *Higley* v. *Disston, Inc.*, a State of Washington court held that a union member may not successfully maintain an action based upon the DFR breach if he or she claimed that the union's alleged negligent failure was to discover and correct unsafe working conditions that led to the injury.[53] In that case, a provision of the collective bargaining agreement provided for a union-employer safety committee, which had general powers to investigate and make recommendations regarding unsafe working conditions. The court held such a provision did not create a duty of reasonable care leading to liability because of a failure to perform as vigorously as it might have, notwithstanding the failure to discover and correct the condition that led to the plaintiff's injury.

Plaintiffs have been unsuccessful in a number of other cases in an effort to sustain similar claims: *House* v. *Mine Safety Appliances Co.* was a third-party complaint by defendant employer dismissed when the court held exclusive duty owed by union to bargaining unit employees with respect to safety provisions in collective bargaining agreement was based upon the DFR obligation, which was not vio-

---

52. 467 F.2d at 5–6, 81 LRRM at 2403–4.
53. 92 LRRM 2443 (Wash. Super. Ct., King Co. 1976).

lated, and the court denied union responsibility for common law negligence tort;[54] *Brooks* v. *N.J. Manufacturers Ins. Co.* held that an injured employee may not maintain action against a union for breach of its DFR obligation because union representatives on plant safety committee were negligent in failing to report and remedy the defective machine that caused injury, in absence of proof of arbitrary, discriminatory, or bad faith conduct;[55] in *Szatkowski* v. *Turner and Harrison, Inc.*, a federal district court remanded the case to state court where the claim by the injured employee was that a dangerous condition resulting from union negligence to perform its duty to inspect the work area resulted in his injury was a pleading of common law negligence (the fact that "the duty of care arises from a contract does not alter the fact that the negligent performance of this duty may give rise to an action in tort");[56] *Burgess* v. *Allendale Mutual Ins. Co.* found no breach of the DFR obligation to an employee injured in a work-related accident despite the contention that the union negligently performed safety condition and inspections, that is, a breach of that obligation does not constitute breach of DFR;[57] *Condon* v. *Local 2944, United Steel Workers* asserted that a union cannot be held liable for negligent performance of a duty it assumed from the health and safety provisions of a collective bargaining agreement and that the DFR is breached only when union conduct is arbitrary, discriminatory, or in bad faith.[58]

In one significant decision, however, *Helton* v. *Hake,* the court sustained a cause of action by survivors of a deceased employee alleging, under Missouri common law, that a union is responsible in tort for its negligent and careless failure to enforce safety rules set forth in a collective bargaining agreement and that a tort may be committed in the nonobservance of contractual duties.[59] If one is committed and does result in death, the court held a survivor may sue under the state's wrongful death statute. The court also held that the cause of action was not preempted under any federal statute, that the union firmly obligated itself by contract when it agreed

---

54. 417 F. Supp. 939, 92 LRRM 3688 (D. Idaho 1976).
55. 103 LRRM 2136 (N.J. Super. Ct., App. Div. 1979).
56. 109 LRRM 2609 (S.D. N.Y. 1982).
57. 111 LRRM 2997 (S.D. Ga. 1982).
58. 683 F.2d 590, 110 LRRM 3244 (1st Cir. 1982).
59. 564 S.W.2d 313, 98 LRRM 2905 (Mo. Ct. App. 1978), *cert. denied*, 439 U.S. 959, 99 LRRM 3033 (1978).

the union steward "shall see that the provisions of these working rules are complied with," and that under the particular collective bargaining agreement, the safety responsibility assumed by the union was separate and distinct from the normal and usual duties involved in the handling of grievances.

The collective bargaining agreement provided in part, "There shall be no work done in the immediate area of high tension lines until the power has been shut off, or the lines insulated, or the safety of the members of bargaining unit otherwise provided for." In the same article, the parties agreed that the union steward would "see that the provisions of these working rules are complied with and report to the Union the true conditions and facts. He shall report the injury of any employees to the proper officers of the Union." Based upon those provisions, the plaintiff's lawsuit asserted a duty was created that the union steward and the union would safeguard the employees from the power line adjacent to the workplace and that the failure to perform that duty constituted a tort for which recovery should be had under the wrongful death statute. A jury trial was held and a verdict returned in favor of plaintiffs against the union and the steward.

Primarily because of the particular language of the provisions, the court, in affirming the judgment in favor of plaintiffs commented,

> We can readily agree that when a union assumes only an advisory capacity with respect to safety and the enforcement of safety regulations so far as the union is concerned is limited to only the usual grievance machinery, then the union is carrying out purely a representative function on behalf of its members and should be limited in its responsibility to performing that representation in a fair and honest manner. In such case, the safety situation would be no different from the many cases cited by defendants where a union has been charged with failure [to perform the DFR].

The court continued,

> Here, however, the Union has chosen to go far beyond a mere advisory status or representative capacity in the processing of grievances. Rather, it has taken over for itself a managerial function, namely the full independent right to enforce safety requirements. With its demand for and successful acquisition of that management right, it must also accept the concomitant responsibility. . . . the safety responsibility assumed by the Union is separate and distinct from the normal and usual duties of a

purely representative nature such as those involved in the processing of grievances.[60]

Thus, that court held the union's duty was one based upon tort but not, under the circumstances of the contractual language, on fair representation.

I have selected these cases because, in spite of what appears to be the consensus that only if a tort is proved, may a union be held liable for a failure with regard to safety conditions or inspections, plaintiffs continue to plead, in part, that the obligation is also an element of the DFR, and if negligently carried out creates that liability. Although accompanied by the usual lack of success, the lawsuits continue to be filed and the theory pursued.

Conclusion

Although predictions are hazardous business, probably most of the federal DFR law has been decided, subject to clarification by the Supreme Court of the standards of conduct constituting DFR negligence and perfunctory handling.

Some international unions, some employer associations, and some commentators are concerned and have expressed the need for congressional action removing the DFR from the authority of the courts and placing it with the NLRB. While I make no brief for the right to use the courts in DFR cases, given the present composition of the National Labor Relations Board and its increasingly proemployer orientation, perhaps some of the crumbs from that feast may be enjoyed by the class of union defendants in DFR cases, should exclusive authority in those cases be given to the Board. One can be certain, however, in that event that the slight opportunity for plaintiffs to be successful will be extinguished unless, of course, the influence of *Bowen* on the Board creates a method for holding the union more responsible when, in fact, the original sin is almost always committed by the employer.

---

60. *Id.*, 98 LRRM 2910.

Exhaustion of Internal Union Remedies after *Clayton* and *Bowen*

David Y. Klein

Those who champion plaintiff's rights in duty of fair representation (DFR) litigation have been the beneficiaries of a double dose of assistance from the United States Supreme Court in a period of a little more than one and one-half years. In April 1981, the Court held in *Clayton* v. *UAW* that the defense of nonexhaustion of internal union remedies would be available only where the remedies provided under the union's constitution could grant "full relief" or reactivate the grievance.[1] Then in 1983, the Court held in *Bowen* v. *U.S. Postal Service* that the trial court in a section 301–duty of fair representation proceeding may apportion back pay liability between a litigant's employer and his union.[2]

The ramifications of these two decisions for those who customarily defend unions and employers in duty of fair representation litigation are substantial. This chapter discusses these ramifications and explores appropriate responses for unions and employers faced with existing or potential duty of fair representation claims.

---

1. 451 U.S. 679, 107 LRRM 2385 (1981).

2. Bowen v. United States Postal Service, 103 S. Ct. 588, 112 LRRM 2281 (1983). It has not been all milk and honey for plaintiffs, however, for in the same period in United Parcel Service, Inc. v. Mitchell, 451 U.S. 56, 107 LRRM 2001 (1981), the Court held that a suit brought under section 301 can most closely be analogized to an action to vacate an arbitration award. Then, just two years later the Court again reexamined the issue, this time concluding that the appropriate limitations period is provided by section 10(b) of the National Labor Relations Act, which established a six-month period for submitting charges of unfair labor practices, including DFR claims, to the NLRB. DelCostello v. Teamsters, 103 S. Ct. 2281, 113 LRRM 2737 (1983). The result has been the dismissal of scores of DFR claims.

While there may not be agreement among trade unionists as to the meaning of the term "duty of fair representation," few, if any, would disagree with the proposition that a trade union does have a responsibility to represent its members fairly. That there is a remedy for the breach of the duty was first definitively established in *Steele* v. *Louisville and Nashville Railroad*,[3] a case arising under the Railway Labor Act[4] that involved claims of racial discrimination. Since that time, the concept that there is a remedy at law for breaches of the duty has been expanded to include claims arising under section 301 of the Labor Management Relations Act and charges filed with the National Labor Relations Board, alleging violations of section 8(b) of the act.[5]

In *Republic Steel Corporation* v. *Maddox,* the Supreme Court held that an employee who seeks to sue his or her employer for a breach of the collective bargaining agreement must first attempt to exhaust contractual grievance procedures before filing an action against his or her employer for breach of the collective bargaining agreement.[6] That requirement is contingent upon the agreement's including a grievance and arbitration procedure. The Court concluded that sidestepping grievance procedures in favor of litigation would deprive the parties of the ability to establish a uniform and exclusive method for orderly settlement of employee grievances. Allowance of a procedure's nonexclusivity would thus result in loss of its desirability as a settlement method. Such a situation, the Court said, "would inevitably exert a disruptive influence upon the negotiation and administration of collective agreements."[7]

The prerequisite of exhausting contractual remedies before initiating a section 301 suit applies equally to the plaintiff union as to the plaintiff individual.[8]

In *Vaca* v. *Sipes,* the Court recognized two exceptions to the exhaustion of contractual remedies requirement. The first occurs

---

3. 323 U.S. 192, 15 LRRM 708 (1944).

4. 45 U.S.C. § 101.

5. 29 U.S.C. § 185(a). The Board has held that section 7 of the act gives employees the right to be free from unfair or irrelevant or invidious treatment by the bargaining agent in matters affecting their employment. *Miranda Fuel Co.,* 140 NLRB 181, 51 LRRM 1584 (1962), *enf. denied,* 326 F.2d 172, 54 LRRM 2715 (2d Cir. 1963).

6. 379 U.S. 650, 58 LRRM 2193 (1965).

7. *Id.* at 653, 58 LRRM at 2194.

8. Mail Handlers, Local 305 v. U.S. Postal Service, 594 F.2d 988, 100 LRRM 3211 (4th Cir. 1979).

"when the conduct of the employer amounts to a repudiation of . . . contractual procedures." A second exception results when the employee plaintiff has been prevented from exhausting his contractual remedies by the union's wrongful refusal to process the grievance. Accordingly, the Court held that a wrongfully discharged employee may bring an action against his employer in the face of the defense based upon the failure to exhaust contractual remedies, provided the employee can prove his union breached its duty of fair representation in the handling of his grievance.[9]

The Court stated the duty of fair representation is breached only when a union's conduct toward its members "is arbitrary, discriminatory, or in bad faith." The Court recognized that while an individual employee does not have an absolute right to have his grievance taken to arbitration regardless of the provisions of the applicable collective bargaining agreement, "a union may not arbitrarily ignore a meritorious grievance or process it in a perfunctory fashion. . . ."[10]

The types of conduct that have been deemed to violate the standards established by *Vaca* are not within the scope of this paper, but conduct that can best be described as negligent,[11] or that which is so acutely perfunctory that the collective bargaining agent fails to attain a basic level of acceptable performance has been found to fall within the penumbra of the standard.[12] It is sufficient to observe that the volume of litigation involving claims of the breach of duty of fair representation has been steadily increasing and that most of these have been hybrid section 301–DFR claims arising out of discharge situations.

The requirement that in order for an employee to sue his or her employer for breach of a collective bargaining agreement, the employee must first prove that the union breached its duty of fair representation in turn created a second exhaustion issue, that is, the exhaustion of internal union remedies. Frequently, the constitution of a union will require that a member first resort to the system of internal remedies provided under the union's constitution before proceeding against the union in a civil court.[13] The courts of the vari-

---

9. 386 U.S. 171, 185, 64 LRRM 2369, 2374–75 (1967).

10. *Id.* at 191, 64 LRRM at 2376–77.

11. Ruzicka v. General Motors Corp., 523 F.2d 306, 90 LRRM 2497 (6th Cir. 1975).

12. Hoffman v. Lonza, Inc., 658 F.2d 519, 108 LRRM 2311 (7th Cir. 1981).

13. *See,* UAW Const. art. 33, § 12 (1977), which provides, "It shall be the duty of

ous circuits split on the question of whether an employee could be required to exhaust internal remedies before instituting a section 301−DFR claim.[14] This issue was resolved by the Court in *Clayton* v. *UAW*.

Clayton Case

In *Clayton*, the Court held "that where an internal union appeals procedure cannot result in reactivation of the employee's grievance or an award of the complete relief sought in his §301 suit, exhaustion will not be required with respect to either the suit against the employer or the suit against the union."[15] The Court rejected the contention of the parties that the exhaustion of a union's internal procedures, like the exhaustion of contractual and arbitration procedures, would further national labor policy, would enable unions to regulate their internal affairs without undue judicial interference, and would promote the broader goal of encouraging private resolution of disputes arising out of the collective bargaining agreement.

The Court noted that it had previously held that the courts have discretion to decide whether to require exhaustion of internal union procedures.[16] It held that in exercising that discretion at least three factors are relevant: first, whether the union officials are so hostile to the employee that he could not hope to obtain a fair hearing on his claim; second, whether the internal union appeals procedures would be inadequate either to reactivate the employee's grievance or to award him the full relief he seeks in his section 301 claim; and third, whether exhaustion of internal procedures would unreasonably delay the employee's opportunity to obtain a judicial hearing on the merits of the claim. If any of these factors is found to exist, the Court said a court may properly excuse the employee's failure to exhaust.[17]

---

any member or subordinate body who feels aggrieved by any action, decision, or penalty imposed upon him or it, to exhaust his or its remedy and all appeals therefrom under the laws of this International Union prior to appealing to a civil court or governmental agency for redress."

14. Johnson v. General Motors, 641 F.2d 1075, 1083, 106 LRRM 2688, 2693 (2d Cir. 1981); Geddes v. Chrysler Corp., 608 F.2d 261, 264, 102 LRRM 2756, 2758 (6th Cir. 1979); Petersen v. Rath Packing Co., 461 F.2d 312, 315, 80 LRRM 2833, 2835 (8th Cir. 1972); Retana v. Apartment, Motel, Hotel, and Elevator Operator's Union, 453 F.2d 1018, 1027 n.16, 79 LRRM 2272, 2278 n.16 (9th Cir. 1972).

15. 451 U.S. at 685, 107 LRRM at 2387.

16. NLRB v. Marine Workers, 391 U.S. 418, 68 LRRM 2257 (1968).

17. Clayton, *supra* note 15, at 689, 107 LRRM at 2389.

It is perhaps somewhat ironic that the defendant union in *Clayton* was the UAW. The UAW is generally acknowledged to have one of the more democratic systems of internal remedies of any North American labor organization,[18] including resort to the union's Public Review Board, comprised of seven "impartial persons of good public repute not working under the jurisdiction of the UAW or employed by the International Union or any of its subordinate bodies."[19] The board has authority to make final and binding decisions on all cases appealed to it,[20] including jurisdiction over appeals involving collective bargaining grievances where the appellant "has alleged before the International Executive Board that the matter was improperly handled because of fraud, discrimination or collusion with management, or that the disposition or handling of the matter was devoid of any rational basis."[21] Furthermore, the union's contracts with employers that employ a majority of the union's members contain provisions that do provide for the reinstatement of grievances if directed as a result of the prosecution of an internal union appeal.[22]

Nevertheless, the Court was critical of the relief that could be afforded under the UAW's system of internal remedies. Part of the rationale advanced by the Court of Appeals for the Ninth Circuit in support of its conclusion that exhaustion should be required of plaintiff Clayton is contained in its comment that the UAW's liability, if any, for breach of its duty of fair representation would depend upon the reasons for the union's withdrawal of the arbitration request. The circuit court noted there was little in the record to indicate why the union's local official changed his mind and withdrew the grievance, but it continued, "The missing motive is precisely the sort of information that an appellate body within the Union would elicit, compiling a record that would greatly assist the Court now."[23]

The Supreme Court, however, criticized this reasoning. First, it noted the union's letter to Clayton, advising him of the withdrawal

---

18. *Cf.*, J. Stieber, W. Oberer, and M. Harrington, Democracy and Public Review —An Analysis of the UAW Public Review Board (Center for the Study of Democratic Institutions 1960).

19. UAW Const. art. 32, § 1 (1980).

20. *Id.*, art. 32, § 3(a).

21. *Id.*, art. 33, § 4(i).

22. *See*, Clayton, *supra* note 15 at 691 n.18, 107 LRRM at 2389 n.18.

23. Clayton v. ITT Gilfillan and UAW, 623 F.2d 562, 566, 104 LRRM 2118, 2119 (9th Cir. 1980).

of his grievance had in fact listed five reasons in support of its decision. But the Court continued, "Since the UAW Constitution does not on its face require any of the decision making panels of the Union to explain the reasons underlying their disposition of an employee's internal union appeal, there is no guarantee that exhaustion will result in a useful interpretation of union rules."[24] The Court noted the restrictions on the jurisdiction of the Public Review Board, stating that it could consider only allegations that the employee's grievance was improperly handled because of fraud, discrimination, or collusion with management. The Court observed, "This standard offers the aggrieved employee less protection than the single 'arbitrary, discriminatory, or in bad faith' standard for breach of the duty of fair representation that we developed in *Vaca vs. Sipes*." The Court concluded its analysis by stating: "Of course, if an allegation cannot be considered by the Public Review Board, no record helpful to a court will be made with respect to that issue. In sum, we conclude that the prospect that exhaustion would create a record helpful to a court in a subsequent §301 action is too speculative to be given much weight."[25]

The jurisdictional standard of the Public Review Board over grievances has been expanded from that considered in *Clayton* to include claims that the handling or disposition of grievances was "devoid of any rational basis."[26] It remains true, however, that the constitution does not require a reviewing panel, including the Public Review Board, to state the reasons for its decision. Whether the expanded grievance appeal jurisdiction allowed to the Public Review Board would have influenced the Court in its analysis is doubtful, at best. In any event, the issue is now academic. Exhaustion will be required only where it can result in the provision of the same relief as sought in section 301 litigation or in the reinstatement of the employee's grievance.

The UAW's collective bargaining agreement with ITT Gilfillan, the defendant employer in *Clayton*, did not contain a provision providing for the reinstatement of collective bargaining grievances. The Court concluded, therefore, that the union's appeals procedure could not result in the reinstatement of Clayton to his job or in the

---

24. 451 U.S. at 693–95 n.24, 107 LRRM at 2390 n.24.
25. *Id.; id.* at 694–95, 107 LRRM at 2391.
26. UAW Const. *supra*, art. 33, § 4(i).

reactivation of his grievance. Accordingly, the Court stated, "The re-lief available through the internal UAW procedures render those procedures inadequate." Clayton had conceded that the UAW's in-ternal procedures were fair and, because of its conclusion as to the inadequacies of the remedies available, the Court did not consider the question of whether the appeals procedure would unreasonably delay the employee's opportunity to obtain a judicial hearing on the merits of his claim.[27]

Decisions since Clayton

Since the issuance of the *Clayton* decision in June 1981, there have been fourteen decisions, reported as of August 30, 1983, in which the claim of failure to exhaust internal union remedies was raised as a defense to an action asserting a breach of the duty of fair represen-tation. All arose out of discharges of the plaintiff employees. Eight of these cases involved the UAW.[28] Of the other six, three involved the Teamsters,[29] and the other three involved the United Trans-portation Union, the Sheet Metal Workers International Associa-tion, and the International Association of Machinists, respectively.[30]

The results obtained in these cases are significant. In all eight of the cases involving the UAW, the motions of the defendants for summary judgment were granted. In each instance, the union's agreement with the employer contained a provision for reinstate-ment of an employee's grievance when directed as the result of the prosecution of an internal appeal. But in the other six cases, only three motions were granted[31] while the other three were denied.

---

27. 451 U.S. at 691–92, 107 LRRM at 2390.

28. Miller v. General Motors Corp., 675 F.2d 146, 110 LRRM 2281 (7th Cir. 1982); Gomez v. Auto Workers, 109 LRRM 3356 (E.D. Mich. 1981); Robins v. Gen-eral Motors Corp., 112 LRRM 2441 (S.D. Ohio 1982); Monroe v. UAW, 113 LRRM 2490 (S.D. Ohio 1982); Nesbitt v. International Harvester, 112 LRRM 3446 (W.D. Tenn. 1982); Hardesty v. Essex Group, Inc., 113 LRRM 2690 (N.D. Ind. 1982); Maine v. General Motors Corp., 111 LRRM 2492 (D. Kan. 1982); Shadday v. Interna-tional Harvester, 112 LRRM 3439 (S.D. Ind. 1983).

29. Tinsley v. United Parcel Service, 635 F.2d 1288, 109 LRRM 2035 (7th Cir. 1981); Rupe v. Spector Freight Systems, 679 F.2d 685, 110 LRRM 3205 (7th Cir. 1982); McKinley v. Kalex Chemical Products, Inc., 108 LRRM 3148 (C.D. Cal. 1981).

30. Rader v. U.T.U., 112 LRRM 2861 (N.D. Ala. 1982); Frenza v. Sheet Metal Workers, 113 LRRM 2619 (E.D. Mich. 1983); Schultz v. Owens Illinois and IAM, Dis-trict 9, 696 F.2d 505, 112 LRRM 2181 (7th Cir. 1982).

31. Tinsley v. United Parcel Service, McKinley v. Kalex Chemical Products, Inc., Rader v. U.T.U., *supra* note 29.

Furthermore, two of these three cases in which motions for summary judgment were granted apparently were based upon a misreading of *Clayton*.[32] Therefore, discounting the two cases that seem to have been incorrectly decided, the results in the other six cases involving unions other than the UAW, the score would stand five-to-one against requiring exhaustion.

The decisive factor in each case where the defense of nonexhaustion of internal remedies was rejected was the court's finding that reinstatement of the grievance could not be obtained as a remedy through resort to the union's internal appeals procedure. The remaining case in which nonexhaustion was successfully asserted as a defense involved the United Transportation Union and arose under the Railway Labor Act under which the employee has the right to go forward with his grievance, including arbitration of that grievance, in the event that his union declines to arbitrate his claim.[33] The removal of the grievance reinstatement issue led the Court to conclude that the plaintiff could have attained complete relief through resort to his intraunion procedures.

Responses to Clayton

When preliminary research indicated that the UAW is faring much better than most other unions in defending against duty of fair representation suits on the basis of asserting as a defense the nonex-

---

32. In Tinsley *supra* note 29, the Seventh Circuit Court affirmed the granting of summary relief by reason of failure to exhaust internal remedies. "[B]ecause Tinsley limited the relief he sought against both the Union and UPS to monetary damages, [citation omitted], the complete relief sought in his § 301 suit was available through the Union appeals procedures." 635 F.2d at 1291, 109 LRRM at 2037. Tinsley had actually sought reinstatement through the grievance procedure. However, the UPS/Local 710 joint grievance committee had advised Tinsley that he would not be reinstated, and the Union declined to submit his grievance to binding arbitration. In his United States district court action, Tinsley sought only damages. Later in Rupe v. Spector Freight Systems, *supra* note 29, the Court overruled its analysis of the exhaustion requirement as stated in Tinsley, noting that Rupe could not have achieved reactivation of his grievance through his resort to his internal union remedies. 679 F.2d at 690, 110 LRRM at 3208. McKinley v. Kalex Chemical Products, Inc., *supra* note 29, also involved the Teamsters Union. In that case, the California district court concluded exhaustion of internal remedies was required, citing the first decision of the Seventh Circuit in Tinsley v. UPS, *supra*, which contained a similar analysis by the Seventh Circuit Court of the exhaustion requirement or that set forth in its second Tinsley decision, later overruled.

33. Rader v. U.T.U., *supra* note 29 (referring to 45 U.S.C. § 153). *Cf.* Andrews v. Louisville and Nashville Railroad, 406 U.S. 320, 80 LRRM 2240 (1972).

haustion of intraunion remedies, I thought it would be useful to survey other unions to determine what response, if any, they were contemplating in light of *Clayton* and its progeny.[34] Accordingly, I sent a letter to the legal departments of all 396 labor organizations listed in the *Directory of U.S. Labor Organizations,* 1982–83 edition, published by Bureau of National Affairs, inquiring whether *Clayton* had stimulated an effort to negotiate reinstatement clauses in their collective bargaining agreements. Thirty-seven unions responded (see Appendix). Of the unions responding, seven indicated that they were still in the process of formulating a policy in response to *Clayton.* Two stated they had attempted to negotiate reinstatement clauses, but without success. Eleven unions stated they have not attempted to negotiate reinstatement clauses and did not plan to do so. Six unions stated that while they have not attempted to negotiate reinstatement clauses, they do plan to do so. Six unions stated that duty of fair representation claims have not been a problem to them. Five unions stated they regarded the reinstatement of grievance issues to be matters for local union consideration. Five unions stated that their system of internal remedies did not provide for appeals involving the disposition of collective bargaining grievances. Finally, three unions stated that they had informal arrangements for the reinstatement of employee grievances, which were usually honored. (For lists of unions giving specific responses, see Appendix).

Of those unions responding that they had not attempted and do not intend to attempt to negotiate reinstatement provisions, several advanced special reasons for their positions. The AAUP observed that grievance processing in higher education tends to have a special character, since peer review grievance mechanisms are often in place even in the absence of collective bargaining. Counsel for the American Flint Glass Workers Union advised that the union's system of internal remedies is not applicable to the disposition of grievances under collective bargaining agreements, and stated that, in his opinion, a provision for the reinstatement of grievances in a collective bargaining agreement would encourage internal appeals, many frivolous. He pointed out that the decision to withdraw a grievance must be made by the international union; local unions do not have this authority. The National Association of Broadcast Employees and

---

34. It would have been of equal interest to obtain the viewpoints of employers; however, I could think of no feasible way of contacting a representative cross section.

Technicians stated that while it did not contemplate negotiating re-instatement clauses, the union intended to be very careful to make sure that each member would receive "his day in court."

On the other hand, the National Treasury Employees Union stated that negotiation of reinstatement clauses is a "major goal" of the union's pending negotiations. Farm Workers' counsel advised that the Farm Workers had a special problem resulting from a recent decision of the California Agricultural Labor Relations Board that UFW members need not exhaust internal union remedies, which includes an appeal to the union's Public Review Board, before the institution of DFR claims with that board. Counsel did indicate that there were special considerations in the Farm Workers association since loss of good standing in the union can result in loss of employment. He indicated that the Agricultural Labor Relations Board decision had been appealed and that he anticipated the case would go to the California Supreme Court, and possibly the U.S. Supreme Court.

Conclusion

It is apparent from the volume of cases reported that litigation based upon claims of an alleged breach of the duty of fair representation are increasing each year. It would seem reasonable to conclude that the Supreme Court's decision in *Bowen* may further stimulate such litigation, since it is now clear there are two defendants who are answerable for monetary damages, including lost wages. It is altogether probable that unions that have not heretofore experienced problems with duty of fair representation claims will in the future encounter such claims with increasing frequency, although unions and employers operating under the Railway Labor Act will not likely find themselves more extensively involved with section 301–DFR claims, regardless of *Bowen* and *Clayton*. This will likely be true, too, for unions and employers operating in such industries as the building trades, in which grievances are a comparative rarity and grievances involving discharge are rarer still.

For unions that are extensively involved in DFR litigation, however, it is apparent that a system of internal remedies that is fair, expeditious, and can result in the provision of the relief available to a plaintiff in a section 301–DFR proceeding or in the reinstatement of a member's grievance will substantially increase chances of successfully defending against DFR claims on the basis of the failure to exhaust internal appeal procedures. Likewise, employers whose collective bargaining contracts contain reinstatement provisions will be able to continue to assert successfully as a defense in section 301–DFR litigation the failure of the plaintiff to exhaust internal union remedies.

Appendix

July 22, 1983

Att: Legal Department

Dear Sirs/Madams:

The purpose of this communication is to elicit information concerning the policies of your union as respects duty of fair representation cases following the issuance of *Clayton vs. Automobile Workers*, 451 U.S. 679, 107 LRRM 2385 (1981). The question with which I am particularly concerned relates to the holding of the court in *Clayton* that:

> "We conclude that the policies underlying Republic Steel are furthered by an exhaustion requirement only where the internal union appeals procedures can either grant the aggrieved employee full relief or reactivate his grievance. . . . If the internal procedures are not adequate to effect that relief, the employee should not be required to expend time and resources seeking a necessarily incomplete resolution of his claim prior to pursuing judicial relief." (107 LRRM 2391)

I will be presenting a paper at a duty of fair representation conference this fall sponsored by the New York State School of Industrial and Labor Relations of Cornell University. What I am attempting to find out is how many unions have attempted to respond to the *Clayton* decision by writing into their collective bargaining agreements a clause that would provide for the reinstatement of an employee's grievance should the employee ultimately prevail during the course of an internal union appeal. It would seem clearly to be in the best interest of both the employer and the union to include in their collective bargaining agreement a clause permitting reintroduction of withdrawn grievances following the successful prosecution of an internal appeal. Certainly, cost considerations alone in defending duty of fair representation suits would seem to support this conclusion.

It is perhaps ironic that *Clayton* should have involved the UAW since that Union for several years now has had agreements with most of the major employers with whom it bargains to reinstate into the grievance procedure grievances previously withdrawn should the aggrieved employee be successful at any stage of his internal appeal in persuading the union that his grievance should not have been withdrawn. In three such cases, the Public Review Board has directed the Union to reinstate an employee's grievance, and to submit that grievance to arbitration.

For example, in a Letter of Understanding between the UAW and Ford Motor Company dated October 5, 1976, the Union and the Company agreed that where, as a result of the submission of an appeal by an aggrieved member of the Union, it is determined by the International Executive Board, the

Public Review Board or the Constitutional Convention Appeals Committee that the disposition of a grievance was improperly concluded by the Union body or representative involved, the grievance may be reintroduced into the procedure. The Letter of Understanding further provides that the Company will not be liable for back pay claims from the time of disposition of the grievance until the time of its reinstitution.

Do your collective bargaining agreements negotiated either before or since *Clayton* contain any similar provision? If not, does your union contemplate negotiating similar clauses in the future? If the answers to both of these questions are negative, I would be interested in learning whether to your knowledge your union has considered the issue.

I would appreciate very much your responding to these questions, or receiving any additional comments you may wish to make.

Thank you for your help and cooperation.

Sincerely,
David Y. Klein
Executive Director
Public Review Board
UAW

Responding Unions

An alphabetical listing of the responding unions follows:

Airline Employees Association
Airline Pilots Association
Aluminum, Brick and Glass Workers International Union
American Association of University Professors
American Federation of State, County and Municipal Employees
American Flint Glass Workers Union
American Postal Workers Union
Association of Flight Attendants
Brotherhood of Locomotive Engineers
Brotherhood of Railway, Airline and Steamship Clerks
Freight Handlers Express and Station Employees
Brotherhood of Railroad Signalmen
Glass, Pottery, Plastics and Allied Workers International Union
Graphic Communications International Union
International Association of Firefighters
International Brotherhood of Electrical Workers
International Longshoremen's Association
International Longshoremen's and Warehousemen's Union
Maryland Classified Employees Association
Mechanic's Educational Society of America
Montana Public Employee's Association

National Association of Broadcast Employees and Technicians
National Association of Postal Supervisors
National Education Association
National Treasury Employees Union
Operating Engineers International Union
Service Employees International Union
Transport Workers Union of America
United Association of Journeymen and Apprentices of the Plumbing and Pipe Fitting
    Industry of the United States and Canada
United Farm Workers of America
United Furniture Workers of America
United Paper Workers International Union
United Mine Workers of America
United Rubber, Cork, Linoleum and Plastic Workers of America
United Steel Workers of America
United Textile Workers of America
United Transportation Union

Responses

Still formulating policy: American Postal Workers Union; Graphic Communications International Union; Service Employees International Union; United Mine Workers; Rubber, Cork, Linoleum, Plastic Workers of America; United Textile Workers of America; United Transportation Union.

Unsuccessful in negotiations: Airline Employees Association; United Paper Workers International Union.

No plans to negotiate: Airline Pilots Association; Aluminum, Brick and Glass Workers International Union; American Association of University Professors; American Flint Glass Workers; Brotherhood of Railroad Signalmen; International Brotherhood of Electrical Workers; International Longshoremen's Association; Mechanic's Educational Society; National Association of Broadcast Employees and Technicians; United Association of Journeymen and Apprentices of the Plumbing and Pipe Fitting Industry of the United States and Canada; United Furniture Workers.

Plan to negotiate: Association of Flight Attendants; International Longshoremen's and Warehousemen's Union; Montana Employee's Association; National Treasury Employees Union; Transport Workers Union.

DFR suits not a problem: Airline Employees Association; American Association of University Professors; Brotherhood of Locomotive Engineers; Brotherhood of Railroad Signalmen; United Mine Workers; United Steel Workers.

Reinstatement is a local issue: American Federation of State, County and Municipal Employees; International Association of Firefighters; International Brotherhood of Electrical Workers; Mechanic's Educational Society; International Union of Operating Engineers.

No grievance appeal provision: Airline Pilots Association; American Flint Glass Workers; International Brotherhood of Electrical Workers; United Association of Journeymen and Apprentices of the Plumbing and Pipe Fitting Industry of the United States and Canada; United Steel Workers.

Informal grievance reinstatement: Brotherhood of Railway, Airline and Steamship Clerks, Freight Handlers, Express and Station Employes; Montana Public Employees Association; United Transportation Union.

The Duty in
the Public Sector

Harold R. Newman

In the predecessor to the present volume, *The Duty of Fair Representation,* the discussion of the public sector was embodied within Benjamin Aaron's general overview: "The application of the duty of fair
representation is somewhat different in the public sector." He hy-
pothesized

> [t]hat when the bargaining representatives in the public sector do achieve
> the same power . . . that is exercised by their private sector counterparts
> . . . they should be held subject to the same duty of fair representation.[1]

It is fair to say that by now the Aaron hypothesis has proven itself.
Even a cursory examination of the reported cases reveals that employee organizations representing public employees are held to at
least a substantially similar, if not identical, standard of conduct vis-
à-vis their unit constituency as that governing their private sector
counterparts. So, too, the fact patterns triggering the litigation in the
public sector trace those prevailing in the private sector.

Along with this similarity in law and fact, the public sector generally faces many of the same problems as affect the private sector.
If there is any difference in this regard, it is that our problems are
accentuated by the somewhat different context in which the duty in
the public sector takes place. For example, litigants appearing be-

---

The invaluable research and editorial assistance of John M. Crotty, Esq., are
gratefully acknowledged—H.R.N.

1. B. Aaron, *The Duty of Fair Representation: An Overview,* in The Duty of Fair Representation 16 (J. T. McKelvey ed., New York State School of Industrial and Labor
Relations, Cornell University 1977).

fore my agency the Public Employment Relations Board (PERB), are typically unrepresented, inexperienced individuals. They are unfamiliar with legal procedures generally and accept with difficulty, and usually not at all, the limited extent of substantive review of an organization's conduct. Moreover, there is only a very limited sifting of the meritorious claims from the frivolous. New York has no prosecution system similar to the general counsel. There is only a limited factual review conducted on receipt of an improper practice charge—which is processed free of charge—and unless the charge fails to state a cause of action on its face, the litigant is entitled to proceed to some disposition of the charge.[2]

These factors, and others, have contributed to the growth of the litigation, the source of the complaint most commonly expressed and one shared by we who labor for government. As evidence of the staggering growth, consider that although a few references to the doctrine can be found earlier,[3] it was not until 1977 that the groundswell of litigation in New York began.[4] In the five-year period since, PERB staff members and I and my colleagues on the board have combined to issue more than 125 formal decisions in cases specifically alleging a breach of an organization's duty of fair representation (DFR), with the majority of these decisions concentrated in 1981 and 1982. This number represents only those cases actually litigated and does not include those that were voluntarily withdrawn or settled or that raised a fair representation claim only tangentially. It is estimated that fair representation cases now account for approximately 20 percent of our yearly case load, and I would imagine, without attempting any scientific verification, that this experience is typical of the docket in other jurisdictions. The

---

2. PERB's Rules of Procedure, 4 NYCRR 204.2, require a determination on receipt of the charge as to whether "the facts as alleged may constitute an improper practice." The charge is dismissible at this point only if "the facts as alleged do not, as a matter of law, constitute a violation."

3. Plainview–Old Bethpage CSD, 7 PERB ¶ 3058 (1974); DeCherro v. CSEA, Inc., 60 App. Div. 2d 743, 400 N.Y.S.2d 902 (1977); Jackson v. Regional Transit Service, 54 App. Div. 2d 305, 388 N.Y.S.2d 441 (1976); Gosper v. Fancher, 49 App. Div. 2d 674 (1975), aff'd, 40 N.Y.2d 867, 356 N.E.2d 479, 94 LRRM 2032 (1976), cert. denied, 430 U.S. 915, 94 LRRM 2798 (1977). See also, Kaufman v. Goldberg, 64 Misc. 2d 524 (Sup. Ct. Kings Co. 1979).

4. It was that year that PERB first "defined" the duty. In Brighton Transportation Assn., 10 PERB ¶ 3090 (1977), the board indicated that the duty is breached by conduct that is improperly motivated, grossly negligent, or irresponsible. Accord, Nassau Educational Chapter, CSEA, Inc., 11 PERB ¶ 3010 (1978).

practitioners among you can perhaps attest to the accuracy of this statement more readily than I.

Given this overwhelming wealth of precedent, it is difficult to establish either a starting or ending point for discussion of the case law. This particular topic is heavily analyzed, and it is not my intention to reexamine issues that have been subjected to extensive analysis already. Indeed, persons better suited to this task than I have offered their insights, legal and personal, into general and specific principles established by the cases. Given the similarity in standards and fact patterns noted, their comments are equally applicable and useful to any analysis of the duty in the public sector. The pros and cons of easing or tightening the organizations' standards of conduct have also been debated extensively. Nonetheless, I am faced with the realization that if my intention to avoid duplication were followed slavishly, I would have to close at this point. Although I understand the brevity might be welcome, the importance of the topic commands slightly lengthier analysis.

In reviewing the literature and case reports, I observed that although there is no shortage of cases or legal critique, there is little discussion of the possible causes for that litigation or the future trends in the development of the duty in either sector of the economy. At the risk of ignoring a consideration of others, I have chosen two aspects of litigation that currently have more significance to the public than private sector.

The first aspect is the effect of union security provisions on the development of DFR litigation.

Effect of Union Security Provisions

As noted, the burst of litigation in New York began suddenly in 1977 and has continued to grow. I do not believe it merely coincidental that 1977 was also the year in which an agency fee authorization was enacted in New York State.[5] This belief that union security

---

5. N.Y. Civ. Serv. Law, ¶ 208.3(a) & (b) (McKinney 1983). Representatives of state employees are entitled to a deduction from the salary of nonmembers equal to its dues. Organizations representing other employees are entitled to negotiate for such a deduction. A refund procedure is required by both subdivisions to permit a nonmember to object to the expenditure of fees for "activities or causes of a political or ideological nature only incidentally related to terms and conditions of employment."

arrangements prompt fair representation litigation is contrary to a basic assumption underlying the traditional rationale voiced by the proponents of the legislation. It is argued that with the financial stability that flows from an obligation imposed on all in the unit to contribute to the costs of representation, organizations will be able to deal with any and all issues on their merits.[6] Organizations, it is argued, would no longer have to be subjected to suit by persons who had good claims left unresolved simply because pursuit of their rights was too expensive.

This rationale—union security provisions might substantially reduce the number of claimed breaches of duty by eliminating one of the underlying causes for complaint—is mistaken for a few reasons. It may be true that, at times, an individual's meritorious claims go unpursued simply because the organization lacks the financial resources to proceed. But these occasions represent only a small percentage of the total complaints filed and are confined mainly to the independent representatives of small units. The argument also overlooks the dynamics and reality of employment, particularly in the public sector. Persons who do not pay for services rendered may content themselves to accept the contractual benefits without question. The imposition of a charge for that service, however, has a natural tendency to increase the level of expectation, and that which may have been acceptable when free is satisfactory no longer. What is common to all employment becomes acute in the public sector because its work force in large part consists of professional, white-collar employees who are more likely and perhaps better able to voice and demand enforcement of their rights.

These observations are not offered as a rationale for opposition to union security provisions. I am not against union security clauses and believe they advantage both union and employer. These observations are made, rather, because public sector union security legislation is new and spreading. DFR litigation should be recognized, particularly by the organizations subjected to the suits, as a likely consequence of the enactment of union security provisions. Benefits rarely are free, and this one appears clearly to have exacted its price.

I would like to move now from cause to trend.

---

6. For a summary of the arguments, *see*, Hanslowe, Dunn & Erstling, Union Security in Public Employment: Of Free Riding and Free Association. Institute of Public Employment Monograph No. 8 (New York State School of Industrial and Labor Relations, Cornell University 1978) at 6–8.

Extent of the Duty

There is no longer, if there ever was, any question that the bargaining agent owes a duty to all unit personnel in the negotiation and administration of the collective bargaining contract. The majority of cases filed still involve alleged breaches of the duty in these areas, particularly the processing of grievances to arbitration. While there is no doubt of the significance of these cases to the particular parties, resolution of this type of case is primarily a factual matter, involving little development of new law or expression of new policy.

There is, however, a new line of cases brought, in New York at least, largely by nonmember, agency fee payers. These test the traditional rationale of the case law and question whether the contract defines the extent of the union's duty to the individual. Questions have been raised as to whether and to what extent a duty of fair representation should be applicable in areas other than negotiation and administration of the contract. Given the myriad civil service laws and regulations governing the employment relationship in the public sector and the universal expansion of union membership programs and benefits, the opportunity to test the length and breadth of the duty is expansive.

A few cases will identify the trend and its development thus far. Although the cases cited are drawn from New York for convenience, the developing case law is not confined to any one state.

It is established in New York that the duty is not limited only to the enforcement of the terms of the contract at least if employment benefits or services are otherwise offered by the union to its members. In *United Federation of Teachers* (*Barnett*), a charge was brought by a nonmember alleging that his bargaining agent had denied him representation at a noncontractual job-rating review proceeding, although representation was given to the union's members.[7] The organization defended its refusal to represent the nonmember on the ground, inter alia, that it was privileged to deny representation because the service was not rendered with respect to a procedure grounded upon the contract. The defense was rejected on the finding that an adverse determination on review could affect the employee's entitlement to a salary increase. Since the review procedure was directly related to the individual's employment relationship and members were given the service, the duty was held to attach.

---

7. 14 PERB ¶ 3017 (1981).

The decision in the *United Federation of Teachers* involved a discrimination in the availability of a noncontractual, job-related benefit based upon the person's union membership status. If there is no improper discrimination involved, it is equally clear that bargaining agents in New York are not required by PERB to affirmatively undertake noncontractual avenues for the redress of an individual's complaint.[8] For example, in *Public Employees Federation (Hartner)*, the board specifically held that an organization's duty of fair representation does not include the obligation, absent discrimination in the rendition of the service, to prosecute lawsuits on behalf of an employee even though the suit is one seeking to challenge an adverse employment decision.[9]

These decisions have involved issues directly or indirectly affecting the individual as employee. There is yet another, and potentially more significant, line of cases spawned by the agency fee enactment that involve denials to nonmember fee payers of benefits that do not arise from nor affect the employment relationship but are offered to union members as internal membership benefits. With increasing frequency, the board is called upon to determine whether the bargaining agent is permitted to withhold the benefit from the nonmember notwithstanding that his fee payments contribute to the general funds from which the benefits are financed.

In the first case to raise that issue with the board, it was determined, in finding a violation, that a duty parallel to that of the duty of fair representation applied to a limited range of member-only benefits financed in part by agency fee payments.[10] In *United University Professions, Inc. (Eson)*, agency fee payers were not covered by certain insurance policies given to the union members, although income from the nonmembers' fees was used to pay for the policies.[11]

---

8. Several other jurisdictions have adopted the same view. *See,* State of New Jersey, 5 NJPER ¶ 10, 223 (1979); Tri-County Education Assn., 13 PPER ¶ 13, 207 (Pa. Lab. Rel. Bd. 1982); Los Rios College Federation of Teachers, 6 PERC ¶ 13, 169, *aff'd,* 6 PERC ¶ 16,188 (Cal. Pub. Emp. Rel. Bd. 1982).

9. 15 PERB ¶ 3066 (1982). *Accord,* Public Employees Federation (Farkas), 15 PERB ¶ 3134 (1982) (appeal pending).

10. Florida has specifically allowed, in the absence of a union security provision, a limitation of internal benefits to union members only. City of Winter Haven, 7 FPER ¶ 12,129, *aff'd,* City of Winter Haven v. Hillsborough County PBA, 8 FPER ¶ 13,029 (Fla. Dist. Ct. App. 1981).

11. 12 PERB ¶ 3117 (1979), *aff'd,* United University Professions, Inc. v. Newman, 80 App. Div. 2d 23 (1981), *mot. for lv. to app. denied,* 54 N.Y.2d 611 (1981).

It should be noted that at the time, the New York State Insurance Department had advised the union that it could not issue the policies to nonmembers, a limitation that has since been removed. In relevant part, the decision reads,

> We conclude that a parallel duty exists under the Taylor Law to protect the agency fee payer from discriminatory use of his funds by his collective bargaining representative. That duty requires that so long as a union is the beneficiary of agency fee payments in amounts equal to dues paid by members, the union must use the funds so obtained in a manner that will accord to both members and agency shop fee payers an equal opportunity to share in substantial economic benefits furnished by the union with such funds.[12]

Although the board was careful to state that this parallel duty attached only to "substantial economic benefits"[13] lest we eliminate all traditional distinctions between members and nonmembers, agency staff are now processing a number of charges seeking a more particularized definition of the standard that will, if past history repeats, end in appeals to the board.[14]

New Jersey has taken recently the ultimate step in the development of this trend. In *PBA Local 199*, the New Jersey Public Employment Relations Commission held that the arbitrary denial of an individual's application for membership in the union was a breach of the organization's duty of fair representation.[15] In concluding, it noted that the result reached was apparently dictated by the enactment of the "service fee" legislation in that state.[16]

Were I once again to gaze into my cloudy crystal ball in search of some conclusion and forecast, I would say that the prospects for a reduction in the volume of yearly litigation of fair representation is-

---

Members-only insurance policies have also been held to breach a union's duty of fair representation in California. King City Joint Union High School District, 6 PERC ¶ 13,065 (Cal. Pub. Emp. Rel. Bd. 1982).

12. 12 PERB ¶ 3117 at 3212.

13. California has similarly imposed a "substantial impact" test in determining whether an organization's internal affairs are subject to the duty. *See*, SEIU, Local 99, 3 PERC ¶ 10,134 (Cal. Pub. Emp. Rel. Bd. 1979).

14. The standard has been held to apply to a medical expense plan, which although costing little, had the potential for substantial payments in the event of catastrophic or repetitive illness or injury. United Federation of Teachers (Barnett), 15 PERB ¶ 3103, *aff'g*, 15 PERB ¶ 4521 (1982). It has been held inapplicable, however, to an organization's distribution of its various newspapers and periodicals. United Federation of Teachers (Barnett), 16 PERB ¶ 4625 (Aug. 30, 1983).

15. 6 NJPER ¶ 11,198 (1980).

16. N.J. Employer-Employee Relations Act, § 34:13A-5.5 & 5.6 N.J. Laws, ch. 477 (1979).

sues are not good. The next five years may, however, show a shift in the concentration of the cases away from claims involving inadequate enforcement of the contract through grievances and arbitration. Were the latter to continue as the trend for the future, a reduction in litigation might be expected because organizations may be able to escape responsibility in this area by affording employees greater participation in the processing of their own grievances and an opportunity to select a personal representative of their choice.[17]

A means to escape exposure to litigation and potential liability is not as available or cost-free, if the hypothesis and trend noted here are correct. If the enactment of union security legislation represents a fundamental cause for the increasing number of cases filed, only by choosing to forgo the benefit that may be essential to its continued financial existence can an organization hope to free itself from some of the charges. So too, if the trend in litigation is toward the filing of cases seeking to impose extracontractual duties upon the bargaining agent or the extension of membership benefits to nonmembers, the organization can avoid or minimize the attacks against it only by not offering or expanding its services in noncontractual areas or by treating the nonmembers as members for benefit purposes. This price may prove too costly for unions seeking to obtain or maintain their status as a bargaining agent or those intent upon preserving themselves as membership organizations.

-----

17. For example, the New Jersey PERC held the duty inapplicable in Licensed Practical Nurse Assn. of New Jersey, Inc., 6 NJPER ¶ 11,111 (1980), *aff'g*, 6 NJPER ¶ 11,081, because the individual had elected to be represented at a civil service hearing by an attorney she had retained privately.

The Duty of
Fair Representation:
A View From the Bench

Harry T. Edwards

I will not pretend to suggest that there is "a view from the bench," as if to distinguish my present perspective from my perspectives as a practitioner, labor law scholar, or arbitrator. Indeed, my views on the duty of fair representation have remained relatively constant, and the cases still look the same to me now as they did five, ten and fifteen years ago. What has changed, however, is the legal framework in which these cases are being considered and, also, the number of cases being heard.

The Increased Numbers of Reported Cases

Most of us assumed that the critical issues surrounding the duty of fair representation were put to rest in 1967 when the Supreme Court issued its landmark decision in *Vaca* v. *Sipes*.[1] Under *Vaca*, the duty of fair representation was thought to be an extremely narrow concept, and any individual employee seeking to invoke it faced a very heavy burden of proof. Today, however, although employee claims still look the same as they did sixteen years ago, the doctrinal branches of the duty of fair representation now extend well beyond

Judge Edwards wishes to acknowledge and express his gratitude for the invaluable collaborative efforts of Susan L. Segal, Esq., in the preparation of this chapter. Ms. Segal is a graduate of the University of Michigan Law School and is presently an associate with Gray, Plant, Mooty, Mooty & Bennett in Minneapolis, Minnesota.
    1. 386 U.S. 171, 64 LRRM 2369 (1967).

Federal DFR Cases

Jurisdiction	1968	1972	1977	1982
Supreme Court	0	0	0	0
Court of Appeals	7	12	17	30
District Court	8	14	24	54
Total	15	26	41	84

both the roots established by the Supreme Court's decision in *Vaca* v. *Sipes* and the germinal seed that was planted with the Court's 1944 decision in *Steele* v. *Louisville & Nashville Railroad.*[2]

In an effort to find any discernible trends in the number of duty of fair representation claims now being heard, I made a limited search for such cases through Westlaw. I selected the years of 1968 (the year after *Vaca* was decided), 1972, 1977 and 1982 (*i.e.*, five, ten and fifteen years after *Vaca*) to determine the number of reported cases in the federal courts involving claims of a breach of a duty of fair representation. My research produced the figures shown in the table. Because it is always extremely difficult to create a fully accurate search on Westlaw and Lexis equipment, there may be some errors in the search data. I doubt, however, that they are significant, especially with respect to the trend of increasing numbers of cases.

In considering these statistics, it is important to recall that the *absolute* numbers of duty of fair representation cases actually being processed in court far exceed the figures that I have cited. My figures are understated because the sample excludes (1) all unreported federal district court cases, (2) all cases in which a suit was settled short of judgment, (3) most public sector cases, (4) many cases prosecuted by the NLRB, and (5) all state court decisions. Nevertheless, albeit limited, the sample does show an increase of 460 percent in the number of reported duty of fair representation cases during the past fifteen years! Even with a margin of error as high as 50 percent (to take account of the cases not included in the sample and any deficiencies in the Westlaw search), the rate of increase in the number of cases would still be quite extraordinary.

My bottom line reaction to these figures is one of dismay, primarily because I think that the increase in cases is related more to a doctrinal expansion in judge-made law than to increased incidents

---

2. 323 U.S. 192, 15 LRRM 708 (1944).

of union breaches of the duty of fair representation. In one narrow sense, we might view this doctrinal expansion as something akin to the recent court decisions that have modified the employment-at-will doctrine. In each instance, the salutary effects of the expanded judge-made law are reflected in enhanced protections for *individual* workers. In the case of an expanded concept of the duty of fair representation, however, the gain may be more illusory than real, for it often comes at the expense of collective bargaining and labor arbitration.

The Potential Threat to Arbitration

I have been on the bench for almost four years and my experiences as a judge and, previously, as an arbitrator and an advocate have served to strengthen my belief that the traditional system of labor arbitration in the United States is an unparalleled means of dispute resolution. Arbitration offers unions, employers and individual employees a relatively quick and inexpensive means of resolving traditional labor disputes. And it provides a forum in which the parties control the selection of the decision maker, the matters to be presented, and the remedies that can be awarded. By contrast, in the judicial system, judges are assigned by the luck of the draw, and matters are judged, and remedies awarded according to principles of external law, not limited by the parameters of a collective bargaining agreement. Arbitration also provides a more flexible process where procedural and technical bars can give way to common sense. The results are an enhanced acceptability of the decision maker and, at least in most cases, an award with which both parties can abide. Thus, in many aspects of employment relations, I am of the belief that arbitration presents a superior method of dispute resolution to that offered by the judicial system.

Moreover, I am not alone in this belief. The growth and acceptance of labor arbitration has been truly phenomenal over the past several decades.[3] In addition, labor arbitration has been favored by the Supreme Court as a preferred means of dispute resolution, and

---

3. Robins, *The Presidential Address: Threats to Arbitration*, in Arbitration Issues for the 1980s, Proceedings of the 34th Annual Meeting, National Academy of Arbitrators 5 (James L. Stern and Barbara D. Dennis eds., BNA 1982).

labor arbitration processes and decisions have been protected from judicial intervention in a manner not accorded other quasi-judicial tribunals.[4] Yet, today, as a result of the increased frequency of duty of fair representation cases, arbitration is being threatened on several fronts. First, I think that it fairly may be maintained that recent judicial decisions have expanded the scope of the duty of fair representation beyond what was ever intended when the doctrine was first enunciated. Second, along with the increase in the number of fair representation cases, courts are deciding the merits of the underlying contract breach claims in more cases and applying judicial interpetations of collective bargaining agreements, rather than remanding grievances to arbitration. Third, union representatives are losing a significant measure of their assumed discretion to administer collective bargaining contracts and to process grievance disputes. A brief examination of some recent judicial opinions will highlight some of these points.

Judge-Made Doctrinal Expansions

The duty of fair representation was initially formulated by the Supreme Court in *Steele* v. *Louisville & Nashville Railroad.* In *Steele,* the Court ruled that a "bargaining representative of a craft or class of employees [has] the duty to exercise fairly the power conferred upon it in behalf of all those for whom it acts, without hostile discrimination against them."[5] The Court stated that this did "not mean that [a union] is barred from making contracts which may have unfavorable effects on some of the members of the craft represented."[6] However, it did mean that "discriminations based on race alone are obviously irrelevant and invidious," and such discriminations are actionable as a breach of the union's duty of fair representation.[7]

---

4. The Steelworkers Trilogy set down a legal framework that favors the jurisdiction of arbitrators and allows for only the most limited review of arbitration awards. *See,* United Steelworkers v. American Mfg. Co., 363 U.S. 564, 46 LRRM 2414 (1960); United Steelworkers v. Warrior & Gulf Navigation Co., 363 U.S. 574, 46 LRRM 2416 (1960); and United Steelworkers v. Enterprise Wheel & Car Corp., 363 U.S. 593, 46 LRRM 2423 (1960).

5. 323 U.S. at 202–3, 15 LRRM at 712.

6. *Id.* at 203, 15 LRRM at 712.

7. *Id.*

From the time of the *Steele* decision until the Supreme Court's decision in *Vaca* v. *Sipes,* the courts routinely held that a breach of the duty of fair representation could be established only by proof of bad faith or discriminatory conduct by a union. Although *Vaca* is a much more expansive judicial statement than *Steele,* it does not abandon the narrow conception of the duty of fair representation. Thus, in *Vaca,* the Supreme Court flatly rejected the suggestion "that every individual employee should have the right to have his grievance taken to arbitration."[8] Rather, the Court first recognized that unions have broad discretion to supervise the grievance machinery and to invoke arbitration, and then held that "a union does not breach its duty of fair representation . . . merely because it settle[s] [a] grievance short of arbitration."[9] To highlight this point, the Court made it clear that a union's decision that a particular grievance lacks sufficient merit to justify arbitration will not constitute a breach of the duty of fair representation because a judge or jury later finds the grievance meritorious.[10] Under *Vaca,* then, an employee is required to prove "arbitrary or bad-faith conduct on the part of the Union in processing his grievance" in order to make out a claim of a breach of the duty of fair representation.[11] This standard is slightly more liberal than the one enunciated in *Steele* but clearly consistent with the notion in *Steele* that a union must have broad discretion to function effectively as a bargaining agent.

Unfortunately, there are enough dicta in *Vaca* to allow for judicial excursions from the basic premises underlying that decision. As a consequence, lower court actions since 1967 have produced increasing, albeit inconsistent, judicial intervention in matters of contract administration, contract interpretation, grievance processing, and arbitration.

One illustration is presented by an Eighth Circuit en banc decision in *Smith* v. *Hussmann Refrigerator Co.*[12] The case involved a union's challenge to the promotion of four junior employees under a contract that said seniority would govern in the event that competing employees were "substantially equal" in ability. The union

---

8. 386 U.S. at 190, 64 LRRM at 2376–77.
9. *Id.* at 192, 64 LRRM at 2377.
10. *Id.* at 192–93, 64 LRRM at 2377–78.
11. *Id.* at 193, 64 LRRM at 2378.
12. 619 F.2d 1229, 103 LRRM 2321 (8th Cir.) (en banc), *cert. denied,* 449 U.S. 839, 105 LRRM 2657 (1980).

brought a grievance on behalf of four senior employees who had been passed over for the job openings. The grievance went to arbitration and two of the grievances were sustained. The arbitrator's award provided that all six employees, the four originally chosen by the company and the two grievants, were entitled to the classification. The union objected to the award on the ground that there were only four openings and, thus, only four of the employees should be awarded the positions.

A meeting was held between the union and management, at which the parties agreed that the four most senior employees were entitled to the jobs in order of seniority. After reaching this agreement, the parties, without notice to the nongrievant employees, resubmitted the case to the arbitrator for "clarification" of which of the six employees were to be awarded the four positions. The parties informed the arbitrator of their prior agreement and presented him with corrected seniority dates and bid sheets. In a supplemental decision, the arbitrator thereafter directed that the jobs should be awarded to the four most senior employees. The nongrievant employees then sued for breach of the duty of fair representation and breach of contract.

The Eighth Circuit, in upholding a jury verdict against the union, found a number of bases upon which to conclude that the union had breached its duty of fair representation. These included the union's decision to press the four grievances on the basis of seniority, the failure to notify the nongrievant employees that the award was being resubmitted to the arbitrator for "clarification," and the union's failure to accept and process grievances from those employees after the arbitration award was "clarified" to their detriment. Although there are alternative grounds stated, it seems clear that the opinion for the court posits a view that the union's decision to process the grievances of the four senior employees, by itself, constituted a breach of the duty of fair representation.

Several judges in *Smith* rejected this latter conclusion, arguing that such a decision by the court improperly interfered with the union's determination of how the seniority clause should be interpreted and applied. It is significant to note that nowhere in the decision was the union found to have acted in bad faith or without a rational purpose. It is also noteworthy that none of the judges in *Smith* even considered remanding the case to arbitration for further proceedings pursuant to proper notice to the plaintiffs.

Another example of the expansion of the obligations encompassed within the scope of the duty of fair representation is reflected in a recent decision of the Ninth Circuit in *Gregg* v. *Teamsters, Local 150*.[13] *Gregg* involved grievances for severance pay under a contract provision that awarded such pay when layoffs were "due to the closing of a plant or depot," but not when a layoff merely resulted from the operation of seniority rules. The employer had closed three of its four depots in the area and reduced the number of drivers at the fourth depot. The union initially processed grievances from employees at all four depots, but later, on advice of counsel, withdrew the grievances of the employees at the fourth depot. The grievants at the fourth depot filed suit for a breach of the union's duty of fair representation. The Ninth Circuit concluded that the union's withdrawal of the grievances constituted a breach of its duty of fair representation. The court affirmed an award of damages against the union in an amount equal to what each of the plaintiffs would have received in severance pay had their grievances been successful.

The rationale underlying the decision in *Gregg* is somewhat surprising. The court appeared to acknowledge that the union had a rational, tactical reason for abandoning the plaintiffs' grievances. The court, nevertheless, determined that the union's reasons were "too insubstantial" to justify its actions. In reaching this conclusion, the court in *Gregg* applied a test tied to the merits of the underlying grievances: "[t]he more important and meritorious the grievance [from the court's perspective], the more substantial the reason must be to justify abandoning it."[14] It is likely that the practical effect of this test is to shift the burden of proof to the union to establish a compelling reason for its actions whenever a plaintiff can show that his or her grievance is colorably meritorious.[15] This would seem to be at odds with the Supreme Court's statement in *Vaca* that an employee is required to prove "arbitrary or bad-faith conduct on the part of the union in processing his grievance." The *Gregg* standard also may be extremely hazardous insofar as it invites a judge to supplant his or her views of the "importance" of a grievance for those of the union. In addition, it is highly noteworthy that the court in

---

13. 699 F.2d 1015, 112 LRRM 2924 (9th Cir. 1983).

14. *Id.* at 1016, 112 LRRM at 2925.

15. In Gregg the Ninth Circuit did not conclude that the plaintiff's grievances were in fact meritorious; the court merely noted that "reasonable and legitimate arguments supported them." *Id.*

Gregg, like the court in *Smith,* failed to consider a remand of the case to arbitration. The net result, again, is a judicially imposed remedy in a situation where there has been no arbitral determination of liability.

In another case from the Ninth Circuit, *Dutrisac v. Caterpillar Tractor Co.,* the court awarded damages against a union for inadvertently failing to file a grievance, even though the court affirmed the district court's ruling that the plaintiff had been terminated for just cause under the contract.[16] The court reached this conclusion on arguably anomalous reasoning that the rejection of the plaintiff's claim by the district court did "not necessarily mean that the arbitrator would have rejected it had [the union] timely submitted it to arbitration."[17]

The expansion of the duty of fair representation to include inadvertent conduct, *i.e.,* conduct that is merely negligent rather than deliberate or in bad faith, as in *Dutrisac,* raises yet additional concerns.[18] The courts finding a breach in these circumstances have generally done so on a negligence or duty of due care theory, although the cases, in language at least, claim to adhere to the view that simple negligence will not constitute a breach of duty.[19] While it is not a startling notion to require unions to process grievances in a timely fashion, the rationale of these cases do hold potential dangers if a duty of due care theory is applied in other types of cases. For example, in several recent cases, employees have claimed that unions have breached the duty of fair representation in allowing unsafe conditions to exist during working hours.[20] The transfer of such a standard to a suit for breach of a union's duty to monitor or enforce plant safety provisions would create a whole new field of tort law that could bankrupt union treasuries.

---

16. 113 LRRM 3532 (9th Cir. 1983).

17. *Id.* at 3536.

18. See also, Ruzicka v. General Motors Corp., 523 F.2d 306, 90 LRRM 2497 (6th Cir. 1975), *modified,* 649 F.2d 1207, 107 LRRM 2726 (6th Cir. 1981); Reid v. Postal Union, 109 LRRM 3065 (S.D. N.Y. 1982). But *see,* Hoffman v. Lonza, Inc., 658 F.2d 519 (7th Cir. 1981).

19. For example, in Dutrisac v. Caterpillar Tractor Co., the Ninth Circuit concluded that the union's failure to file the grievance on time constituted not merely simple negligence, but "reckless disregard for the rights of the plaintiff." 113 LRRM at 3534.

20. *See,* Condon v. Local 2944, United Steelworkers, 683 F.2d 590, 110 LRRM 3244 (1st Cir. 1982); Burgess v. Allendale Mutual Ins. Co., 111 LRRM 2997 (S.D. Ga. 1982).

The net impact of certain of the decisions that I have discussed, and others like them, is to create a confusing system of constraints on union conduct. The problem is exacerbated by the fact that a great many of these cases are subject to jury trials, in which the subtleties of national labor policy are easily lost.

Litigation of the Merits of the Underlying Grievances

My point about jury trials leads me to a related concern, having to do with what happens to a duty of fair representation case once a union breach has been found. From all appearances, it seems that the courts have ignored the federal labor policy of nonintervention in the arbitral process and have proceeded wholesale to decide the merits of the underlying grievances rather than returning the cases to arbitration. I am of the view that this practice not only alters the parties' bargain but threatens havoc with labor contract administration.

In many (if not most) cases in which a breach of the duty of fair representation has been found, appropriate relief is an order requiring the parties to proceed under the grievance procedure in their contract. When courts avoid this approach, and undertake to decide the merits of grievances, they cause harsh and unnecessary intrusions into the parties' private system of governance and dispute resolution. This thesis was expertly developed by David Feller in 1973, in his seminal article entitled "A General Theory of the Collective Bargaining Agreement."[21] Feller argued that, in the typical labor contract, an important part of the bargain is the agreement that disputes between the parties will be governed by the rules contained in the contract as may be interpreted and applied by an arbitrator. When the courts intervene and supply their own interpretation of the agreement, this undermines a critical basis of the parties' bargain.

As developed in Feller's article, a collective bargaining agreement does not create a contract between the employer and any employee, the breach of which may be redressed by a court suit by the employee. Thus, Feller argues, a collective bargaining agreement is

---

21. Feller, *A General Theory of the Collective Bargaining Agreement,* 61 Calif. L. Rev. 663 (1973).

not a promissory undertaking between employer and employee; rather, it is a set of rules to govern employer and employee conduct. The remedy for a violation of the rules must be provided by the agreement, not notions of public law or policy external to the agreement. Feller maintains that management agrees to the restrictions contained in a collective bargaining agreement "only as those restrictions on its rights may be interpreted and applied by an arbitrator in case of a disagreement."[22]

The arbitrator's role, as emphasized in a more recent speech by Feller,[23] is to determine what remedies are cognizable under the parties' agreement. This view is consonant with a position espoused by Theodore St. Antoine in his thoughtful paper on the arbitrator as a "contract reader."[24] St. Antoine reasons that, "[s]o long as [the arbitrator] is dealing with a matter duly submitted to him, . . . [he] is speaking for the parties, and his award *is* their contract."[25] Under this view, the arbitration process holds out the advantage of providing the parties with some certainty and control over the penalties and remedies to which they may be subject for a breach or violation of their compact.

As Feller points out in his article, the logical extension of these views is that a union breach of the duty of fair representation should be remediable only in a suit to compel the union to proceed with the grievance procedure under the parties' collective bargaining agreement. Thus, courts should not take jurisdiction to determine the merits of the employee's grievance in the first instance. Under the Feller thesis, the bargain between the parties is enforcement of the agreement. Interpretation of the agreement by a court or jury and the imposition of damages flowing from formulas provided in external law are beyond the parties' agreement and constitute unjustified intrusions into the arbitration process; such intrusions are particularly egregious because we normally seek to protect the arbitration process from judicial interference pursuant to firmly established principles of federal labor policy under the Steelworkers' Trilogy.

---

22. *Id.* at 775–76.

23. Feller, *Remedies in Arbitration: Old Problems Revisited,* in Arbitration Issues for the 1980s, Proceedings of the 34th Annual Meeting, National Academy of Arbitrators 109 (James L. Stern and Barbara D. Dennis eds., BNA 1982).

24. St. Antoine, *Judicial Review of Labor Arbitration Awards: A Second Look at Enterprise Wheel and Its Progeny,* in Arbitration—1977, Proceedings of the 30th Annual Meeting, National Academy of Arbitrators 29 (Barbara D. Dennis and Gerald G. Somers eds., BNA 1978).

25. *Id.* at 35.

Despite the obvious force of these arguments, many courts nowadays regularly proceed to the merits of the underlying contract claims in duty of fair representation suits. The authority for such an approach is found in *Vaca* v. *Sipes,* where the Supreme Court briefly touched upon the question. In *Vaca,* the Court acknowledged that an order compelling arbitration "should be viewed as one of the available remedies when a breach of the union's duty is proved."[26] The Court, however, refused to hold that a remand to arbitration was the sole remedy for a breach of a duty of fair representation. The problem is that, in construing *Vaca,* the lower courts appear to have gone overboard in declining to utilize the arbitration remedy in duty of fair representation cases.

There are some important reasons why a court might not opt to remand a case to arbitration once a union has been found guilty of a breach of its duty of fair representation. One is the potential of hostility between the complaining employee and the union agent who will be assigned to represent him in arbitration. Another is that, after the Supreme Court's decision in *Bowen* v. *U.S. Postal Service,*[27] bargaining agents may have a reduced incentive to succeed in arbitration, knowing that an arbitral victory for the employee may result in an assessment of damages against the union. Furthermore, it has been argued that, in part because arbitrators may lack authority to assess damages against the union, it is a waste of judicial resources to "split" duty of fair representation cases between courts and arbitrators.[28]

Feller convincingly argues that many of these contentions are inconsequential,[29] and I would agree. It certainly is not unusual for the courts to "split" cases with arbitrators, for this is done all the time in cases arising under the Steelworkers' Trilogy or in *Boys Markets*[30] suits to enforce contractual no-strike provisions. If a court is seriously concerned about adequate representation for the individual employee at the arbitration hearing, separate counsel may be assigned the employee, with the court retaining jurisdiction over the matter. A court might also retain jurisdiction to apportion damages

---

26. 386 U.S. at 196, 64 LRRM at 2379.

27. 103 S. Ct. 588, 112 LRRM 2281 (1983).

28. *See,* Segarra v. Sea-Land Service, Inc., 581 F.2d 291, 296, 99 LRRM 2198, 2202 (1st Cir. 1978).

29. Feller, *supra* note 21, at 814–15.

30. *See,* Boys Markets, Inc. v. Retail Clerks Local 770, 398 U.S. 235, 74 LRRM 2257 (1970).

between the company and the union under *Bowen* in the event that the arbitrator finds in favor of the individual employee. In other words, there are numerous possibilities available to a court to protect the rights of individual employees short of judicial interpretation of the agreement. And if we are able to ensure the protections given to individual employees under *Vaca* without destroying important principles and processes of *collective* bargaining, we should seek to foster such accommodations.

Conclusion

In reading some of the recent judicial decisions in duty of fair representation cases, one vaguely perceives a new body of law interpreting collective bargaining agreements. The most troubling aspect about this is that the judge-made law appears, at times, wholly divorced from traditional arbitral precedent. The Ninth Circuit, in the *Dutrisac* opinion, acknowledged this phenomenon with a passing observation that "[c]ourts and labor arbitrators do not always consider the same factors when deciding whether a contract has been breached."[31] This might not be so bad except that it highlights my central point, that the parties are not getting what they bargained for when a court usurps the arbitral function and decides the underlying contract claim in a duty of fair representation case.

At a time when we are terribly concerned about overworked judges and overcrowded judicial dockets, it is ironic to observe judges embracing ever-expanding conceptions of the duty of fair representation and reaching to decide the merits of cases that properly may be decided in another forum. It may be that, in the United States, we have begun to react to legitimate and heightened concerns about the rights of *individuals* in the workplace. In particular, we may now be more prepared than ever before to ensure some form of just cause determination for any discharged worker. This certainly has been suggested by the recent judicial excursions in the employment-at-will cases. Likewise, when presented with appealing cases, judges and juries have found it easy to expand the duty of fair representation to address individual claims.

The problem with this approach is that it relies on piecemeal

---

31. Dutrisac v. Caterpillar Tractor Co., 113 LRRM at 3536.

and confusing judicial opinions in lieu of legislative reform. Once the concept of the duty of fair representation has been expanded, it will reach not only individual discharge cases, but also cases brought by individuals affecting the collective rights of all employees in the workplace. Such cases, involving seniority, layoffs, and job assignments, go to the heart of collective bargaining; an erroneous decision on a contract interpretation issue can have a significant impact on the rights of both parties and all workers covered by the agreement. This, of course, explains the Court's firm reluctance in *Vaca* to limit union discretion in contract administration and grievance processing.

Unfortunately, trends such as the one that we are now witnessing with respect to duty of fair representation cases tend to take on a life of their own. *Bowen* v. *U.S. Postal Service* is a striking example.[32] Other authors in this volume will discuss *Bowen* in detail, so I will not prolong the analysis. It is enough for me to say that I have yet to square the result in *Bowen* with the mandate of *Vaca* v. *Sipes*. I have yet to understand, on the undisputed facts of the case, why the national union's considered determination not to appeal Bowen's case to arbitration was found to be a breach of the duty of fair representation. Nor do I understand why the case was not remanded to arbitration if the union was indeed guilty of a breach. The Supreme Court's decision in *Bowen* focuses solely on the damages apportionment issue, and claims no retreat from the principles enunciated in *Vaca* v. *Sipes*. Nevertheless, the result in *Bowen* stands in curious contrast to previously established precedent.

As is now apparent, I think that the present state of the law poses some serious problems for collective bargaining. The burden now lies with employer and union representatives to reach some accommodations that will stem the tide of judicial intrusions into matters of collective bargaining.

---

32. *Supra* note 27.

The Parties

A Union Advocate's View

Seymour M. Waldman

The Expanding Duty Owed by Unions to Their Members

From the perspective of a labor organization, the duty of fair representation presents what may fairly be described as a no-win situation. As the scope of that duty expands through recent court decisions, the union advocate may reasonably query: what course of conduct will satisfy the standard and steer the union clear of liability?

If the union does not arbitrate a grievance because it regards the claim as lacking in merit, then it may be liable to the prospective grievant for "arbitrary" representation.[1] If it processes the grievance to the final stage but loses the arbitration, it may be liable to the grievant for "perfunctory" representation.[2] If it hires lawyers to handle some but not all arbitrations, on the reasonable premise that some disputes involve larger, more important issues with significant precedential effect, it may be liable to a grievant to whom it has not

The invaluable research and editorial assistance of Robert B. Stulberg, Esq., are gratefully acknowledged—S.M.W.

1. *See,* Bowen v. United States Postal Service, 103 S. Ct. 588, 112 LRRM 2281 (1983); Vaca v. Sipes, 386 U.S. 171, 64 LRRM 2369 (1967).

2. *See,* Hines v. Anchor Motor Freight, Inc., 424 F. 554, 91 LRRM 2481 (1976); Holodnak v. Avco Corp., 381 F. Supp. 191, 87 LRRM 2337 (D. Conn. 1974), *aff'd in part and rev'd in part,* 514 F.2d 285, 88 LRRM 2950 (2d Cir. 1975), *cert. denied,* 423 U.S. 982, 90 LRRM 2614 (1975).

assigned counsel.[3] If it does not engage an expert witness to testify at an arbitration because it does not deem such expertise necessary for proper presentation of the case, it may be liable if a judge—or a jury[4]—subsequently disagrees with its strategic decision.[5] Even if the union overcomes these theories of liability and prevails in the state or federal court or before the National Labor Relations Board, it will nevertheless have expended considerable time and money in defending itself. Those expenditures cannot be recaptured for the benefit of the union treasury—although, in the converse situation, a successful grievant may recover from the union not only costs and attorney's fees, but also back pay lost from the time of a hypothetical arbitration.[6]

Moreover, the scope of the duty of fair representation is not limited to the grievance-arbitration arena. Unions must be prepared to defend themselves against fair representation challenges to amendments to the unions' constitution and bylaws, to the negotiation of collective bargaining agreement provisions, to referrals under a hiring hall or union referral system, or to any union action or decision that may be deemed to affect a member.[7] But even this is too narrow a formulation. The union may also be liable under the duty of fair representation theory to individuals in the bargaining unit who are not union members and from whom the union generally derives no financial support.[8] Thus, a union, though hard-

3. See, Del Casal v. Eastern Airlines, Inc., 465 F. Supp. 1254, 101 LRRM 2059 (S.D. Fla. 1979), aff'd, 634 F.2d 295, 106 LRRM 2276 (5th Cir. 1981).

4. See, Cox v. C. H. Masland & Sons, Inc., 607 F.2d 138, 102 LRRM 2889 (5th Cir. 1979).

5. See, Curtis v. U.T.U., 102 LRRM 2961, 2962 (E.D. Ark. 1979) ("When . . . a case is not routine but requires, by its nature, expert representation of the worker in order to adequately present his claim, the union must provide such expert representation if it is not to be held guilty of unfair representation").

6. Bowen v. United States Postal Service, supra note 1.

7. See, e.g., Humphrey v. Moore, 375 U.S. 335, 55 LRRM 2031 (1964); Branch 6000, National Assn. of Letter Carriers v. NLRB, 595 F.2d 808, 100 LRRM 2346 (D.C. Cir. 1979); NLRB v. General Truck Drivers, I.B.T., Local 315, 545 F.2d 1173, 93 LRRM 2747 (9th Cir. 1976); Local 13, ILWU v. Pacific Maritime Assn., 441 F.2d 1061, 77 LRRM 2160 (9th Cir. 1971), cert. denied, 404 U.S. 1016, 79 LRRM 2182 (1972).

8. See, Steele v. Louisville & Nashville Railroad, 323 U.S. 192, 202–3, 15 LRRM 708, 711 (1944); Republic Steel Corporation v. Maddox, 379 U.S. 650, 653, 58 LRRM 2193 (1965); Vaca v. Sipes, supra note 1; Del Casal v. Eastern Airlines, Inc., supra note 3; Deboles v. Trans World Airlines, Inc., 552 F.2d 1005, 1016, 94 LRRM 3237, 3242 (3d Cir. 1977), cert. denied, 434 U.S. 837, 96 LRRM 2514 (1977).

pressed to find the funds needed to service to its own members, must provide service to others in the unit who provide nothing in return.

If this be deemed a paranoid view of the dilemmas confronting labor organizations, then one need only read the advance sheets in recent years to appreciate the astonishing number of adjudicated cases involving duty of fair representation claims. The rapid expansion of litigation in this area has placed the doctrine of fair representation in the forefront of union concerns and has gone to the very heart of the grievance-arbitration system.

The Adverse Impact upon the Grievance-Arbitration Process

The impact upon the grievance-arbitration process of the dramatically increasing invocation of the doctrine of fair representation has been substantial. Some unions that undoubtedly were too casual in evaluating and prosecuting employee grievances are now devoting more attention to their grievance handling responsibilities. That is all to the good. But, in the far larger group that has traditionally taken these responsibilities seriously and conscientiously, the spate of litigation has induced a kind of defensive conduct that, in my view, undermines and denigrates the entire grievance-arbitration process.

The basic concept of arbitration—and its traditional appeal to the participants in the labor relations arena—was that arbitration would be a prompt, efficient method of resolving disputes, conducted under relatively informal procedures by lay representatives who were basically responsible for contract administration. As such, arbitration would permit the utilization and consideration of the "common law" of the shop, which might not appear fully in the collective bargaining agreement itself. The arbitrator's award would be final and binding and would terminate the dispute. If contract interpretations were involved, then the parties could be guided by the interpretations embodied in the award.[9]

---

9. Steelworkers Trilogy, *see,* United Steelworkers v. American Mfg. Co., 363 U.S. 564, 46 LRRM 2414 (1960); United Steelworkers v. **Enterprise** Wheel & Car Corp., 363 U.S. 593, 46 LRRM 2423 (1960); United Steelworkers v. Warrior & Gulf Naviga-

The doctrine of the duty of fair representation, in its practical application, has undermined virtually every one of these objectives. Faced with the possibility of substantial damages or, at the very least, substantial litigation costs, all too many unions have felt compelled to adopt the obvious, protective strategy of taking virtually every grievance to the final step, even if the employee claim be deemed meritless and frivolous. Presentations are often made more elaborate than is warranted by the nature of the case. Professionals, rather than lay union representatives, are used more than would otherwise be justified. And the result is neither final in itself nor a reliable guide to future conduct until any duty of fair representation claim has been barred by the statute of limitations or finally determined. In short, the specter of fair representation lawsuits has resulted in more, but less conclusive, arbitrations, lengthier and more contentious hearings, greater formality and more procedural niceties, and a tendency to advance every conceivable argument, however flimsy it may appear, for fear that failure to do so will later result in liability to the union.

Ironically, when the union takes most or all grievances to arbitration, it imperils its ability to act as a responsible negotiator, mediator and adjudicator in fashioning a sound, consistent interpretation and application of the collective agreement for the entire shop. When the union submits to arbitration important contractual issues —such as transfer, promotion, or seniority—in the context of weak or damaging individual facts, it jeopardizes the contractual rights of the entire bargaining unit, which will necessarily be affected by an adverse arbitration award.

Despite formulations of the duty of fair representation that appear to permit considerable leeway in union decision making,[10] the refusal to arbitrate in the face of a grievant's insistence on doing so is particularly risky. The reason, in my judgment, lies in the traditional judicial approach toward the role of the advocate. Under the National Labor Relations Act, an exclusive bargaining agent is the

---

tion Co., 363 U.S. 574, 46 LRRM 2416 (1960). *See also,* Cox, *Reflections upon Labor Arbitration,* 72 Harv. L. Rev. 1482 (1959); Cox, *Current Problems in the Law of Grievance Arbitration,* 30 U. Colo. L. Rev. 24 (1958). *See also,* Waldman, *The Duty of Fair Representation and Arbitration,* New York University Conference on Labor (1976).

10. *See,* Ford Motor Co. v. Huffman, 345 U.S. 330, 31 LRRM 2548 (1953); Vaca v. Sipes, *supra* note 1; Humphrey v. Moore, *supra* note 7.

"employee's representative."[11] It is easy and natural for a judge to equate *representative* with *advocate.* At that point, the judge, particularly one unfamiliar with labor relations, tends to apply the litigation model. Under that model, the advocate's duty is to present, as best he can, his client's cause; it is not his function to pass judgment upon or to "decide against" his client. That is the role of the judge, the umpire, the neutral. The advocate, to use a popular phrase, is a hired gun.

When this model is applied to a union's refusal to arbitrate an employee's grievance, it is obvious that the union representative will not have complied with the advocate role to which the judicial mind is accustomed. Therefore, despite legal formulations to the contrary, the union will, in many cases, have to overcome this practical hurdle in justifying its decision not to arbitrate. Unfortunately, many unions, wary of duty of fair representation complaints, have begun to lean toward the advocate model, to the detriment of the grievance-arbitration process.

The harmful effects of this approach to labor relations extend well beyond the arbitration; they undermine and eviscerate the pre-arbitration process as well. This is particularly unfortunate, for the most important ingredient in a successful grievance resolution process is not the ultimate arbitration but the pre-arbitration stages. In the more fruitful industrial relationships, most grievances are resolved before arbitration; arbitration is the exception, not the rule. The touchstone of such a relationship is a willingness on the part of the principal representatives of labor and management to decide against their own subordinate representatives if they believe the other side is correct. Thus, upper-level management must be prepared to decide against its low-level supervisors, and upper-level union representatives must be willing to overrule their own subordinates.

One of the most damaging consequences of the outpouring of duty of fair representation claims is that the participants in the pre-

---

11. 29 U.S.C. § 159; Miranda Fuel Co., Inc., 140 NLRB 181, 184, 51 LRRM 1584, 1586 (1962), *enf. denied,* 326 F.2d 172, 54 LRRM 2175 (2d Cir. 1963) ("the privilege of acting as an exclusive bargaining representative derives from Section 9 of the Act, and a union which would occupy this statutory status must assume 'the responsibility to act as a genuine representative of all the employees in the bargaining unit' [citation omitted]").

arbitration stage are deterred from making such honest, good-faith judgments when they conclude that the other side is right. For if union representatives must take virtually all disputes to arbitration lest they expose the union to a large monetary judgment, then the prearbitration stage becomes an empty process in which disputes are invariably passed on to the arbitrator. It is too much to expect that management representatives, confronted with this kind of defensive conduct by their union counterparts, will undertake to overrule their own subordinates and decide grievances in favor of the union, without some sign of reciprocity.

I am not suggesting that meritorious grievances should be swapped or traded off. I am suggesting that the more sophisticated representatives of both sides should recognize that, in many instances, the positions taken by their own subordinates are untenable and unjustified; and if the parties are deterred from acting on that conviction, then the entire process will suffer.

Conflict between the Duty and Other Statutory Provisions

One of the ironies of the duty of fair representation doctrine is its fundamental inconsistency with other statutory and case law principles which tend to undermine a union's efforts to discharge its duty and protect itself from liability. The major federal labor statutes were enacted in 1935, 1947, and 1959 and thus predate the judicial evolution of the duty of fair representation in the mid-1960s.

One prominent example is the union election provision contained in Title IV of the Labor-Management Reporting and Disclosure Act of 1959 (LMRDA), as judicially construed.[12] In order to discharge its duty of fair representation, a union should have experienced officials with a background in the industry, familiarity with contract provisions, and some minimal educational qualifications. But any efforts by the union to require the kinds of qualifications for elected officials that would best serve the duty of fair representation cut against the LMRDA's policy of preserving maximum democratic choice to the membership and narrowing the "reasonable qualifications" that a union may impose upon candidates for office.[13]

---

12. 29 U.S.C. § 481 *et seq.*
13. 29 U.S.C. § 481(e).

Thus, courts have struck down union constitutional provisions requiring of candidates for office a specified period of time in the union,[14] attendance at a particular proportion of union meetings,[15] or competency "to perform the duties of the office."[16] To the defense that these qualifications better ensure more capable, experienced and qualified officials, courts have responded that these are all considerations to be put to the electorate but that, if the membership chooses to elect inexperienced, unqualified candidates, such is their democratic and statutory right.[17] That may all be very well and entirely consistent with the underlying objective of the LMRDA, but it is these very same members who are then entitled to seek recovery from the union treasury when the unqualified representatives they have elected perform as might be anticipated in handling grievances.

Similarly, the extent of a union's ability to represent bargaining unit employees is in many cases dependent upon the quality of the shop steward, the union's representative in the shop and the person primarily responsible for the development of the grievance at its earliest, and often most critical, stage. It is at this stage that contractual time limits are imposed, evidence preserved or lost, and cases made or "blown." In order to ensure the continued availability of an experienced shop steward, unions have sought to negotiate superseniority provisions in their collective bargaining agreements. However, the NLRB and the courts, fearful of violating other statutory policies against rewarding union membership, have severely restricted unions' ability to protect shop stewards.[18]

In order most effectively to handle grievances and process arbitrations, a union also needs an adequate treasury. The hiring of professionals, which may become a practical—if not a legal—necessity in at least some arbitrations, cannot be accomplished without suf-

---

14. See, Wirtz v. Operating Engineers, Local Unions Nos. 406, et al., 254 F. Supp. 962 (E.D. La. 1966).

15. Steelworkers, Local 3489 v. Usery, 429 U.S. 305, 94 LRRM 2203 (1977); Marshall v. ILA, Local 1402, 617 F.2d 96, 105 LRRM 2694 (5th Cir. 1980).

16. See, Donovan v. Laborers, Local 120, 683 F.2d 1095, 110 LRRM 3183 (7th Cir. 1982).

17. See, Steelworkers, Local 3489 v. Usery, supra note 15, at 312, 94 LRRM at 2206; Donovan v. Laborers, supra note 16, at 1104–5, 110 LRRM at 3188–90.

18. See, Dairylea Cooperative, Inc., 219 NLRB 656, 89 LRRM 1737 (1976), enf'd, 531 F.2d 1162, 91 LRRM 2929 (2d Cir. 1976); Gulton Electro-Voice, 266 NLRB No. 84, 112 LRRM 1361 (1983).

ficient resources. But the LMRDA imposes strict limitations on a union's ability to raise dues. Although the union as an institution owes a duty of fair representation to its members, it lacks the ability to raise funds to discharge that duty without the approval of those same members.[19] If, however, the members refuse to raise their own dues, the union is not relieved of its institutional duty of fair representation to them.

As a final example of statutory policies counterproductive to the effective discharge of the duty of fair representation, section 14(b) of the National Labor Relations Act of 1935 authorizes state right-to-work laws.[20] The number of states adopting these statutes has been rising in recent years.[21] The duty of fair representation is owed to nonmembers of the union who are a part of the bargaining unit.[22] Although this is often a costly obligation, nonmembers in right-to-work states cannot be required to pay the dues necessary to bear their fair share of the cost. Although some service charge is permissible, the current state of the law does not, in my view, permit the union to levy charges sufficient to fully recover the cost to the union of the grievance-arbitration process.

Thus, while the courts and the NLRB have been imposing upon unions higher standards of performance in the administration of the grievance-arbitration mechanism, they have been restricting unions' ability to meet those standards. If unions are to be held to the expanding duty of fair representation, they should, at the very least, be given the flexibility to manage their affairs in a way that will increase their effectiveness and strength.

---

19. 29 U.S.C. § 411(a)(3). *See,* Burroughs v. Operating Engineers, Local 3, 686 F.2d 723, 111 LRRM 2501 (9th Cir. 1982).

20. 29 U.S.C. § 164(b).

21. As of 1980, twenty states had statutes or constitutional provisions that, in some degree, prohibited union security provisions that would otherwise be permitted under the NLRA. *See generally,* Morris, The Developing Labor Law, vol. 2 (2d ed. 1983) at 1391–92 n.196.

22. *Supra* notes 8 and 11.

What Employers Can Do about DFR Suits

Andrea S. Christensen

The primary focus of the preceding chapters has been a legal analysis of the historical development of the duty of fair representation doctrine: questions such as how to define the duty of fair representation, how it should be exercised in the grievance and arbitration procedure of collective bargaining agreements; who presently has authority to define it; and who should have such authority are all highly significant to the employer's participation in the collective bargaining process. For the purposes of this discussion, however, I am assuming that unions and employers will continue for some time to be exposed to the burden of defending duty of fair representation litigations in a variety of forums. As a defense mechanism, unions will continue to process meritorious as well as nonmeritorious grievances to arbitration.

As a practitioner—and a management one at that—I would like to examine the means by which the parties to a grievance and arbitration procedure can try to reduce the number of occasions when it will be perceived by a grievant that the union has failed to meet its duty of fair representation. I will focus not so much on how to win the postarbitration cases but on how to avoid them in the first instance.

A review of current case law indicates that when a question of fair representation is raised, the primary issue is the union's conduct. Nonetheless, often either the employer or arbitrator or both could have adjusted their conduct in such a way as to have prevented a subsequent challenge to the proceedings.

An employer's primary interest is to obtain finality. That was what the employer bargained for when it agreed to binding arbitration. Employers are also interested in maintaining credibility in the grievance and arbitration procedure. This result can be obtained only if the employees perceive that the process as a whole is fair, that they have an equal chance to prevail, and that the results cannot easily be overturned. Every successful challenge to an arbitration award merely tempts additional challenges and heightens uncertainty as to the viability of the process. Thus, in addition to the risk of having to underwrite a portion of the back pay awarded as a result of a union's failure to meet its duty of fair representation, the employer risks challenge to future awards.[1] The success of a duty of fair representation suit in one instance impairs the certainty of the result in future arbitrations.

Employers have been outspoken in their criticism of an employee's opportunity to have "two bites at the apple" under the National Labor Relations Act, Title VII of the Civil Rights Act, and the Federal Age Discrimination in Employment Act.[2] Duty of fair representation litigation provides yet another opportunity to generate such multiplicity of litigation and to give the grievant another chance.

In determining the employer's role in the arbitration process, it should be noted that in a duty of fair representation case, a plaintiff can often obtain free counsel or retain counsel on the basis of a contingency fee arrangement. Employers and unions do not normally have the same access to counsel.

Though the focal point of duty of fair representation litigation is the union's role in the proceedings under challenge, both the participating employer and arbitrator have a meaningful interest in insulating the arbitration process from such subsequent challenges. No adjudicator relishes the thought of being reviewed by a judge or jury. An arbitrator whose award has been overturned or who has been the subject of litigation has diminished acceptability with the same parties in future disputes.

Moreover, arbitrators can be subpoenaed and deposed to disclose their perception of the union representative's conduct at the hearing. An arbitrator cannot charge study days for this activity and

---

1. *See*, Bowen v. United States Postal Service, 103 S. Ct. 588, 595, 599, 112 LRRM 2281, 2284–86 (1983).

2. *See*, Alexander v. Gardner-Denver Co., 415 U.S. 36, 7 FEP Cases 81 (1974).

cannot recover legal fees.[3] In *Bliznik* v. *International Harvester Company,* the plaintiff sought to depose the arbitrator to establish the union's breach of its duty of fair representation in the prior arbitration.[4] The arbitrator moved to quash the deposition subpoena. It was agreed that the arbitrator's testimony would be restricted to his factual recollection of the conduct of the union's representative at the arbitration hearing. The plaintiff's subpoena also sought all correspondence, briefs, exhibits, the arbitrator's notes, all materials utilized by the arbitrator in reaching his decision, and copies of all the arbitrator's decisions issued over the previous thirteen years in disputes between the parties involving the discharge of employees with fifteen years of service.

The district court denied the arbitrator's motion to quash the subpoena. The court directed that the deposition could solicit testimony only as to the union's conduct at the arbitration hearing. More important, the court found no immunity for arbitrators in this type of case. The court equated the deposition of an arbitrator to calling a former juror to testify in an attorney malpractice case: "[A]n arbitrator who is paid for his services does not need to be accorded any more protection from the burden of giving testimony than an ordinary citizen."[5] The court granted the document request with the exception of the arbitrator's notes, his decisional materials, and his decisions over the past thirteen years, not because the documents were not relevant but because their production would be too burdensome. The arbitrator was also directed to bring his notes to the deposition to refresh his recollection.

It is thus clear that it is in the interest of all participants in the arbitration process to avoid future litigation as to perceived procedural defects.

During the Grievance Procedure

The dilemma for an employer commences with the grievance procedure itself. Many duty of fair representation cases arise out of the union's failure to file for arbitration. Obviously, the employer's role

---

3. *See,* Calzarano v. Liebowitz, 550 F. Supp. 1389, 1391 (S.D. N.Y. 1982).

4. 87 F.R.D. 490 (N.D. Ill. 1980).

5. *Id.* at 492.

at this stage is very limited, but the employer is not required to be a silent bystander. Since the employer can be a victim of the union's failure to process the grievance to arbitration, the employer should be alert to evidence of the union's misconduct and intercede where there is a high risk of further litigation. Absent extraordinary circumstances, it cannot be less expensive to litigate a duty of fair representation case in court than to arbitrate the underlying dispute.

Where the grievance involves a discharge or a dispute as to the application of the collective bargaining agreement's seniority provisions, the employer should carefully investigate its position on the grievance to ensure that its view will most likely prevail, regardless of the forum. In this regard, an employer must keep in mind that in a duty of fair representation case, a jury may evaluate a just-cause standard quite differently than an arbitrator. If the risk of a duty of fair representation suit appears to be high, it may be prudent for an employer to try to persuade the union to proceed to arbitration.

If the employer views its chances of prevailing to be problematical, it may be more prudent for the employer to wait and see if a duty of fair representation suit is actually filed. If such a suit is commenced, the employer may elect to enter into an agreement with the union and grievant to submit the case to arbitration. The choice of options here will obviously depend upon the employer's assessment of the merits of its case and the likelihood that there will subsequently be a challenge to the union's conduct.

In cases where the time limitations under the collective bargaining agreement have expired, the employer's choice may be a more difficult one. The employer has bargained for specific time limits in the grievance and arbitration procedure. In discipline cases where the employer carries the burden of proof, the availability of witnesses and their ability to recall relevant events are critical to the employer's ultimate success. Furthermore, if the employer waives the contractual time limits to avoid a duty of fair representation litigation, the waiver may be viewed by subsequent arbitrators as being applicable to future grievances. On the other hand, the employer's liability for back pay and costs in a duty of fair representation suit is clear, and the employer's insistence that the contractual time limits control may increase his back pay liability if a court finds in favor of the grievant.[6]

---

6. *See,* Bowen, *supra* note 1, at 595, 599, 112 LRRM at 2284–86.

Therefore, particularly if an employer perceives the case to be a close one and a duty of fair representation action is threatened, the employer should consider waiving the contractual time limits in the grievance and arbitration procedure, but for that case only. This can be accomplished by executing a nonprecedential stipulation with the union that the employer agrees to submit the grievance to arbitration, despite the acknowledgment by both the company and union that the grievance is untimely. Such a stipulation should specifically provide that the waiver relates only to the case at issue, that it is not applicable to any subsequent grievances, and that both parties agree that the agreement's time limits continue to be operative.

Though, as a general rule, formal prehearing discovery is not available to the parties to an arbitration, section 8(a) (5) of the National Labor Relations Act, as amended, requires an employer to provide the union with the information necessary to perform its duty to investigate grievances.[7] Arbitration awards have been overturned where a union could not perform its duty of fair representation because of the employer's refusal to provide information determined subsequently to be relevant to the arbitration. This is not to suggest that the time-consuming and costly techniques of courtroom discovery be introduced into the arbitration process, but during the initial phase of the grievance procedure, the union should be given enough information to permit evaluation of the case and to fulfill its duty of fair representation. In some cases, voluntary disclosure of relevant material can be helpful in persuading the union representative, and possibly even the grievant, that the grievance is not meritorious. Moreover, appropriate disclosure should be made with the recognition that in a subsequent duty of fair representation litigation, the documents withheld by an employer during the grievance procedure will be made available to the union, the grievant, or both under the broad rules of discovery that pertain in any judicial litigation.

According to the Sixth Circuit, one type of evidence that an employer need not divulge to the union in advance of arbitration is the identity of the witnesses whose testimony will be used at the hearing to sustain the employer's position. In *Buckeye Cellulose Corp.* v. *District 65, U.A.W.*, an arbitrator granted reinstatement without back pay even though he found the grievant to be guilty of the conduct char-

---

7. NLRB v. Acme Industrial Co., 385 U.S. 432, 436, 64 LRRM 2069 (1967).

ged.[8] The arbitrator justified the reinstatement on the grounds that the termination was excessive because of the employer's refusal to disclose the identity of its witnesses before the arbitration hearing.

The Sixth Circuit set aside the award on the grounds that the arbitrator's decision was based on his view of the fundamental fairness of the process and not on any found violation of the contract. The court concluded that the arbitrator was improperly dispensing his own brand of industrial justice and was not acting within the limits of his jurisdiction, i.e., the provisions of the collective bargaining agreement. Other arbitrators and courts may view this problem differently than the Sixth Circuit. It is certainly arguable that in some circumstances, refusal to disclose the identity of key witnesses can be perceived as adversely affecting a union's ability to prepare its case. Therefore, depending upon the likelihood that identified witnesses might be subjected to prehearing harassment, the employer may want to respond affirmatively to a union request for identification.

Obviously, the procedures used by the parties to select the arbitrator must be beyond challenge. The selection must be conducted in good faith with the duty of fair representation in mind. In this regard, the parties should weigh the possible ramifications of selecting different arbitrators for cases with the same or similar facts. The recent United States Supreme Court decision in *W.R. Grace and Co.* v. *Local Union 759* is an example of a case in which different arbitrators came to opposite decisions on the same basic fact pattern.[9] In this situation, the losing party in either case has a compelling argument for challenging the award on the grounds that a violation of the duty of fair representation has occurred.

Once the arbitrator is selected, communications with the arbitrator including meetings of the union, company, and arbitrator in the absence of the grievant should be undertaken with the knowledge that such activities may be subject to disclosure in a duty of fair representation suit.[10] Though trial judges frequently engage in ex parte communications and side bar discussions, when they are asked to review another adjudicator's conduct, they may well take a stricter view of such communications. Therefore, when participating in such communications, it should be kept in mind that today's conversation

---

8. 689 F.2d 629, 111 LRRM 2502 (6th Cir. 1982).

9. 103 S. Ct. 2177, 113 LRRM 2641 (1983).

10. Teamsters v. E. D. Clapp Corp., 551 F. Supp. 570, 576 (N.D. N.Y. 1982).

may subsequently be the subject of full disclosure and litigation in another forum.

When to Object

The stage of the process in which the employer can most effectively function to ensure its finality is the arbitration hearing. There is little an employer can meaningfully do when a union refuses to process the grievance or processes it in an untimely manner. At the hearing, however, the employer has the opportunity to try to ensure that the hearing itself is not procedurally defective. This is primarily the responsibility of the arbitrator, but if the arbitrator does not intervene the parties' representatives should assume the responsibility.

In cases where the grievant or grievants are not present at the hearing, the risk that the resulting award will be challenged is manifold. The absence of the grievant can of itself serve as grounds for vacating the award.[11] Absent extraordinary circumstances, the arbitrator should in the first instance decline to open the hearing, even if there is no motion to adjourn by the company or union. If the arbitrator does not question the grievant's absence, the employer should object and insist that the grievant be produced.

The absence of the grievant can be critical evidence in a subsequent duty of fair representation suit. Moreover, the grievant's participation in the hearing may persuade him or her that the case lacks merit or, at a minimum, the difficulty of proving to the contrary. It is also advisable for the employer to expressly object to the grievant's absence at the hearing so as to preserve its right in any subsequent duty of fair representation litigation to argue that it was not a willing participant to this situation and, therefore, should not be required to share in the costs if the award should be overturned. In *Tatum* v. *Frisco Transportation Co.*, the Eighth Circuit reversed the decision of the Missouri-Kansas Drivers Council in a case in which the grievant had not been notified of the scheduled hearing and the union had not presented any witnesses or affidavits at the hearing.[12] A jury verdict reinstating the grievant and assessing damages of $20,000

---

11. Grane Trucking Co., 241 NLRB 133, 137–38, 100 LRRM 1624 (1979); Saginacio v. Attorney General of New Jersey, 87 N.J. 480, 435 A.2d 1134, 111 LRRM 2701 (1981).

12. 626 F.2d 55, 104 LRRM 3089 (8th Cir. 1980).

against the employer and $325 against the union was affirmed by
the circuit court on the grounds that the union's omissions "seriously
prejudiced the injured employee's right . . . and subverted the arbitral process."[13] The court concluded that the employer was not protected from relitigation by the finality provisions of the agreement
and that the drivers council's decision was reviewable on its merits.

It is not necessarily in the employer's best interest to object to a
grievant being represented by private counsel. The presence and
even participation at the hearing by the grievant's representative
make it far more difficult for the grievant to subsequently challenge
the results on the grounds that he was not properly represented at
the hearing. The potential disadvantage for the employer is the
risk that participation by the grievant's representative will prolong
the hearing. But, even an additional hearing day will prove far less
costly than a subsequent defense of a duty of fair representation
complaint.

When the identified grievants are present but other employees
who may be adversely affected by the award are not present at the
hearing, the employer should consider whether to insist upon their
presence or, in the alternative, to call them as its own witnesses. In
seniority cases, the employer is often less concerned as to which
conflicting group prevails than that a final decision be obtained.
Furthermore, the employer is more likely to obtain finality if all significant interests that will be affected by the result are at least represented at the hearing and are allowed to participate. Though courts
are not in agreement, there are instances where denial of a motion
to intervene by employees who were not represented by the union
has led to reversal of the award.[14] Also, when a union announced at
the beginning of a hearing that it did not represent the grievant, the
arbitrator's failure to require that the grievant's interests be represented resulted in an unenforceable award.[15]

When Not to Object

Obviously, an employer cannot and should not try the union's case,
but the employer should not insist upon procedural technicalities

---

13. *Id.* at 59, 104 LRRM at 3092.

14. Sedita v. Board of Education, 82 Misc.2d 644, 371 N.Y.S.2d 812 (Sup. Ct.
1975), *aff'd in part*, 53 App. Div.2d 300, 385 N.Y.S.2d 647 (4th Dep't 1976), *rev'd on
other grounds*, 43 N.Y.2d 827, 373 N.E.2d 365, 402 N.Y.S.2d 566 (1977).

15. Russ Togs, Inc., 253 NLRB 767, 768, 106 LRRM 1067, 1069 (1980).

that thwart the introduction of relevant or even only arguably relevant evidence. Participants to the process know that arbitrators will take most evidence "for whatever it is worth." With the proliferation of duty of fair representation cases, arbitrators will become even more reluctant to exclude proffered evidence if it has any conceivable relevance to the case. When an employer objects to the introduction of such evidence, an assessment should be made as to whether the exclusion of such evidence is worth a possible future litigation.

If it becomes evident during the arbitration hearing that the union either cannot or will not represent the grievant properly, in my view, the arbitrator should intervene. If the circumstances warrant such intervention, the arbitrator should examine witnesses and even request that certain witnesses or other evidence be produced. It is not recommended that an arbitrator call his own witnesses, as he could be perceived to have become one of the litigants and thereby impair the participants' faith in his impartiality. If, however, the arbitrator becomes convinced that certain additional evidence is essential, he should discuss his concerns with the company and union representatives.

As the United States Supreme Court made clear in the lead case of *Hines* v. *Anchor Motor Freight, Inc.*, the presentation of inaccurate or incomplete facts may lead to a reversal of the award.[16] The arbitrator should render his decision solely on the basis of his perception of the facts. He should, therefore, ensure that he has a thorough understanding of the facts and that appropriate evidence has been introduced as to all the facts necessary to render a decision. Arbitral awards that rely upon incorrect facts or evidence that was not introduced at the hearing are frequently subject to challenge.

Current duty of fair representation litigation raises the same questions as to whether there should be a transcript of the hearing as those raised in the Title VII litigation after the Supreme Court's decision in *Alexander* v. *Gardner-Denver Co.*[17] There is no question but that a transcript will significantly increase the cost and length of the process. But in cases in which a challenge to the union's representation appears likely the existence of a transcript may actually save both money and time. It is certainly more likely that a duty of fair representation suit can be dismissed in a motion for summary judg-

---

16. 424 U.S. 554, 570–71, 91 LRRM 2481, 2487 (1976).
17. *Supra* note 2.

ment proceeding if a transcript of the arbitration hearing is part of the moving papers. In *Bliznick,* the court implied that an arbitrator could not be deposed if a transcript of the proceedings were available.[18] Of course, the existence of a transcript may raise questions subsequently if the grievant demands a free copy of the transcript.[19]

A transcript is helpful to both the employer and union as a basis for challenging the grievant if he alters his testimony at a subsequent duty of fair representation trial. It should be noted, however, that a transcript cannot be used to challenge a witness's credibility if the witness was not sworn at the original hearing. Thus, though I hesitate to recommend any device that will increase the cost of arbitration, a transcript may actually reduce the employer's exposure in a subsequent litigation. A transcript may provide helpful evidence that the employer did not do anything at the hearing to impair the union's ability to execute its duty of fair representation. A transcript can be equally helpful to a union in proving that it executed its duty properly.

More obviously flagrant procedural defects, such as refusal to allow one side to submit a brief or to cross-examine a witness or to postpone a hearing where good cause is shown, have all resulted in duty of fair representation suits and reversal of the award. In these situations, it may be advisable for the employer not to press too vigorously its technical rights. Accordingly, if the employer utilizes procedures that unnecessarily increase the cost of arbitration the union will not process what it perceives to be close cases but the grievant may well do so, on his own, in court. It is, in fact, the close cases that provide the greatest risk that a judge or jury will apply a set of standards in conflict with the normal industrial rules.

Perception of Fair Process

The arbitrator's conduct at the hearing is critical to ensuring that the participants perceive the process to be fair. Gratuitous comments about the merits of the case during the hearing should be avoided. An arbitrator should not try to mediate the case, particularly before

---

18. *Supra* note 4.
19. Grovner v. Georgia-Pacific Corp., 625 F.2d 1289, 1291, 105 LRRM 2706 (5th Cir. 1980).

all the evidence has been presented. Arbitrators who initiate settlement discussions at the close of the opening statements or of one side's case leave the impression that the case has been prejudged. If the arbitrator's mediation efforts fail, the loser can argue that the unsolicited mediation efforts constitute evidence of arbitral bias.

The arbitrator should take care to ensure that the grievant has had a full opportunity to present his case. A grievant who believes he has been heard and treated fairly—even if he loses—will be less likely to try to relitigate his case. Indeed, in cases where the arbitrator or union specifically ask the grievant at the conclusion of the hearing if he believes he has been fairly represented, courts have cited the grievant's affirmative response as evidence in support of its decision to refuse to set aside the award.[20] The grievant's choice as to how to answer such a question in the presence of the arbitrator and the union may not be an easy one, but its utility in any subsequent duty of fair representation suit is unquestionable. The same question should be directed at the grievant's attorney—even if the attorney has not been permitted to participate in the hearing. At a minimum, a negative response from the grievant or his attorney will provide the parties and arbitrator with an opportunity to evaluate, and possibly, eliminate in a timely fashion the grievant's grounds for challenging the representation.

Though convincing arguments can be made that neither the courts nor the NLRB should be permitted to interject their influence into the arbitration process, as a practical matter, duty of fair representation suits are a persistent reality, and they will continue to be a problem for both companies and unions. Federal legislation that would provide for a uniform method for challenging an arbitral award would certainly be helpful, but in the interim, the parties must take steps to reduce their exposure. The participants should therefore seek methods by which they can limit the influence of outside interests by persuading the participants to the process of the ultimate fairness and inviolability of the process itself.

---

20. Hart v. National Homes Corp., 668 F.2d 791, 794, 109 LRRM 2938, 2940 (5th Cir. 1982).

The Plaintiff's Perception of Litigation

Paul H. Tobias

This chapter sets forth the views of a lawyer who specializes in representing individual employees complaining of unfair representation and seeking judicial relief for breach of contract claims. My views are very different from those of union and employer advocates. In addition, I disagree with most NLRB officials, arbitrators, judges, and commentators who seem overly supportive of the labor-management establishment and the system it fosters.

My theme is the bitterness felt by the victims of unfair representation. Ninety percent of their lawsuits are defeats. Their high expectations of justice in the courtroom are usually unfulfilled. Their lawyers share their disappointment with the legal system.

Employee Awareness of Contract Rights

The number of section 301–DFR lawsuits increases.[1] Now, more than ever, individual workers are sensitive to legal matters and are determined to protect their rights.

In the past twenty-five years, legislatures have passed many new statutes bestowing employment rights and benefits on special inter-

---

1. Section 301–DFR litigation is a hybrid suit brought by an individual employee against an employer for breach of a labor agreement under section 301(a) of the Labor Management Relations Act and against a union for breach of the duty of fair representation.

est groups and regulating the workplace. The concept of due process and the right to a fair hearing have been highly publicized in the media. Pursuit of self-interest through legal proceedings is considered normal and proper. New public agencies, such as the Equal Employment Opportunity Commission, encourage workers to register complaints against their employer. The doctrines of self-assertiveness and looking out for Number One have overshadowed older concepts of cooperation, self-denial, and sacrifice. For better or worse, Americans have become a litigious people. Rank-and-file employees are now willing to take on city hall.

Employees in union shops focus their attention on the labor agreement. Employers and unions traditionally speak of the contract as the Bible, which is to be obeyed by all. Unions organize non-union shops by bragging about "rights" gained in contracts and enforced through a grievance-arbitration procedure. Thus, employees rely upon the sanctity of the labor agreement.

But individuals hurt by contract violations often learn to their dismay that unions fail to help them. For example, unions, for a variety of reasons, often do not arbitrate meritorious claims. The result is that contract rights that appeared to be cast in marble often turn out to be written in sand.

It is wrong not to arbitrate for a long service employee with a good work record who has been unfairly discharged. A citizen accused of a traffic violation has the absolute right to a hearing and several appeals if convicted. Yet, the victim of a wrongful termination, who has lost everything, may never get a day in court.

Unfortunately, there is inadequate legal protection for victims of unfair representation. The record of section 301–DFR plaintiffs in court is abysmal.[2] There are only a few reported verdicts that have been affirmed. As a practical matter, individual rights remain illusory.

Rank-and-file employees do not understand the rationale of existing law, which appears to favor the labor-management establishment at the expense of individual rights—neither does the public, which is sympathetic to the growing trend of judicial erosion of the

---

2. NLRB records show a greater percentage and number of victories for individual victims of section 8(b)(1)(A) violations. But, such statistics are unrealistic, since it is believed that over 90 percent of all DFR charges are dismissed by the Regional Directors. Also, the employer is usually not a party to NLRB proceedings, and the remedy, therefore, is often inadequate.

employment-at-will doctrine and protection of job rights in the non-union sector.[3]

Plaintiffs' Frustration and Anger

Defendants often characterize section 301–DFR plaintiffs as paranoid. But if the latter's view of the labor-management world is a little distorted, it is no wonder. Employees who have been wronged by their employer and abandoned by their union usually become hostile, bitter, and emotionally upset. Their former allies—foremen, personnel directors, stewards, business agents, and co-workers have turned against them. They tend to see union and management groups as a monolith, working together to defeat their reasonable objectives.

As the worker's case moves from the factory and union hall to the courtroom, the list of adversaries grows. By then, an arbitrator, a joint committee, the EEOC, an unemployment or workers' compensation agency, or the NLRB has usually denied one of the claims. They attribute their defeats to conspiracy and other improper motives.[4] They suspect the defendants may have tampered with the tribunals that have issued adverse decisions.

An employee's last hope is the private bar and a United States district court. These institutions usually fail him. The court usually agrees with the company and union and dismisses the case on some technical legal point unrelated to the merits of his grievance. Most lawyers refuse to take his case. The lawyer he finally obtains often seems more preoccupied with obtaining a fee than with helping him. His lawyer's original enthusiasm for the case usually becomes blunted by time, the difficulties of the litigation, and the ferocity of the defense efforts. Plaintiff's attorney, with his business suit and friendly rapport with opposing counsel, seems allied with the system that he is fighting.

In a typical case, the company has violated plaintiff's rights as set forth in the labor agreement. The union has mishandled his grievance. Yet, despite an obvious injustice, he loses in court. Thus,

---

3. These views are also expressed in an article of mine, *The Plaintiff's View of 301–DFR Litigation*, 5 Employee Rel. L. J. 510 (1980).

4. Plaintiffs typically voice unverified suspicions that union officials have been "paid off" by the company.

plaintiff's paranoia is reinforced by the adverse result. The reasons for the defeat usually do not make sense, e.g., retroactive application of an unforeseen short statute of limitations, lack of exhaustion of remedies unknown to him, or failure to show more than "mere" negligent representation.

Plaintiff's counsel sometimes shares a distorted view of the workplace. His clients are the exception—those who have been rejected by both employer and union. The lawyer only sees the system broken down, e.g., a grievance procedure that is tainted or ineffective. The union is perceived as an adversary and reacts as an enemy, rather than in its traditional role as champion of the employee.

Plaintiff's counsel is usually a general practitioner and not a labor law expert. After a brief investigation, he is convinced that the employer has acted unfairly. He hears powerful evidence of carelessness, laziness, and often hostility on the part of the union. The initial high expectations are usually dashed upon the obstacles of litigation: great expense, long delay, protracted discovery, technical motions, an exceptionally high burden of proof, massive obstinate resistance by defendants, and an unsympathetic judge.

Plaintiff's attorney emerges from the litigation with a nuisance settlement or a defeat, little or no fee, and often with a disgruntled client who owes him money for unpaid expenses. Like the grievant, he seeks an outlet to vent his disappointment and frustration. The labor-management establishment and the court system, which have adopted its views, become the targets.

Recent events reinforce the disillusionment of the plaintiffs' bar. In spite of the terrible track record of employees in section 301–DFR cases, defendants view these suits with an alarm that almost reaches hysteria. Faced with serious economic problems resulting from automation, foreign imports, and the recession, big labor and big management are frustrated. They unite in their antagonism towards outsiders, dissidents, and individual employees who seek to interfere with their internal dispute-resolution system, the grievance-arbitration procedure. Plaintiffs in section 301–DFR suits are a natural scapegoat.

One of the leading groups representing the labor-management establishment is the American Bar Association (ABA) Section of Labor and Employment Law, with more than ten thousand lawyers representing primarily employers and unions. At the mid-winter 1981 meeting of the ABA section's governing body in the Domini-

can Republic, there was unprecedented unanimity favoring new legislation, which would drastically diminish the rights of plaintiffs in
section 301–DFR suits.

A few weeks later, the prayers of the ABA were answered. On
April 20, 1981, the Supreme Court announced its decision in *United
Parcel Service* v. *Mitchell*.[5] For thirty-five years, lawyers and scholars
believed that plaintiffs had several years to file suit and were governed by breach of contract, tort, and other miscellaneous state statutes of limitations.[6] Out of the blue, the Supreme Court declared
that short arbitration statutes, usually no more than ninety days
in duration, governed suits against the employer like *Hines*.[7] The
lower federal courts, thereafter, routinely dismissed pending section
301–DFR suits against both company and union, even where no arbitration had been held, and even though in *Mitchell* the union was
not a party.[8]

The lower courts were almost unanimous in applying *Mitchell*
retroactively.[9] The result was the brutal, wholesale dismissal of
cases. Hundreds of plaintiffs, who had relied in good faith upon
long statutes of limitations and whose cases had often been pending
for several years, were unfairly denied a right to trial.[10]

The federal courts have been overwhelmed by the increasing
number of new filings and resultant backlogs. Federal judges have
adopted the notion that the grievance-arbitration procedure is the
panacea for labor problems and that the federal courts are not the
place to resolve an individual's labor disputes.[11]

---

5. 451 U.S. 56, 107 LRRM 2001 (1981).

6. *See*, Note, *Statute of Limitations Governing Fair Representation Action against Union
When Brought with Section 301 Action against the Employer*, 44 Geo. Wash. L. Rev. 418
(1976) and Boyce, Fair Representation, the N.L.R.B. and the Courts 90–95 (Univ. of
Pennsylvania, Wharton School 1978).

7. Hines v. Anchor Motor Freight, Inc., 424 U.S. 554, 91 LRRM 2481 (1976).

8. *See, e.g.* Badon v. General Motors Corp., 679 F.2d 93, 110 LRRM 2562 (6th
Cir. 1982).

9. *See, e.g.*, Lawson v. Teamsters Local 100, 698 F.2d 250, 112 LRRM 2553 (6th
Cir. 1983); Stevens v. Gateway Transportation Co., 696 F.2d 500, 112 LRRM 2177
(7th Cir. 1982). *Cf.* Singer v. Flying Tiger Line, Inc., 652 F.2d 1349, 108 LRRM 2392
(9th Cir. 1981).

10. Chevron Oil Co. v. Hudson, 404 U.S. 97 (1971), holds that a dramatic change
in the law that was not "clearly foreshadowed" should not be retroactive where substantial inequity results.

11. The Steelworkers Trilogy is traditionally cited by courts as containing the rationale for judicial abstention, *e.g.*, Steelworkers v. Warrior & Gulf Navigation Co.,
363 U.S. 574, 46 LRRM 2416 (1960). Federal judges tend to be impressed by the

For these reasons, the courts do not look with favor upon section 301–DFR suits. Their attitude, recently articulated by the Seventh Circuit, is that these cases are often "trivial" and "prevent not only federal judges but unions and employers from getting on with more important matters."[12] The *Mitchell* case and its progeny provided a method for the courts to clear their dockets of numerous jury trials, a trend that is likely to continue in the post-*DelCostello* era.[13] The retroactive application of *Mitchell* and *DelCostello* is an example of the courts callous attitude towards section 301–DFR plaintiffs.[14]

No Adequate Remedies

The Supreme Court heralded the duty of fair representation as "a bulwark to prevent arbitrary union conduct against individuals stripped of traditional forms of redress."[15] The plain truth, however, was more realistically expressed by Clyde Summers, who stated that the "law still is almost without exception a form of words which holds the promise to the ear and breaks it to the heart."[16]

The recent *DelCostello* case established a six-month uniform federal statute of limitations, rather than the shorter state arbitration statutes resulting from *Mitchell*.[17] No other category of civil court litigants with an original action is faced with a statute of limitations of less than one year.

unity of expert counsel for the union and employer concerning the issues of a section 301–DFR case.

12. Dober v. Roadway Express, Inc., 707 F.2d 292, 113 LRRM 2595 (7th Cir. 1983). Recently, unsuccessful section 301–DFR plaintiffs have been subjected to the almost unheard of award of attorney fees against them if the court finds the suit "was filed in bad faith." Perichak v. IUE, 715 F.2d 78, 114 LRRM 2134 (3rd Cir. 1983); McCandless v. A&P, 697 F.2d 198, 112 LRRM 2794 (7th Cir. 1983).

13. DelCostello v. I.B.T., 103 S. Ct. 2281, 113 LRRM 2737 (1983).

14. See, e.g., Andrews v. Richards, 114 LRRM 2374 (D.Mo. 1983); Curtis v. I.B.T., Local 299, 716 F.2d 360, 114 LRRM 2355 (6th Cir. 1983); Perez v. Dana Corp., 545 F. Supp. 950, 112 LRRM 2617 (DC Pa. 1982), aff'd, 718 F.2d 581, 114 LRRM 2814 (3d Cir. 1983); Edwards v. Sea-Land Service Inc., 720 F.2d 857 (5th Cir. 1983); Rogers v. Lockheed—Ga. Co., 720 F.2d 1247 (11th Cir. 1983).

15. Vaca v. Sipes, 386 U.S. 171, 64 LRRM 2369 (1967).

16. Summers, *Individual Rights in Collective Agreements and Arbitration*, 37 N.Y.U. L. Rev. 362, 410 n.188 (1962).

17. The analogy of the Court in DelCostello to the six-month 10b statute of the National Labor Relations Act is unfair, since the charging party need not retain a lawyer to file an unfair labor practice charge with the NLRB.

Six months is simply not enough time for a terminated employee to find and retain competent counsel to handle his case. Ninety-five percent of all labor law specialists represent either companies or unions and decline to represent individual employees with section 301–DFR cases. The average plaintiff may have to contact four or five lawyers before finding a maverick employee rights specialist or general practitioner with the special courage to undertake a complex case that does not appear a sure winner.[18]

Six months is an inadequate time to complete the investigation, fact-finding, legal research, reflection, notice to defendants, and settlement discussion that should precede the filing of a law suit. Furthermore, the short limitations period conflicts with other important national policies favoring prior exhaustion of administrative and internal union remedies before going to court.

Counsel typically requires an advance retainer of at least $1,000 to cover start-up expenses, part of the fee, or both. Many employees who have been terminated naturally have financial difficulties and typically need more than six months to raise the money for counsel. In sum, the short statute makes it extremely difficult for a discharged employee without special resources to commence a timely lawsuit.

For the few plaintiffs fortunate enough to retain a good lawyer within six months, the litigation path is strewn with almost insurmountable legal hurdles.

The Supreme Court still clings to the idea that the union owns the grievance and should be able to control what happens in the grievance procedure. The union control theory remains the lynch pin for its decisions.[19] Recently, the Court reaffirmed its belief that "union discretion [in grievance handling] is essential to the proper functioning of the collective bargaining system."[20]

The lower courts are reluctant to interfere with a union's decisions concerning grievance handling. Plaintiffs must show unfair representation to gain standing to sue the employer. Grievants who

---

18. Employee rights specialists now concentrate on more lucrative age discrimination and nonunion employment-at-will discharge cases and are extremely wary of taking a new section 301–DFR case.

19. The term union controlled grievance theory is found in Comment, *The Union's Duty of Fair Representation: Group Membership Interests v. Individual Interests,* 16 Duq. L. Rev. 779, 787 (1977–78).

20. IBEW v. Foust, 442 U.S. 42, 60 L. Ed.2d 698, 101 LRRM 2365 (1975).

have meritorious claims but are denied access to arbitration have no judicial remedy, unless they can prove outrageous union misconduct. The rationale is that some individuals must be sacrificed in order to prop up the union's prestige and to achieve more important union policies involving collective interests.[21]

The focus of the current debate on the definition of the DFR, unfortunately, remains on the issue of union liability, rather than the issue of when plaintiffs should be able to obtain a de novo hearing of the contract claim in court. Victims of a swap, whose grievances have been dropped or improperly compromised solely in order to benefit other grievants and others who have not received adequate representation because of a union conflict of interest are often unable to obtain relief.[22] Moreover, the largest American union, the Teamsters, often cooperates with employers to deny their members fair and unbiased hearings. The decisions of Teamster joint employer-union committees are frequently governed by political deals and prejudged at secret ex parte conferences.[23] Yet, individual Teamsters have no practical remedy for relief from the abuses of the joint committee system.[24] Furthermore, unjustly discharged employees whose unions are without funds to underwrite arbitration are routinely denied a court hearing on the merits.[25]

Unlike all other fiduciaries, a union can be negligent without incurring liability for damages. In cases of personal or political hostility, violence, racial animosity, and other forms of malice, victims of a tort traditionally can recover punitive damages. But, the recent *Foust* case eliminates the possibility of an award of punitive damages

---

21. "If you believe in the principle of collective bargaining you must believe in the collective interest and not the individual interest." Associate General Counsel of the United Steelworkers of America, Carl B. Frankel, quoted in *Business Week,* Aug. 13, 1979, p. 76. However, recent surveys show that contrary to what their lawyers say, most union leaders in fact believe that individual rights are paramount and should not be sacrificed. Schwartz, *Different Views of the Duty of Fair Representation,* 34 Lab. L. J. 415 (1983).

22. Buchholtz v. Swift & Co., 609 F.2d 317, 102 LRRM 2219 (8th Cir. 1979), *cert. denied,* 444 U.S. 1018, 103 LRRM 2143 (1980).

23. Azoff, *Joint Committees as an Alternative Form of Arbitration under the NLRA,* 47 Tul. L. Rev. 325, 328–30 (1973).

24. Davis v. Ryder Truck Lines, Inc., 113 LRRM 2072 (S.D. Ohio 1982); Early v. Eastern Transfer, 699 F.2d 552, 112 LRRM 3381 (1st Cir. 1983).

25. "The mere fact that the union is inept, negligent, unwise and insensitive or ineffectual will not standing alone, establish a breach of the duty." Statement of NLRB general counsel. Quoted with approval in Kleban v. Hygrade Food Products Corp., 102 LRRM 2773 (E.D. Mich. 1979).

against a union, even in the most aggravated unfair representation cases.[26] Also, in spite of the recent *Clayton* case, plaintiffs, under some circumstances, may still be required to go through the motions of exhausting complicated, obscure, time-consuming, biased, and unknown internal union remedies to gain standing to sue not only the union but also the employer.[27]

Bowen v. *United States Postal Service* has reduced the possibility of out-of-court settlements of section 301–DFR actions.[28] Unions are now faced with the lion's share of the liability, i.e., breach of contract damages beginning from the date of the hypothetical arbitration award, plus attorneys fees. The maximum liability of an employer in the average discharge case is only about nine months back pay.

Before *Bowen,* some plaintiffs often made token settlements with the union or did not sue the union at all, hoping for the union's cooperation in prosecution of the claim against the employer. Previously, plaintiffs with a strong case against a "deep pocket" employer could anticipate the possibility of a modest settlement, since the employer bore the greatest financial exposure. Such scenarios are no longer viable. Unions, for a variety of political, economic, and policy reasons, are much less likely to settle cases than employers. Since *Bowen,* it has been almost impossible for plaintiffs with large damage claims to obtain a reasonable settlement. As a result, lawyers are even less likely to represent plaintiffs with bona fide claims on a contingency basis.[29] Another result is that settlement of plaintiff's claim by arbitration becomes impossible in some cases unless the union is joined as a party defendant.[30]

---

26. IBEW v. Foust, 442 U.S. 42, 101 LRRM 2365 (1979).

27. Clayton v. UAW, 451 U.S. 679, 107 LRRM 2385 (1981). Illustrative post-Clayton cases are Tinsley v. United Parcel Service, 635 F.2d 1288, 109 LRRM 2035 (7th Cir. 1981); Rios v. UAW, 98 LC 10,308 (C.D. Calif. 1982).

28. 103 S. Ct. 588, 112 LRRM 2281 (1983).

29. A recent article cogently points out that in wrongful discharge cases the contingency fee system discourages suits for plaintiffs "whose lower levels of lost income results in a lower level of damages and hence smaller expected returns for attorneys." Note, *Protecting Employees at Will against Wrongful Discharge: The Public Policy Exception,* 96 Harv. L. Rev. 1931, 1943 (1983). Experienced lawyers usually will not represent employees with grievances involving nonmonetary issues or small claims. There is little incentive for a lawyer to accept a discharge case which has a settlement potential of less than $10,000 when faced with a hundred hours of work to achieve the settlement.

30. An arbitration in which both union and employer are hostile to the employee's claim would be an unfair tribunal for plaintiff since most professional arbitrators would be reluctant to rule against the hand that feeds them.

In practice, the federal courts are for the well-to-do. Governments, large corporations, and wealthy individuals, battling among themselves, can obtain justice there. But for a section 301–DFR plaintiff, the expense of complex litigation against powerful, well-heeled adversaries is usually more than he can bear. For example, the cost of taking and transcribing five days of depositions is more than $3,500. Photocopying, travel, telephone, subpoena fees, investigation, and other miscellaneous costs usually total at least $1,000. These out-of-pocket expenses are usually out of reach of the average unemployed dischargee. Counsel may be willing to take the case on a contingency basis but usually is unwilling to advance such costs.

Even if plaintiff has the law and facts on his side, he and his counsel will have difficulty sustaining the burden of years of struggle in discovery, trial, appeal, and retrial.[31] Motions for summary judgment are inevitable and are difficult to overcome. The defendants control most of the important witnesses and documentary evidence. The union presents a united front with the company concerning critical questions of contract interpretation and past practice. The delays are monstrous. Many plaintiffs literally do not survive the decade or so that may be necessary to prevail in protracted litigation.[32]

Bright Spots for Plaintiffs

The section 301–DFR scene is not all bad. First of all, the law is now more settled, well known, and available to the labor relations community.[33]

There have been a number of verdicts favorable to plaintiffs.[34]

---

31. Examples of large plaintiff verdicts recently overturned by the court of appeals are: Freeman v. O'Neal Steel, 609 F.2d 1123, 103 LRRM 2398 (5th Cir. 1980); Anderson v. Paperworkers, 641 F.2d 574, 106 LRRM 2513 (8th Cir. 1981); Self v. I.B.T., Local 61, 620 F.2d 439, 104 LRRM 2125 (4th Cir. 1980); Findley v. Jones Motor Freight, 639 F.2d 953, 106 LRRM 2420 (3d Cir. 1981).

32. Scott v. I.B.T., Local 377, 548 F.2d 1244, 94 LRRM 2505 (6th Cir. 1977), *cert. denied*, 431 U.S. 968, 95 LRRM 2643 (1977); Gray v. Asbestos Workers, Local 51, 447 F.2d 1118, 78 LRRM 2291 (6th Cir. 1971). Scott and Gray, like plaintiffs Hines and Owens in the Hines and Vaca cases, never lived to see the results of their claims.

33. *See, e.g.,* Morris, 2 The Developing Labor Law 1285–1358 (2d ed. BNA 1983), devoted exclusively to section 301–DFR suits.

34. *See, e.g.,* Tatum v. Frisco Transp. Co., 626 F.2d 55, 104 LRRM 2089 (8th Cir. 1980); Bryne v. Buffalo, 98 LC 10,279 (2d Cir. 1983); Seymour v. Olin Corp., 666

There have been notable settlements. Counsel and trial judges are more familiar with the applicable case law. Jury instructions are no longer a novelty. The outcome is more predictable. Counsel and their clients now have sufficient experience to work out reasonable settlements, if they desire.

More important, section 301–DFR litigation has dramatically affected the unions' attitude towards the grievance procedure. Unions now pay more attention to grievance handling. Also, unions now place a greater emphasis on educating business agents and stewards about the investigation and presentation of grievances. Union lawyers are routinely consulted about whether to arbitrate. The result is that grievants are receiving better representation. Also, fear of lawsuits has caused a marked increase in the number of arbitrations. The *Bowen* case, with its added financial exposure for unions, will undoubtedly accelerate the trend toward more arbitrations.

The scope of the duty has expanded. The majority of the circuit courts now hold that it is not necessary to prove bad faith to show unfair representation.[35] Gross negligence, as well as unexplained, irrational, and unreasonable inaction have recently been held to be prohibited.[36] The mere fact that a union's decision is in good faith or made for what is thought to be good union policy will not immunize its conduct if there is objective evidence of arbitrary representation.[37] The Supreme Court's use of the word *perfunctory* in *DelCostello*, along with "arbitrary, discriminatory, and bad faith," potentially strengthens plaintiff's position that gross negligence violates the duty. In addition, there is a trend toward development of the duty of fair representation in the negotiation and ratification of

---

F.2d 202, 109 LRRM 2728 (5th Cir. 1982); Lowe v. Pate Stevedoring Co., 595 F.2d 256, 101 LRRM 2357 (5th Cir. 1979); and Harrison v. U.T.U., 530 F.2d 558, 90 LRRM 3265 (4th Cir. 1975), *cert. denied*, 425 U.S. 958, 92 LRRM 2168 (1976).

35. *See, e.g.*, Poole v. Budd Co., 706 F.2d 181, 113 LRRM 2493 (6th Cir. 1983). *See also*, Morgan, *Fair Is Foul, and Foul Is Fair—Ruzicka and the Duty of Fair Representation in the Circuit Courts*, 11 U. Tol. L. Rev. 335 (1980), regarding the different standards used in each circuit.

36. Ruzicka v. General Motors, 649 F.2d 1207 (6th Cir. 1981); Milstead v. I.B.T., Local 957, 580 F.2d 232, 99 LRRM 2150 (6th Cir. 1978); Dutrisac v. Caterpillar Tractor Co., 113 LRRM 3532 (9th Cir. 1983).

37. Wyatt v. Interstate & Ocean Transp. Co., 623 F.2d 888 (4th Cir. 1980); Miller v. Gateway Transp. Co., Inc., 616 F.2d 272, 103 LRRM 2591 (7th Cir. 1980); NLRB v. Postal Workers, 618 F.2d 1249, 103 LRRM 3045 (8th Cir. 1980).

labor agreements. For example, numerous violations have been sustained where the union has failed to communicate properly with employees concerning contract proposals.[38]

Issues for the 1980s

Over the next few years, plaintiffs will be urging that the courts adopt the following positions:

1. The filing of an internal union appeal of unfair representation, the filing of section 8(b)(1)(A) unfair labor practice charges with the NLRB, or a request for a rehearing of an adverse joint committee or arbitration decision tolls the statute of limitations during the pendency of these procedings.[39]

2. The statute of limitations does not run against company or union until the plaintiff has actual knowledge of the acts constituting unfair representation; and fraudulent concealment of the breach of the DFR tolls the running of the statute.[40]

3. When there is a conflict of interest between individuals and groups, such as disputes over allocation of overtime, seniority rights, and fight cases, the union has a duty to give reasonable advance notice to all interested employees of any grievance meetings or arbitration affecting the rights of either party.[41] The union should give advance notice of the position it intends to take, in order that the person or group not favored by the union may take steps to protect themselves. If the union actively favors one group, the other unrepresented group should be able to ob-

---

38. Parker v. Local 413, 657 F.2d 269 (6th Cir. 1981); Trail v. I.B.T., 542 F.2d 961, 93 LRRM 3076 (6th Cir. 1976).

39. Pesola v. Inland Tool and Mfg. Inc., 423 F. Supp. 30, 93 LRRM 2458 (E.D. Mich. 1976); Dent v. U.S. Postal Service, 542 F. Supp. 834, 113 LRRM 3343 (S.D. Ohio 1982). In addition, the statute is no bar where there is continuing misconduct. Angulo v. Levy Co., 113 LRRM 2335 (N.D. Ill. 1983).

40. Brown v. College of Medicine, 101 LRRM 3019 (N.J. Super. Ct. 1979).

41. For seniority cases with varying results, *see,* Bell v. I.M.L. Freight, Inc., 589 F.2d 502, 100 LRRM 2219 (10th Cir. 1979); King v. Space Carriers, 608 F.2d 283, 102 LRRM 2590 (8th Cir. 1979); Humphrey v. Moore, 375 U.S. 335 (1964); and Smith v. Hussmann Refrigerator Co., 100 LRRM 2238 (8th Cir. 1979). Examples of fight cases are Prude v. Drackett, 27 EPD 32,334, 93 LC 13,296 (N.D. Ill. 1981) and Amalgamated Clothing & Textile Workers, 259 NLRB No. 152, 109 LRRM 1087 (1982).

tain a de novo hearing of a meritorious grievance in court without further proof of unfair representation.

4. The court cannot consider or admit an NLRB dismissal or withdrawal of a section 8(b)(1)(A) unfair labor practice charge as evidence concerning the breach of DFR issue.[42]

5. A decision of a Teamsters joint committee is not accorded the same weight as a decision of ᵒ professional arbitrator and a plaintiff need not show unfair representation to obtain judicial review of the merits if plaintiff has been denied a fair hearing before a joint committee.[43]

6. Expert testimony concerning the practices of the parties with respect to arbitration is admissible, but expert opinion as to the ultimate breach of duty issue is not admissible.[44]

7. The union should continue to be responsible for attorney fees and litigation expenses as part of compensatory damages or under the "common benefit–private attorney general theory."[45]

8. The union can be liable for refusal to process a grievance or other forms of unfair representation, even if there is no breach of contract or finding against the employer, for example, where it is established that there was a lost possibility of a settlement with the employer.[46]

9. In extreme cases of intentional breach of the DFR, plaintiffs can recover damages for emotional distress.[47]

---

42. Smith v. Hussmann Refrigerator Co., 100 LRRM 2238 (8th Cir. 1979).

43. At present, a joint committee decision cannot be vacated unless there is unfair representation; the court gives an employee standing to bring action to vacate under the U.S. Arbitration Act and fraud, bias, or collusion can be shown; or the award fails to draw its essence from the agreement or the committee exceeds its powers. Davis v. Ohio Barge Line, Inc., 535 F. Supp. 1324, 28 FEP Cases 1723 (W.D. Pa. 1982), *vacated and rem'd,* 112 LRRM 2892 (3d Cir. 1983); Barrentine v. Arkansas–Best Freight System, Inc., 615 F.2d 1194, 103 LRRM 1732 (8th Cir. 1980).

44. *See,* Freeman v. O'Neal Steel, 436 F. Supp. 607, 95 LRRM 3212 (D. Ala. 1977), *rev'd on other grounds,* 609 F.2d 1123, 103 LRRM 2398 (5th Cir. 1980).

45. Emmanuel v. Omaha Carpenters, 560 F.2d 382, 95 LRRM 3320 (8th Cir. 1977); Scott v. I.B.T., Local 377, 548 F.2d 1244, 94 LRRM 2505 (6th Cir. 1977), *cert. denied,* 431 U.S. 968, 95 LRRM 2643 (1977).

46. Harrison v. U.T.U., 530 F.2d 558, 90 LRRM 3265 (4th Cir. 1975), *cert. denied,* 425 U.S. 958, 92 LRRM 2168 (1976).

47. Kaiser v. Local 83, 577 F.2d 642, 99 LRRM 2011 (9th Cir. 1978); Farmer v. A.R.A. Services, 660 F.2d 1096, 108 LRRM 2145 (6th Cir. 1981).

10. Reliance on the advice of its attorney concerning the dropping of a grievance does not insulate a union from DFR liability.[48]

11. The court may order reinstatement or in lieu thereof "front pay," prospective damages from the date of trial to the expected date of retirement. If the employer successfully argues that reinstatement is an improper remedy, the employer, rather than the union, should be liable for the prospective damages.

12. The fact that a union's decision not to arbitrate is made or ratified by a vote of the membership does not insulate the union's decision from careful scrutiny.[49]

13. Upon request, a union has a DFR concerning enforcement of a favorable arbitration award in court and vacation of an illegal award.[50] A union also has the duty to act in good faith concerning the handling of unfair labor practice charges filed with the NLRB.

14. A union that pleads poverty as the reason for failure to arbitrate but fails to permit the grievant to pay the costs is guilty of unfair representation, and the employee has a right to trial of a section 301–DFR claim.

15. Failure to notify a grievant of an arbitration, joint committee hearing, or contractual grievance meeting concerning his or her grievance is unfair representation.[51]

16. Failure to follow contractual time limits for filing, processing, or arbitrating grievances is unfair representation as a matter of law, permitting plaintiff to obtain a de novo hearing on the merits of his grievance.

---

48. Gregg v. I.B.T., Local 150, 699 F.2d 1017 (9th Cir. 1983); Hughes v. I.B.T., Local 683, 554 F.2d 365, 95 LRRM 2652 (9th Cir. 1977).

49. Branch 6000 National Ass'n of Letter Carriers v. NLRB, 595 F.2d 808, 100 LRRM 2346 (D.C. Cir. 1979); NLRB v. I.B.T., Local 315, 545 F.2d 1173, 93 LRRM 2747 (9th Cir. 1976); and Alvey v. General Electric, 622 F.2d 279, 104 LRRM 2838 (7th Cir. 1980).

50. *Cf.*, Sear v. Cadillac Auto Co., 501 F. Supp. 1350, 105 LRRM 3366 (D. Mass. 1980).

51. Bond v. I.B.T., Local 823, 521 F.2d 5, 89 LRRM 3153 (8th Cir. 1975); Tatum v. Frisco Transp. Co., 626 F.2d 55, 104 LRRM 2089 (8th Cir. 1980); *cf.*, Whitten v. Anchor Motor Freight, Inc., 521 F.2d 1335, 90 LRRM 2161 (6th Cir. 1975), *cert. denied*, 425 U.S. 981, 94 LRRM 2201 (1976).

17. A union that merely "goes through the motions" without proper investigation or presentation of argument is guilty of perfunctory unfair representation.[52]

18. Under some circumstances, an international union may be liable for unfair representation, even if it is not a party to the labor agreement.[53]

19. Plaintiffs are entitled to trial by jury.[54]

20. A plaintiff should not be required, against his will, to accept an arbitration controlled by defendants as the sole remedy for breach of contract and the DFR without provision for payment of plaintiff's fees and other safeguards assuring a fair hearing.[55]

Suggestions for Reform

Some state courts now hold that nonunion employees discharged in bad faith, or in violation of company rules or contrary to public policy, have standing to sue. These nonunion employees do not have the protection of a labor agreement and its just-cause clause. Nevertheless, they have an absolute right to a judicial determination of the merits of their claims of wrongful discharge. Ironically, this recent judicial erosion of the employment-at-will doctrine means that many nonunion employees will have greater legal protection than union employees.[56] The plight of the wrongfully discharged employee,

---

52. Curtis v. U.T.U., 102 LRRM 2961 (E.D. Ark. 1979), 486 F. Supp. 966, 103 LRRM 2779 (E.D. Ark. 1980), rev'd, 648 F.2d 492, 107 LRRM 2442 (8th Cir. 1981). See, Printing and Graphic Communication, Local 4, 267 NLRB No. 78, 114 LRRM 1026 (1983) (following Tenorio v. NLRB, 680 F.2d 598, 110 LRRM 2939 (9th Cir. 1982).

53. Donahue v. L.C.L. Transit Co., 492 F. Supp. 288, 105 LRRM 3491 (W.D. Wis. 1980).

54. Minnis v. UAW, 531 F.2d 850, 91 LRRM 2081 (8th Cir. 1975); Cox v. C.H. Masland & Sons, 607 F.2d 138, 102 LRRM 2889 (5th Cir. 1979).

55. Hiller v. Liquor Salesman's Local 2, 338 F.2d 778, 57 LRRM 2629 (2d Cir. 1965); Carlisle v. ILGWU, Local 122, 102 LRRM 2804 (N.D. Ga. 1979); Chapman v. Southeast Region ILGWU, 280 F. Supp. 766 (D. S.C. 1978); Wyatt v. Interstate & Ocean Transp. Co., 96 LRRM 3095 (E.D. Va. 1977).

56. See, e.g., Lamb v. Briggs Mfg., 97 LC 55,390 (7th Cir. 1983) (union employees do not have protection of the new statute in Illinois protecting victims of retaliatory discharges). Cf., Peabody Galion v. Dollar, 666 F.2d 1309, 109 LRRM 2068 (10th Cir. 1981).

abandoned by his union and denied the right to an impartial hearing in arbitration or court, becomes even more desparate.

The most desirable solution is to guarantee every worker with a nonfrivolous claim of wrongful discharge a fair hearing in some tribunal—either arbitration, administrative agency, or court. Section 9(a) of the National Labor Relations Act[37] should be interpreted or, if necessary, amended to permit employees to arbitrate their own grievances and pay the costs themselves, if the union will not represent them. If employees are denied the right to process grievances, they should be able to petition a United States district court for the appointment of a master to act as the arbitrator of the grievance. Another alternative would be to give a new branch of the NLRB exclusive jurisdiction over wrongful discharge cases, if a union refuses to arbitrate or the employee fears unfair representation. A similar system prevails for discharged federal employees, who must elect whether to have their appeals arbitrated by the union or heard by the Merit System Protection Board (MSPB).[38]

The prospect for legislative reform is bleak. Individual employees have no lobbies in Washington or champions in Congress to support them. Management and labor have the political clout to defeat any proposals harmful to their interests. Individuals can look only to courageous federal judges for creative development and interpretation of the law.

In most cases, the federal courts do not provide industrial justice. The real beneficiaries of section 301–DFR litigation are not the plaintiffs, but those employees who have received improved representation in the grievance procedure as a result of union fear of DFR suits.

Job rights have escalated in economic, social, and psychological importance. To the average American, freedom from wrongful termination may rank higher than the liberties protected by the United States Constitution. The current trend of section 301–DFR litigation approves substandard union representation and subordinates the role of the individual to the collective interest of the union. This

---

57. Section 9(a) of the act states, *inter alia*, that employees "shall have the right at any time to present grievances to their employer and to have such grievances adjusted without the intervention of the bargaining representative. . . ."

58. *See*, Civil Service Reform Act, 5 U.S.C. §§ 4301, 7121 (1978).

pattern runs counter to the public's view of industrial justice, while the direction of state court decisions in employment-at-will cases is more in tune with the times.

Existing remedies for the victims of unfair representation are plainly inadequate. The American legal system should find a way to bring its decisions in line with the expectations of our citizens.

Measuring the Union's Duty to the Individual: An Analytic Framework

Clyde W. Summers

How do we measure the duty owed by a union to an individual employee when it represents that employee in the grievance procedure or in arbitration? The adjectives of *Vaca* v. *Sipes*—"arbitrary, discriminatory or in bad faith"—describe results more than define boundaries.[1] The more explicit directions of the Court—"a union must in good faith and in non-arbitrary manner, make decisions as to the merits of particular grievances," and "a union may not arbitrarily ignore a meritorious grievance or process it in a perfunctory manner"—provide, at best uncertain guidance.[2]

My purpose is to get beyond the adjectives and generalities and to develop a framework of analysis that builds on the rights involved and distinguishes between categories of cases. The union's duty varies depending on the particular function it is performing and failure that is claimed. I cannot work out all the variations. I can at most construct the framework, fleshed out by a few illustrations.

The Underlying Premise of Individual Contract Rights

The starting point for building an analytic framework to measure the union's duty is the starting point used by the Court in *Vaca* v. *Sipes*—the individual's right under the collective agreement. The

---

1. 386 U.S. 171, 190, 64 LRRM 2369, 2376 (1967).
2. *Id.* at 194, 191, 64 LRRM at 2378, 2377.

basic premise of *Vaca* v. *Sipes,* built upon *Smith* v. *Evening News,*[3] is that an individual employee acquires legal rights under the collective agreement which he can enforce under section 301.[4] This was made explicit by the Court in the following terms:

> let us assume a collective bargaining agreement that limits discharges to those for good cause and that contains no grievance, arbitration or other provisions purporting to restrict access to the courts. If an employee is discharged without cause, either the union or the employee may sue the employer under Section 301. . . . Smith v Evening News Ass'n, 371 U.S. 195.[5]

The logic of *Vaca* was that the individual had a legally enforceable contract right, subject only to exhaustion of the procedures provided by the contract. To excuse exhaustion, the individual must show that he attempted to exhaust the procedures but was prevented from doing so by the union's failure to represent him fairly.

When the employee sues the employer, violation of the duty of fair representation is not the basis of the action. The suit is for violations of contract, and fair representation by the union is a bar to that suit. The union's duty is a separate legal duty enforceable by a separate cause of action, with a separate measure of damages. The union's liability under *Bowen* may include some of the damages for violation of the employee's contract right. Thus, in discharge cases this includes the additional wages or other contractual rights lost because of the delay in the individual obtaining a remedy due to the union's failure to meet its statutory duty to represent the employee. The underlying right, however, is the contract right, and the substantive damages are for violation of that right.

The starting premise was underlined by *Hines* v. *Anchor Motor Freight,* in which the Court again started with a restatement of *Smith* v. *Evening News,*

> Section 301 contemplates suits by and against individual employees as well as between unions and employers.[6]

Discharging for theft an employee who was in fact not guilty was a violation of that employee's contract right not to be discharged without cause. The employee could sue the employer under section 301, and the employer's only defense was that the employee was fairly represented in the arbitration proceedings. The union's failure to

---

3. 371 U.S. 195, 51 LRRM 2646 (1962).
4. 29 U.S.C. § 185.
5. 386 U.S. at 183, 64 LRRM 2374.
6. 424 U.S. 554, 562, 91 LRRM 2481, 2484.

investigate removed the employer's defense, and the employer was liable to the employee for violating his contract right, even though the employer had no part in the union's failure to represent fairly. Not even an arbitration award stands as a bar to the employee's action when the union has failed in its duty:

> We cannot believe that Congress intended to foreclose the employee from his Section 301 remedies otherwise available against the employer if the contractual processes have been seriously flawed by the union's breach of its duty.[7]

The right the Court sought to protect was the individual employee's contract right under the collective agreement. The employee was to be foreclosed from his section 301 remedies only by the union's proper processing of it as his representative.

The premises and reasoning of *Smith, Vaca,* and *Hines* make three propositions doubly clear—propositions that reject too often accepted assumptions.

First, the obstacle to individual suits under collective agreements does not arise from the union's statutory status as exclusive representative; the obstacle is erected by the union and the employer when they provide that their grievance procedure and arbitration shall be the exclusive means for remedying breaches of contract. In *Smith* v. *Evening News,* the Teamsters union was the statutory representative, but this did not give it exclusive right to enforce contract rights. In the absence of such a provision in the collective agreement, the individual employee could sue. In *Vaca* v. *Sipes* the individual's suit was barred because, as the Court repeatedly emphasized, the collective agreement provided that the union had sole power to invoke the higher stages of the grievance procedure and demand arbitration. It was the union's assertion, with the assent of the employer, of exclusive control over contractual procedures that foreclosed the individual from his section 301 remedies.

Second, the union does not "own" the grievance. The union may, by agreement with the employer, assert control over access to the contractual procedures and insist on being the exclusive representative in those procedures. The individual, however, continues to have rights under the collective agreement and can bring suit

---

7. *Id.* at 570, 91 LRRM at 2481.

in his own name to enforce those rights. That suit is barred only if the union has represented him fairly in the contractual procedures over which it has asserted control.

Third, the union's role in grievance handling is completely different from its role in negotiation. In negotiations, the union is creating rights, rights the individuals did not otherwise have. The union's duty is not to discriminate unfairly among employees in creating those rights, and the individual's claim is only for a fair share. In grievance settlement and arbitration, the union is administering a procedure for enforcing rights that the individuals have. The union's duty is to act as their representative in those procedures to enforce their rights, not deprive them of their rights. In negotiations there are no basic guidelines for what rights should be created; in grievance settlements the basic guideline is the contract right.

Starting with the basic proposition that the individual employee acquires legal rights under the collective agreement, rights which he or she can individually enforce in court under section 301 but for the union's asserting exclusive power to act as representative, how should we measure the union's duty to represent the individual in the grievance procedure and arbitration over which it asserts exclusive control? Answering that question requires that we examine separately the union's duty when it resolves or settles disputes as to contract interpretation and when it resolves and settles disputes as to factual issues. Regardless of whether the issue is one of contract interpretation or one of fact, there is the additional question of the union's duty to follow certain procedures in processing the grievance. These are the three major categories of fair representation cases, and the underlying premise is applicable to each category in quite different ways.

This framework of analysis will not reconcile all the cases, because they are hopelessly irreconcilable. Nor will it necessarily reach results consistent with the so-called majority view, if that exists anywhere except in the astigmatic eyes of the viewer. The mirage of appealing adjectives has led courts far into an uncharted wasteland. The most that can be done here is to mark out the paths that the underlying premise of *Vaca* and *Hines* provide and that track the complex of individual and collective rights to which those paths lead.

Cases of Contract Interpretation

In the contract interpretation cases it is necessary to distinguish between two broad types: first, thoses cases with which there is no substantial dispute as to the meaning and application of the relevant term of the contract, and second, those cases in which the meaning and application of the provision are unclear and unsettled.

Where there is no substantial dispute as to the meaning and application of the agreement, the union's refusal to process a grievance constitutes a refusal to enforce the individual's contract right and a total denial of that right. For example, in *Lerwill* v. *Inflight Motion Pictures,* the collective agreement clearly defined the workday and workweek and required premium pay for overtime.[8] The employer failed to pay the premium for overtime hours, but the union refused to process a grievance. The union claimed that if the right to overtime premium were enforced, the employer would shorten the workweek, with a reduction in earnings, and some employees wanted the extra hours. The employees had an undisputed contract right to overtime pay, and this was a legally enforceable right. The court upheld the employees' suit against the employer. The union, which assumed the role of exclusive representative to enforce such rights, cannot refuse to enforce them on the employees' behalf and at the same time bar the individuals from enforcing them in their own behalf.

To take another case, the collective agreement requires that after the probationary period employees must be paid the regular rate. The employer continues to pay the probationary rate for a year after the probationary period has ended, but the union refuses to process a grievance on the claim that the employer would otherwise dismiss employees before the end of the probationary period and hire new employees. In the terms used by the Court in *Vaca,* the union has not made a good-faith judgment as to the merits of the grievance, for the merits are not in dispute. The union has arbitrarily ignored a meritorious grievance; its action is arbitrary in the most elemental sense of that word, as not being in accord with rule or principle.

Where the meaning of the collective agreement is not in dispute,

---

8. 582 F.2d 507 (9th Cir. 1978).

the individual employee has a clear contract right. The union's duty as representative of the employee is to enforce, not destroy, that contract right. For the union to do any less is not just a failure to represent fairly, it is a failure to represent at all. Indeed, it is to act against, rather than on behalf of the employee it has undertaken to represent.

The union may, of course, negotiate amendments to contractual provisions that it finds unwise or undesirable,[9] and the fairness of that amendment will be judged by the good-faith standard of *Steele* and *Huffman,* rather than the contractual right or meritorious grievance standard of *Vaca.*[10] But until the agreement is amended by procedures prescribed by union rules for amendment, the union should be bound to follow the substantive rules established by its collective agreement and enforce the rights those rules create.

This result does no more than fulfill the expectations all the parties had when the contract was negotiated. Before an explicit provision is agreed upon, the union and management representatives at the bargaining table have weighed the various interests and competing claims and determined the rights to be created and benefits to be allocated. They expect that the provision agreed upon will govern cases arising during the life of the contract. Also, the union members who approve the agreement, either by referendum or through a committee, expect that they will enjoy the rights created by the provision.

Cases in which the meaning and application of the collective agreement is unclear and unsettled present quite different considerations. If the agreement is ambiguous or leaves a gap, then the union and employer have in fact not agreed upon a governing rule. The ambiguity may be deliberate or the presence of the gap plainly recognized, the parties preferring to leave the terms unsettled than risk impasse or postpone signing the contract until they can negotiate out the unsettled term. More often the potential ambiguity or gaps are not recognized because the parties are unable to foresee the

---

9. *See, e.g.,* Dwyer v. Climatrol Industries Inc., 544 F.2d 307, 93 LRRM 2728 (7th Cir. 1976), *cert. denied,* 430 U.S. 932, 94 LRRM 2962 (1977), where the court upheld the union's formal amendment of a pension agreement to meet the problem of a plant closing.

10. Steele v. Louisville & Nashville RR Co., 323 U.S. 192, 15 LRRM 708 (1944); Ford Motor Co. v. Huffman, 345 U.S. 330, 31 LRRM 2548 (1953); Vaca v. Sipes, 386 U.S. 171, 64 LRRM 2369 (1967).

myriad variations of problems that may arise during the life of the contract. Regardless of the reasons for the ambiguity or gap, the agreement is in fact not complete. Some terms remain unsettled; as to those terms, there is no contract. In such cases, the individual has not acquired a contract right, for the parties have not agreed upon the relevant term.

When grievances raise issues involving unsettled contractual terms, the function of the grievance procedure is to provide a forum for the parties to negotiate settlements of disputed terms. If the parties are unable to agree, then the arbitrator resolves the ambiguity or fills the gap. The grievance procedure and arbitration is the process adopted by the parties to complete the agreement. The process is essentially one of negotiating a term in the collective agreement, and the union's duty should be substantially the same as in negotiating the agreement itself, so long as the settlement comes within the range of ambiguity of the contractual provision.

Two examples may help illuminate the point. In *Rupe* v. *Spector Freight Systems* a collective agreement prohibited discharge of employees without just cause.[11] This was clearly applicable to regular seniority employees, was clearly not applicable to probationary employees, and was silent as to its applicability to casual employees who could not acquire seniority. When a casual employee was discharged, the union agreed with the employer that the employee was more comparable to the probationary employee, and only employees who had seniority should be protected against discharge. The reality here is that when the collective agreement was negotiated, the union and employer left unsettled the rights of casual employees not to be discharged. The casual employee could not claim that he had acquired a contract right not to be discharged except for just cause because no such term was agreed upon. The union, in settling the grievance, completed the contract by filling in the missing term, and the term it agreed upon was not unreasonable nor inconsistent with the collective agreement. The union did not refuse to enforce a contract right. It only refused to create one. The measure of its duty was that of *Steele* and *Huffman,* not *Vaca.*

In *Tedford* v. *Peabody Coal Company,* the collective agreement provided that employees granted leave of absence for union busi-

---

11. 679 F.2d 685, 110 LRRM 3205 (7th Cir. 1982).

ness should retain their seniority and continue to accrue seniority during their leave.[12] The contract did not state whether, at the end of their leave, they were entitled to return to the job they had held or whether they could use their accrued seniority only to move into vacancies that occurred. The union took the position that such an employee could not claim his old job but only vacancies according to his accrued seniority. The union's grievance settlement was again a completion of the collective agreement. It did not take away any established contract right of the individual, but instead defined and established contract rights that were previously undefined. The union weighed the interest of the employee against the burden his bumping back into his old job would place on other employees and made a rational choice. Its choice was within the range of ambiguity of the contractual provision, for it recognized his accrued seniority and was a plausible reading of the provision.

When there is no substantial dispute as to the meaning and application of the collective agreement, the function of the union as representative of the employee is to enforce his or her established contract rights. When there are ambiguities or gaps leaving the term unsettled, the function of the union is to define and establish the contract rights. The union's responsibility as representative of the individual employee in the two cases is quite different; the fairness of the union's representation of the employee must be measured by the function it is charged with performing.

Whether a term in the collective agreement is to be considered settled or unsettled does not depend on the words of the agreement alone. Terms may become defined and established by past practices manifesting a mutual understanding as to the governing rule. Grievance settlements and arbitration awards may establish precedents the parties consider controlling. Such practices or precedents define and settle contract terms as if these terms were explicitly stated in the collective agreement, and they establish equally enforceable rights in the individual employee. A union's refusal to obtain for one employee benefits of an established practice enjoyed by other employees is as discriminatory as refusal to enforce express terms of the agreement. For a union to settle a grievance of one employee contrary to a precedent established to govern all employees is to deny equal protection of contract rights. But the union remains free to

---

12. 533 F.2d 952, 92 LRRM 2990 (5th Cir. 1976).

define ambiguous terms and fill in missing terms in its process of completing the contract. The union's function and responsibility as representative depend on whether there is a substantial dispute as to the meaning and application of the contract term.

Cases of Factual Dispute

The second major category of cases comprises those in which the dispute concerns the facts, not the meaning and application of the agreement. The decision whether or not to press the grievance raises no question of collective bargaining policy, other than how vigorously to enforce contract rights; and the outcome of the case creates no precedent defining the substantive rights of others. The paradigm of the factual case is the disciplinary grievance in which the question is one of guilt, or what in fact happened. In such cases, the union's duty in representing the disciplined employee has two facets: first, the duty to investigate and discover the relevant facts; second, the duty to weigh the available facts in deciding whether to pursue the grievance.

In measuring the union's duty to investigate, it is important to remember that the union has assumed the responsibility to represent the employee, and the employee relies on the union to protect him from unjustified discharge. The union, having assumed that responsibility to represent can scarcely deny that it has any duty to find out the facts necessary to defend the employee. Thus in *Hines* v. *Anchor Motor Freight*, a truck driver was discharged because the receipt for his motel bill was larger than the amount shown on the motel books as actually paid.[13] The court of appeals held that the union had a duty to make at least a minimal investigation to determine whether the motel clerk, rather than the truck driver, had falsified the records and pocketed the difference.

In *Tenorio* v. *NLRB*, two employees were discharged for engaging in a barroom brawl with a fellow union member.[14] The union, without interviewing the two grievants but relying on other witnesses, decided not to pursue the grievance to arbitration. The court

---

13. 506 F.2d 1153, 87 LRRM 2971 (6th Cir. 1974), 424 U.S. 554, 91 LRRM 2481 (1976).

14. 680 F.2d 598, 110 LRRM 2939 (9th Cir. 1982).

of appeals reversed the NLRB and held that the union had violated its duty of fair representation. Said the court:

> To comply with its duty a union must conduct some minimal investigation of grievances brought to its attention . . . by making no effort to hear [the grievants'] explanations of events that resulted in their discharge, the union showed a reckless disregard for their rights and thereby breached its duty of fair representation.[15]

The difficult question is how to define the standard of care required of the union. Some unions have very limited resources and place the major burden on the grievant to investigate and develop the facts, but other unions customarily make investigations on their own. Generalized standards such as "reasonable care" or "negligence" provide little guidance and would tend to impose on all unions the same burden.

Two more specific and appropriate guides, however, are available. First, the union should fulfill the reasonable expectations of the grievant. If the union leads the employee to believe that it will investigate or that investigation is unnecessary, as in *Hines*,[16] then the employee may be induced to rely on this and not pursue his own investigation. The union must then be responsible at least for the lack of evidence which the employee might have developed on his own. Second, the union should make substantially equal efforts to investigate similar grievances. In *Tenorio* v. *NLRB*, the court pointed out that the union had departed from its policy of interviewing all discharged employees to obtain their story before processing grievances.[17] The union can no more discriminate against an employee by not investigating his grievance than by refusing to enforce his contract rights. Each employee has equal claim on the union's resources, depending, of course, on the nature of the grievance, the costs and foreseeable benefits of investigation, and other relevant considerations. Fairness requires evenhandedness.

After investigation, a decision must be made as to whether the grievance is worthy of processing and, as it moves up the steps of the grievance procedure, whether it is worth appealing, ultimately to arbitration. These decisions must be made by the union because it controls the grievance procedure. Its duty is to consider all the relevant

---

15. *Id.* at 601, 110 LRRM at 2941. *See also,* Figueroa de Arroyo v. Sindicato de Trabajadores Packinghouse, 425 F.2d 281, 74 LRRM 2028 (1st Cir. 1970), *cert. denied sub nom,* De Arroyo v. Puerto Rico Tel. Co., 400 U.S. 877, 75 LRRM 2455 (1970).

16. *Supra* note 13.

17. *Supra* note 14.

facts available and to make a rational decision as to the merits of the grievance. The union cannot, while purporting to act as representative of the grievant, deprive him of his contract rights under the guise of finding that the grievance has no merit, but it is not obligated to pursue a grievance that it reasonably believes has no merit. The court cannot reweigh the evidence and substitute its judgment; it can only inquire whether the union's decision-making process was adequate and its substantive judgment had a rational basis.

This statement of the union's duty obscures the most crucial and difficult problem. If there is any substantial dispute as to the facts, the union's decision as to the merits of the grievance can seldom be made in absolute terms that it has merit or does not have merit. The decision must often be in relative terms of the likelihood that the grievance will be won or lost in arbitration. The question then becomes, What must be the likelihood of winning before the union is obligated to go forward?

If the union's judgment is that there is little or no hope of winning in arbitration, the union would normally have no obligation to proceed. One exception would be where the union has a practice of carrying all discharge cases to arbitration, regardless of merit. The union cannot fairly deny to one employee the chance enjoyed by others to win a seemingly hopeless case or to obtain a reduction of penalty—a chance of proven substantial value. This would discriminate against the employee denied that chance. In the absence of such a practice, however, the union is not required to appeal cases it reasonably believes it has no hopes of winning. This does not deny the employee of a contract right, for in the absence of proof of violation, the employee has no rights to be vindicated.

Does the union have any obligation to proceed if there is anything less than a substantial certainty of winning? When an employee has been discharged, the loss to the employee can be so severe that the union may have a duty to carry the case to arbitration even if there is only a 25 percent—or less—chance of winning. The union's resources, however, may be so limited that it may reasonably decide to conserve its resources for more promising cases.[18] If the discipline is a two-week suspension, the union may decide that even a 75 percent chance of winning does not justify the expenditure. Other unions may have greater resources or different priorities and

18. Curth v. Faraday, Inc., 401 F. Supp. 678, 90 LRRM 2735 (E.D. Mich. 1975).

carry bare reprimands to arbitration. The union's duty obviously cannot be measured by a mathematical formula, but the union can be required to meet the standard of equal protection. It cannot carry the disciplinary grievances of some employees to arbitration and refuse to carry equally substantial and meritorious grievances of other employees to arbitration. The union is entitled to establish its own priorities, but those priorities cannot be discriminatorily applied. Again, fairness requires evenhandedness.

Equal treatment, however, may be inadequate. If the union decides it has resources to carry to arbitration only those discharge cases it is almost certain to win, employees with less certain but substantial cases will find themselves unable to obtain a determination of their contract rights. They are barred from suing in court because the union, as exclusive representative, claims it cannot afford to take the case to arbitration. It is one thing for the union to determine how it will use its resources; it is quite another thing for the union to negotiate for exclusive control over grievances and arbitration and then use its lack of resources as a reason to bar an employee from obtaining an adjudication and remedy for his contractual right to his job. The union cannot fairly insist on exclusive control when it is unable or unwilling to provide a procedure or remedy. If the union is unable or unwilling to expend its resources, the individual ought to at least be allowed to use his resources.[19] If the individual believes his grievance is worth the cost of obtaining an adjudication and is willing to pay for the arbitration, how can the union refuse to proceed because of cost?

Discipline cases, in practice, commonly involve not only questions of fact, what happened, but also the question of whether the grievant's conduct was just cause for the discipline imposed. Conceptually, this is a question of contract interpretation—what is the meaning of *just cause*? Some meanings of just cause may be defined by posted plant rules or past practices. Others may be settled by precedents of grievance settlements or arbitrations. As with other ambiguous terms, the union is entitled to define the term, working out piece by piece its content through the grievance procedure. Much, however, always remains unsettled, and in practical opera-

19. In Encina v. Tony Lama Boot Co., 448 F.2d 1264, 78 LRRM 2382 (5th Cir. 1971), the court approved the union's refusal to accept arbitration unless the employee would pay the expenses of arbitration because the union believed that there was little chance of winning.

tion, the test of fair representation in the union's refusal to pursue the grievance because it believes that the reason for discipline is justified is the test of equal treatment. If the union's practice or policy is to appeal all discharges for possession of alcohol on the first offense, the union cannot refuse to process the grievance of a particular first offender, absent the showing of special facts that set the case apart. If the union has consistently taken the position in fighting cases that only the aggressor is subject to discharge, it cannot, without a plausible explanation, refuse to process the grievance of an employee who claims he was the victim without investigating as to who was the aggressor. The same general principles are applicable when the question is the reasonableness of the penalty.

In cases other than discipline cases, the union's duty as to factual issues is substantially the same. The union has a duty to make at least a minimal investigation, which includes seeking the grievant's version of the facts and his suggestions as to relevant evidence. The nature and extent of the investigation depend, of course, upon the nature of the grievance, but the controlling context is that the union has assumed the responsibility for representing the employees and they rely upon it to fulfill that function in enforcing their rights under the collective agreement. As minimum standards, the union should make such investigation as it has led the grievant and other employees to rely upon, and it should not discriminate against certain grievants or grievances in allocating its investigative resources.

In weighing the evidence, the union's duty is substantially the same in discipline and nondiscipline cases. The union has the same responsibility to consider all relevant facts and to make a rational decision as to the merits. The nondiscipline cases present the same problem of how much merit the grievance must have to obligate the union to proceed. Where contract interpretation is involved, however, it is important to keep separate the interpretation and factual issues. A grievance settlement or arbitration decision as to the meaning of the agreement creates a precedent that resolves an ambiguity or fills gaps with a certain settled meaning. The union can properly refuse to process a grievance that has a high probability of winning, but that would win by filling in a term contrary to the union's interest. The union could also properly refuse to process a grievance that, if won, would fill in a desired term because it feared that the case might be lost and establish an unfavorable precedent.

If the dispute is factual and the decision as to the facts will create no precedent, the union lacks these justifications for refusing to process a potentially winning grievance or barring an employee from obtaining an adjudication of his contract rights. If the union is unable or unwilling to expend its resources on a grievance the employee believes is worth litigating, the union ought not be able to use its lack of resources to prevent the employee from using his resources in an effort to vindicate his contract rights.

Cases of Procedural Default

The third major category of cases consists of those in which the individual's grievance is lost, not because of the union's interpretation of the agreement or its weighing of the facts, but because of the union's method of handling the case in the grievance procedure and arbitration. In this category of cases, the claimed default does not involve any exercise of judgment but is a purely mechanical or ministerial failure.

The most common case is one in which the grievance is barred because the union failed to file or appeal the grievance within the time limits prescribed by the collective agreement. In *Ruzika* v. *General Motors Corp.*, the discharged employee filed a grievance and the union processed it to the third step, but the union then inexplicably failed to file the statement required to invoke arbitration and allow the final deadline to pass without ever having decided the merits of the grievance.[20] The effect was to forfeit the employee's grievance. The court of appeals, borrowing language from *Vaca*, declared,

> Such negligent handling of the grievance, unrelated as it was to the merits of the Appellant's case amounts to unfair representation. It is a clear example of arbitrary and perfunctory handling of a grievance.[21]

In *Dutrisac* v. *Caterpillar Tractor Co.*, the business agent failed to keep track of the time limits for requesting arbitration and filed two weeks late, thereby barring arbitration of a discharge grievance.[22] In response to the argument that the union's failure to file was not intentional but only negligent, the district court said,

---

20. 523 F.2d 306, 90 LRRM 2497 (6th Cir. 1975).

21. *Id.* at 310, 90 LRRM at 2500. *See also,* Schum v. South Buffalo Ry., 496 F.2d 328, 86 LRRM 2459 (2d Cir. 1974).

22. 511 F. Supp. 719, 107 LRRM 2195 (N.D. Cal. 1981), *aff'd,* 113 LRRM 3532 (9th Cir. 1983).

that the union's negligent failure to timely file plaintiff's grievance for arbitration, thus precluding him from access to the mandatory dispute process even though Union had determined the grievance should be submitted to arbitration, was arbitrary and therefore constituted a breach of the Union's duty of fair representation to the plaintiff.[23]

Other courts have held that losing the grievance file, or engaging in unnecessary correspondence that led to the grievance being filed two days late amounted to "arbitrary and perfunctory handling of the grievance."[24]

The flexible word *arbitrary* has been bent to different results by some courts declaring that the union's conduct must be something more than "simple negligence" or "ordinary negligence."[25] One court attempted to place *arbitrary* more precisely on the continuum by saying that it is "somewhere between negligence and gross negligence—but closer to gross negligence."[26]

In contrast, two circuits have discarded the words arbitrary and perfunctory for quite different adjectives describing a point beyond the end of the customary tort spectrum. In *Hoffman* v. *Lonza, Inc.*, the union simply "forgot" to appeal the grievance within the required five days.[27] The Seventh Circuit, in finding no failure of the duty of fair representation, borrowed language from *Motor Coach Employees* v. *Lockridge*,[28] and declared that proof of a violation

carries with it the need to adduce substantial evidence of discrimination that is intentional, severe and unrelated to the legitimate union objectives . . . [the] distinction . . . between honest, mistaken conduct on the one hand, and deliberate and severely hostile and irrational treatment, on the other, needs to be strictly maintained.[29]

Similarly, the Fifth Circuit in *Coe* v. *Rubber Workers,* held that the union's negligence in appealing a grievance by number without any description and using the wrong number, thereby forfeiting the employee's grievance, did not violate its duty to represent the em-

---

23. *Id.* at 727, 107 LRRM at 2200.

24. Respectively, Reid v. New York Metro Area Postal Union, 109 LRRM 3065 (S.D. N.Y. 1982); Foust v. IBEW, 572 F.2d 710, 97 LRRM 3040 (10th Cir. 1978), *rev'd on other grounds*, IBEW v. Foust, 442 U.S. 42, 101 LRRM 2365 (1979).

25. *See, e.g.*, Ruzicka v. General Motors Corp., 649 F.2d 1207, 107 LRRM 2726 (6th Cir. 1981).

26. Seeley v. General Motors Corp., 520 F. Supp. 542, 110 LRRM 2884 (E.D. Mich. 1981).

27. 658 F.2d 519, 108 LRRM 2311 (7th Cir. 1981).

28. 403 U.S. 274, 77 LRRM 2501 (1971).

29. Hoffman v. Lonza, Inc., *supra* note 27 at 522, 108 LRRM at 2314.

ployee. This "carelessness or inadvertence" was not "deliberate and severely hostile and irrational treatment."[30]

If we look past the pliant and perjorative adjectives to the underlying rights and relationships involved, we can more responsibly measure the union's duty of care in representing employees in the grievance procedure.

We come back to our basic proposition: the individual employee has contractual rights that he can personally enforce under federal law but for the union's assertion of exclusive control over the enforcement procedures. The union is not given exclusive control over grievance by the statute, but obtains it only by negotiating for it with the employer. In simplest terms, the union has voluntarily asserted that it shall be the exclusive representative of the employee in enforcing the employee's contract rights, whether the employee consents or not, thereby barring the employee from any remedial process. The union, which thus imposes itself as the employee's representative, must owe at least as substantial a duty of care as an agent voluntarily selected and continuously controlled.

On what logic can the union as self-appointed agent with irrevocable authority not be responsible for reasonable care in filing grievances and making appeals within its own agreed procedure?[31] As the court of appeals in *Dutrisac* pointed out in distinguishing those cases in which the courts should accord substantial deference to union decisions,

> When the challenged conduct, however, is based not on any decision about how to handle the grievance, but on the failure to perform ministerial acts, judicial deference to the union serves no purpose. A requirement that the union timely pursue those grievances it has decided to pursue does not interfere with union decision making.[32]

The union's self-declared status as sole guardian and enforcer of a nonconsenting individual's contract rights is an anamoly in the law. For courts to hold that a union asserting such status does not owe the duty of ordinary care in performing its function is to impose a Kafkaesque mutation.

---

30. 571 F.2d 1349, 1350–51, 98 LRRM 2304, 2305 (5th Cir. 1978).

31. "I believe that a total failure to act, whether negligent or intentional, except for a proper reason, is behavior so egregious that, as in the case of bad faith, hostile discrimination, arbitrariness or perfunctoriness, the union should be held responsible." Judge McCree concurring in Ruzicka v. General Motors Corp., *supra* note 20 at 316, 90 LRRM at 2505; *see also*, Ruggerello v. Ford Motor Co., 411 F. Supp. 758, 92 LRRM 2228 (E.D. Mich. 1976).

32. Dutrisac v. Caterpillar Tractor Co., *supra* note 22, 113 LRRM at 3533.

I am not contending here that the union should be held to a standard higher than ordinary care, although an argument for a more exacting standard can be made. And ordinary care should be measured by what is expected of ordinary, reasonable union officers, and particularly what is expected by the employee represented in the particular situation. Thus, the failure to appeal within the contractually stated time limits may meet the standard of ordinary care where extensions in the past have been freely given and time limits have been regularly waived.[33] Similarly, the failure to file a written grievance within a certain time may meet the standard where a reasonable reading of the contract clause led the union steward to believe that her oral presentation was sufficient.[34] A subsequent surprising interpretation by the arbitrator that the oral presentation did not preserve the grievance should not make the union liable.

Such a standard of care, to be sure, places a substantial obligation on the union, for the union must rely on shop stewards, plant committees, and union officers, many of whom may be poorly trained. But how can the union properly assert exclusive control over enforcing the employees' rights if it is not prepared to perform the function? The union is not required to assume responsibility or assert control; it can allow the employee to retain control over enforcing his contract rights. Who should bear the risk of incompetence or carelessness of union stewards, committees, and officers? The employee, who has been barred by the union from enforcing his contract rights? Or the union, which has insisted on exclusive control?

The same problems are presented and the same principles applicable to the union's presenting evidence or argument in the grievance procedure or arbitration. The union's duty to investigate has already been discussed, and there the union's duty is bounded by reasonable care, but it is also bounded by the limits on union resources and reasonable priorities as to the use of those resources. The union may shrink its obligation to investigate by placing some of the responsibility and burden on the grievant. But when the union has obtained or been provided with the evidence, presentation of that evidence is under the exclusive control of the union, and it owes a concomitant duty to represent the employee.

---

33. Ruzicka v. General Motors Corp., *supra* note 25.
34. Ethier v. United States Postal Service, 590 F.2d 733, 100 LRRM 2390 (8th Cir. 1979), *cert. denied*, 444 U.S. 826, 102 LRRM 2440 (1979).

The union's duty to the employee in presenting her case can be described in the same general terms as its duty to comply with the time limits, but application of the standard is often more difficult, for there may be questions of judgment as to what evidence and arguments will be effective. But it can at least be said that when there is an unexplained failure to present directly relevant evidence and argument, the union does not meet its responsibility as sole spokesman. For example, in *Baldini* v. *Auto Workers,* a grievant who had been discharged gave the union the names of four possible alibi witnesses.[35] The union failed in the grievance procedure to present them or give their names to the employer. This failure, without any explanation, could amount to a breach of the union's duty. In *Miller* v. *Gateway Transportation Co.,* the union representative did little better, and not well enough to meet the union's duty.[36] His presentation of a discharge case to the joint council consisted, in the words of the court, of a "perfunctory reading of Miller's *pro se* grievance," and did not argue that the employer had failed to give a warning letter before discharge. And in *Milstead* v. *Teamsters Local 957,* a seniority grievance was lost before the joint council because the business agent presenting the case failed to read the relevant contract closely enough to notice that the provision relied on by the employer was missing from the contract. In the words of the court,

> Certainly the duty of fair representation may be breached whenever a union ineptly handles a grievance because it is ignorant of those contract provisions having a direct bearing on the case.[37]

The courts recognized in all three of these cases that the mere fact that the union did not present certain facts or arguments was not a *per se* violation of its duty. If the union considered the facts and arguments but decided that they would not be persuasive, that the grievance was without merit, or that there was some other reational reason for not presenting the particular facts or arguments, the court would not substitute its judgment for the union's.[38] The union's default in each of these three cases was in its negligence, incompetence, or perfunctory treatment of the grievance without consideration of its merits on the basis of the facts or arguments avail-

---

35. 581 F.2d 145, 99 LRRM 2535 (7th Cir. 1978).

36. 616 F.2d 272, 103 LRRM 2591 (7th Cir. 1980).

37. 580 F.2d 232, 236, 99 LRRM 2150, 2153 (6th Cir. 1978).

38. *See, e.g.,* Cannon v. Consolidated Freightways Corp., 524 F.2d 290, 90 LRRM 2996 (7th Cir. 1975).

able. This is certainly not placing an inappropriate responsibility on a self-appointed agent that insists on being the sole spokesman for an individual's contract rights.

The duties imposed on unions to use reasonable care in investigating grievances, processing them in accordance with the contractual procedures, or presenting facts and arguments need not create an unduly burdensome liability, for the union has ways of mitigating its liability. If the employee claims that the union has defaulted at any point in the processing, the union will know of it—at the latest when suit is brought—within six months.[39] When the union becomes aware that a steward or shop committee has bungled, it can notify the employer that the employee has the basis for a suit for breach of contract and ask that the grievance be reinstated. If the employer refuses to reinstate the grievance or contests the individual's suit, then the employer relies on its claim that it has not breached the contract. If the employer loses that suit, then it would seem that under the rationale of *Vaca* and *Bowen* that the back pay accruing during the period the employer contests the claim would be assessable against the employer, not the union.[40] The union would be liable at most for the legal costs of enforcing the individual's contract right.

This result can be reached in a more direct and less contentious way. The parties who negotiated the union's exclusive control over the grievance procedure can negotiate a solution when that procedure goes astray. The collective agreement can provide, as some agreements now do, that if the union determines that it has failed to handle the grievance properly, then it can reinstate the grievance with responsibility only for damages due to the delay caused by its failure to fairly represent the employee. This would, of course, not allow the union to escape cost-free, but would limit its liability to a bearable amount.

Conflicting Interests

The framework of analysis developed here is useful in sorting out, if not deciding, cases in which the union has conflicting interests. Two

---

39. United Parcel Service, Inc. v. Mitchell, 451 U.S. 56, 107 LRRM 2001 (1981); DelCostello v. IBT Local 577, 103 S. Ct. 2281, 113 LRRM 2737 (1983).

40. Bowen v. United States Postal Service, 103 S. Ct. 588, 112 LRRM 2281 (1983).

quite different types of cases are principally involved—first, cases in which the union trades one grievance for another or engages in block trading; second, cases such as seniority and promotion disputes in which the union, by supporting the claims of one employee, inescapably opposes the interests of another.

Grievance trading has many variations, too many to work out here, but some samples may illustrate the analysis. If both grievances involve interpretation of ambiguous or unsettled terms of the collective agreement, then the parties by trading grievances are simply filling in or giving meaning to terms not negotiated before signing the agreement.[41] As pointed out in discussing contract interpretation cases, the union should have as much freedom to negotiate away ambiguities or fill in missing terms as to negotiate the agreement itself. It should be able to trade such grievances much the same as it can trade demands at the bargaining table.

If one of the grievances involves a clear and settled term and the other an ambiguous or unsettled term, the union can trade away the grievance with the unsettled term, thereby filling out the contract and settling the term. No employee's contract rights are bargained away, for, until the undefined term is given a definite meaning, the employee acquires no defined contract right. The union, however, cannot trade away the grievance based on the term about which there is not substantial dispute as to its meaning. That would destroy the individual's contract right and deny him equal treatment under the agreement, for the union would be giving the agreement one meaning as to him and another as to other employees. The fact that the union obtained a benefit for other employees by trading away his contract right only increases the inequality.

Trading grievances that involve questions of fact rather than interpretation of the agreement raises somewhat different problems, particularly where one or both of the grievances implicates no general rule or policy, as in discipline cases where the issue is what happened. It is clear that the union is obligated to investigate each grievance and weigh each grievance on its own merits. The union cannot trade away a grievance, any more than it can refuse to process a grievance, without making a judgment as to whether it is meritorious. Further, if the union's judgment is that the grievance is clearly

---

41. Local 13, ILWU v. Pacific Maritime Ass'n, 441 F.2d 1061, 77 LRRM 2160 (9th Cir. 1971), *cert. denied*, 404 U.S. 1016, 79 LRRM 2182 (1972).

meritorious, it cannot trade away the individual's contract right in order to obtain extra benefits for another employee. The union, as representative of all employees, cannot rob Peter to make a gift to Paul, or even a dozen Pauls. On the other hand, if the union's judgment is that the grievance is not meritorious enough to justify further processing, it can, of course, trade it for whatever it may bring rather than simply surrendering it.[42]

In practical terms, however, the situation is often not so simple, for many grievances are neither sure winners nor hopeless losers. It is the trading of these middle-ground grievances that raises the most difficult problems. If each of two grievances is judged by the union to have enough merit to take to arbitration, but neither have a high probability of being won, can the union surrender one in exchange for the other? If the union would have arbitrated both of the grievances considered separately, it is not clear why the union should act differently because the two grievances happen to coincide in time. In principle, if such a trade is made, the one who benefits from the union's choice should compensate the one whose grievance is sacrificed for his benefit, but such a solution is probably impractical.

If any trading under such circumstances is to be allowed, there are some guides that would seem appropriate. One, assuming that the interests of the employees at stake are equal, it would seem unfair to trade away the grievance with the greater probability of success to gain the grievance with the lesser probability of success. Such a trade would indicate that some other factor influenced the choice —an inference of arbitrariness.[43] Two, if both of such grievances have a better than even chance of success, it would seem unfair to take away one employee's better-than-even chance in order to give the other employee a sure thing. Three, if the employee's interest at stake is a vital one, such as continued employment, it would be inappropriate to trade that away for the benefit of another employee, particularly for any less vital interest of that employee.

From this discussion, certain broad principles emerge and are reasonably clear. First, the union cannot trade away clearly meritorious grievances; to do so would be to trade away contract rights of one employee to give advantages to another. Second, the union can trade away grievances based on genuinely disputed questions of in-

---

42. *See, e.g.,* Miller v. Greyhound Lines Inc., 95 LRRM 2871 (E.D. Pa. 1977).

43. *See, e.g.,* Harrison v. UTU, 530 F.2d 558, 90 LRRM 3265 (4th Cir. 1975), *cert. denied,* 425 U.S. 958, 92 LRRM 2168 (1976).

terpretation, as a part of the process of completing or filling out the unsettled terms of the agreement. Third, the union can trade away grievances that lack the merit to warrant arbitration. Beyond this, the guides are unclear, but the ones stated give the union substantial freedom of action. Courts will not likely substitute their evaluation of the facts and of the likelihood of success in arbitration for that of the union unless this is clearly erroneous or specious. The union will have little difficulty persuading the court that it has stayed within the guidelines suggested.

The other category of conflicting interest cases arise typically in promotion and seniority cases involving relative rights between employees. For example, in *Smith* v. *Hussman Refrigeration Co.,* the employer promoted four employees on the basis of their superior skill and ability.[44] The union was, in effect, processing a grievance on behalf of some employees against other employees. The fact that the union is generally charged with representing all employees does not immobilize it because there are competing claims. The union's responsibility is to make a rational judgment as to the merits of the competing claims under the agreement and support the one that it concludes has the greater merit.[45] The court's criticism of the union in *Hussman* was that it did not judge the relative skill and ability, the standard prescribed by the contract, but gave sole consideration to seniority.

A separate question is whether the employees whose interests the union opposes are entitled to participate in the arbitration proceedings. If the union has decided to represent one of two employees with conflicting interests, it is difficult to understand how the union can claim that it is representing an employee whose interest it directly opposes. The underlying principle is self-evident; how lawyers, especially, could argue otherwise is puzzling. The union may, by the collective agreement, obtain the exclusive right to represent employees in the grievance procedure and arbitration, but that exclusiveness must have an implied exception when the union has a direct conflict of interest. As the court stated in *Hussman*, employees whose promotion the union is attempting to take away in an arbitration proceeding must be entitled to notice of the arbitration and an opportunity to represent their own interests.

---

44. 619 F.2d 1229 (8th Cir. 1980).

45. Belanger v. Matteson, 115 R.I. 332, 346 A.2d 124, 91 LRRM 2003 (R.I. Sup. Ct. 1975).

The solution suggested here is simple in principle: when the union processes a grievance directly adverse to one or more employees, they are no longer represented by the union but can represent themselves. This will not be burdensome on the parties or the process. Allowing such employees to participate in the arbitration, either personally or through a representative, will not increase the number of arbitrations or add substantially to the proceeding. Certainly, the arbitration process, which is prized for its flexibility and informality, should be able to adapt to a single issue, three-party procedure when courts and administrative agencies manage much more complex multiple-party, multiple-issue litigation. Resistance to allowing employees not represented by the union to intervene in arbitration is based less on practical objections than to *passé* premises that the union "owns" the grievance and that arbitration is solely between union and management, premises that were repudiated by *Vaca* and *Hines*.

Conclusion

The framework of analysis suggested here for measuring the union's duty in grievance handling does not give automatic, or even definite, answers in all of the wide variety of cases in which the union's performance is questioned. The framework, however, serves two fundamental purposes. First, it makes visible two underlying premises or propositions which are often obscured by the cloud of adjectives: (1) Each employee acquires individual contract rights under the collective agreement, and those contract rights are legally enforceable by the individual under section 301, but for the union's status as exclusive representative of the employees. (2) The union's status as exclusive representative in grievance handling is not granted or imposed by section 9(a), but is voluntarily sought by the union and granted by the employer. The end result is that individual employees, without consent, are barred from enforcing or obtaining an adjudication of their contract rights and are compelled to accept the union as their legal representative and sole spokesman. By keeping these propositions in the forefront, we can more sensibly measure the duty of the union to the individual employee.

The second fundamental purpose of the framework is that it helps distinguish between different categories of cases and different measures of the union's duty. The union's function, and therefore its duty, in contract interpretation cases is quite different when the contractual provision is clear and settled than when it is ambiguous or incomplete and unsettled. The measure of the union's duty to consider the facts available is different from the measure of its duty to investigate the facts, and both are very different from the measure of its duty in weighing conflicting or disputed evidence. The standard of care and competence required of a union in performing the mechanical functions of processing a grievance is not the same as that required in presenting evidence or argument. All of these are separate from the measure of a union's duty in deciding whether a case is worthy of carrying to arbitration. The crucial point is that there is not one duty of fair representation that can be described with a single string of adjectives, no matter how long and colorful. There is a collection of duties of fair representation, each with its own size and shape. The need is to determine the proper measure for each of the different categories or types of cases.

Beyond these two broad purposes, the framework of analysis does provide relatively clear answers, for some types of cases. With a risk of oversimplification, some of the more obvious answers might be summarized as follows:

1. The union must determine the merits of the grievance on the basis of the collective agreement and the available facts.

2. If the collective agreement and the facts are clear and show a breach of the individual's contract right, the union cannot ignore and thereby destroy that contract right.

3. If the collective agreement is unclear and unsettled, the union has a wide range of reasonableness in resolving ambiguity or filling gaps, so long as the agreement is applied consistently to all employees.

4. If the union's action requires exercise of judgment, such as weighing conflicting evidence, determining the likelihood of winning in arbitration, or determining the facts and arguments to be used in arbitration, the measure of the union's exercise of judgment is only that it must have a rational basis and be evenhandedly applied.

5. If the union's action involves a policy decision, such as the resources to be expanded in investigation or carrying cases to arbitra-

tion, then the decision must again only have a rational basis and be consistently applied.

6. In performing the mechanical functions of processing grievances, the union owes the standard of at least ordinary care, taking account of the nature of the process and the expectations of those represented.

7. When the union, in representing one employee's individual contract rights, directly opposes another employee's contract rights, as in seniority or promotion cases, the union cannot claim the exclusive right to represent the one whose interest it opposes, but must allow him to represent his own interests.

I have deliberately avoided resort to the worn-out, amorphous adjectives, because they cloud the analysis and are often unnecessary. The terms invidious, hostile and bad faith carry connotations of evil motive, but as is clear from the analysis, the union's duty to represent in many situations requires more than good intentions. Bad motive is not an essential element where the contract and the facts are clear, where there is little or no effort to learn the facts, where the grievance file is lost or the appeal date forgotten, and many other situations. This does not mean that motive is irrelevant. Evidence of hostility to the grievant may add credibility to claims of perfunctory processing or other procedural defaults. More important, where the union is claiming an exercise of judgment or policy decisions, proof of bad motive may cast doubts on those claims and remove the courts' reluctance to intervene. In those cases, proof of bad motive may be an essential element, and the adjectives underline that element.

The analysis here does not pretend to be comprehensive. There are unlimited variations of situations, and each must be examined separately to measure the union's duty. Generalizations will have unanticipated exceptions, and relatively clear answers will have blurred boundaries. What is presented here is no more than a framework on which to build in the future.

The Duty in Other Forums

Fair Representation
in Arbitration

Robert J. Rabin

The noted ethologist Konrad Lorenz says, "it is a good morning exercise for a research scientist to discard a pet hypothesis every day before breakfast. It keeps him young."[1] The reported cases on the duty of fair representation have led me swiftly to this hypothesis: the duty of fair representation doctrine has been misapplied in cases in which the union agrees to take the individual's case to arbitration. When the union aligns itself with the individual's cause in arbitration, it is enough to insist that its performance not be arbitrary, discriminatory, or in bad faith. It is unnecessary, and indeed wrong, to require also that the union's performance be something better than perfunctory. Such a standard is unworkable and requires inappropriate supervision by the courts of the quality of the union's representation.

Although hardly a research scientist, I have, in Lorenz's spirit after many a breakfast and much rumination, rejected my initial hypothesis. I now conclude that while the perfunctory standard raises many theoretical and institutional problems, on balance our system is better off with it than without it. You, dear reader, are invited to disagree with me. But I want you to consider my assertion carefully,

---

I am grateful to my research assistants, Christine Hickey and John Ryan, for their invaluable help. My thanks once again to my friend and colleague Bob Koretz for starting me on this topic when we prepared a paper together for the American Arbitration Association's 1975 Wingspread conference, The Future of Labor Arbitration in America. (1976 American Arbitration Association).

1. K. Lorenz, On Aggression 12 (Harcourt Brace and World, 1966).

for it is the heart of the issue in determining how to apply the duty of fair representation to arbitration.

The union's duty to represent an individual fairly in arbitration has its roots in the language of *Vaca* v. *Sipes,* which involved a union's decision not to take an individual's grievance to arbitration.[2] The Court held that the union breaches its duty if its decision not to proceed to arbitration is "arbitrary, discriminatory, or in bad faith." While holding that the individ.al has no absolute right to have his case carried to arbitration, however, the Court said, "we accept the proposition that a union may not arbitrarily ignore a meritorious grievance or process it in a perfunctory fashion."[3] As others have observed, the difficult cases focus not on the discriminatory and bad faith elements of the test, but on the more elusive criteria of arbitrary and perfunctory treatment. The latter term, especially, allows courts to scrutinize union decisions that do not deliberately disadvantage an individual but achieve the same result through inadvertence or carelessness.

Not until almost a decade later did the Court apply the *Vaca* standard to a completed arbitration. *Hines* v. *Anchor Motor Freight* involved truck drivers whose union unsuccessfully challenged their discharges in arbitration.[4] The drivers sued both the union and the company, contending that the union breached its duty towards them and that, as a result, the arbitration award in the company's favor could not stand. While the Court's decision was predicated upon a breach by the union of its duty of fair representation, the novel aspect of the decision was the creation of an exception to the hallowed rule of arbitral finality. Said the Court, "it is quite another matter to suggest that erroneous arbitration decisions must stand even though the employee's representation by the union has been dishonest, in bad faith or discriminatory."[5]

Hines surprisingly did not decide what level of union dereliction may result in overturning a completed arbitration. At the risk of repeating what the reader may already know, let me briefly summarize what happened in *Hines.* The company discharged several truck drivers whom it claimed padded their motel receipts, claiming more

---

2. 386 U.S. 171, 64 LRRM 2369 (1967).
3. *Id.* at 190, 191, 64 LRRM at 2376, 2377.
4. 424 U.S. 554, 91 LRRM 2481 (1976).
5. *Id.* at 571, 91 LRRM at 2487.

for reimbursement for overnight lodging than they actually paid the motel. The drivers contended that it was the motel clerk who was skimming off a profit by charging the drivers more than the going rate (and giving them a receipt for what they actually paid), entering a lower figure in the books, and pocketing the difference. The employees suggested this theory to the union, but were told there was nothing to worry about. Not only did the union make no effort to investigate the employees' contentions, but the drivers, who relied upon the union's assurances, did not hire their own attorney to follow up their claim.

The union presented the drivers' grievances before a joint committee, a device peculiar to the trucking industry. Under this system, grievance decisions are made by a panel consisting of equal numbers of union and management representatives, typically three each. If the panel deadlocks, the case is taken before a neutral arbitrator. But neither the union nor company panel members are bound to uphold the position of their constituency, and if the panel reaches agreement, the case goes no further and is the equivalent of a final, binding arbitration award.[6] The *Hines* grievants lost their claim before the joint committee. The grievants then decided it was time to get their own attorney. She dug up evidence that, although not overwhelming, at least supported the grievants' theory. The evidence did not establish that the clerk padded the bill, but showed that the motel owner could not be sure that the clerk recorded accurate receipts. Despite this new evidence, the joint committee refused to reconsider its decision. At this point, the grievants challenged the union's conduct as a breach of its duty of fair representation.

The district court granted the union's motion for summary judgment. While the Sixth Circuit agreed that a failure to investigate is not enough to establish a breach of the duty of fair representation, since it shows no more than negligence or poor judgment, neither of which violates the standard, it noted that the plaintiffs alleged bad faith, based upon the union's political animosity toward the grievants. The Sixth Circuit concluded that the plaintiffs' allegation that "because of political animosity, local union officials processed their

---

6. Joint committees are discussed in Azoff, *Joint Committees as an Alternative Form of Arbitration under the NLRA*, 47 Tul. L. Rev. 328 (1973). Court cases dealing with specific problems raised by joint committees are collected in footnote 13.

grievance in a perfunctory manner," raised issues of fact precluding summary judgment.[7]

It is important to recognize that the Supreme Court did not review the Sixth Circuit's determination regarding the union's breach of its duty. The union did not appeal the Sixth Circuit's decision to let the question go to trial on the fair representation issue, and the grant of certiorari was limited to the question whether, assuming a breach of the duty, this was grounds to set aside an arbitration award. Thus, the Court has never squarely addressed the precise scope of the duty of fair representation owed by a union in arbitration. Even if the Court implicitly endorsed the Sixth Circuit's conclusions as to fair representation, the finding was of perfunctory treatment resulting from hostility. In other words, the lower court decision rests on the discriminatory and bad faith aspects of *Vaca*.

Despite the narrow issue, the Court could not avoid characterizing the union's performance. As in so many of the lower court decisions, the Court straddled the various branches of the *Vaca* test, and what is dictum at best can only be characterized as waffling.[8] If it is possible to capture this waffling in a few words, errors and bad judgment will not invalidate an award, but a serious or fundamental malfunction of the process will. Perhaps the most telling, but most open-ended, statement of the Court is that it demands a minimum level of integrity in the arbitration process.

---

7. Hines v. Teamsters Local 377, 506 F.2d 1153, 1154–55, 87 LRRM 2971 (6th Cir. 1974).

8. The Court sent out a number of conflicting signals in Hines v. Anchor Motor Freight, 424 U.S. 554, 91 LRRM 2481 (1976). It stated: "the facts demonstrated at most bad judgment on the part of the Union, which was insufficient to prove a breach of duty" (at 559, 91 LRRM at 2483). Also, "Maddox [an earlier case requiring the individual to exhaust his contract remedies before suing in court] nevertheless distinguished the situation where 'the union refuses to press or only perfunctorily presses the individual's claim'" (at 563, 91 LRRM at 2484).

The union's breach removes the bar of finality "if it seriously undermines the integrity of the arbitral process" (at 567, 91 LRRM at 2486). The bar against relitigating an arbitral decision does not apply where "the process has fundamentally malfunctioned by reason of the bad-faith performance of the union" (at 569, 91 LRRM at 2487). The individual remedy under section 301 is not foreclosed "if the contractual processes have been seriously flawed by the union's breach of its duty to represent employees honestly and in good faith and without invidious discrimination or arbitrary conduct" (at 570, 91 LRRM at 2487). Proving a violation "involves more than demonstrating mere errors in judgment" (at 571, 91 LRRM at 2487). "The grievance processes cannot be expected to be error-free" (at 571, 91 LRRM at 2487). "Congress . . . anticipated . . . that the contractual machinery would operate within some minimal levels of integrity" (at 571, 91 LRRM at 2487).

Lower courts have understandably seized upon the dictum in *Hines,* merely replicating the ambivalence of that opinion. This leads to a largely unsuccessful search for that delicate line between conduct that is merely erroneous, careless, or negligent and performance that falls into that elusive realm of "perfunctory."[9]

Decisions Involving Arbitration

Before returning to my initial thesis that we would be better off to drop the term perfunctory, with all its permutations, from the fair representation lexicon, I want to take a closer look at the lower court decisions that have worked with the *Hines* standard. My research assistants and I canvassed fair representation decisions involving arbitrations over a period of roughly the last six years.[10] We do not claim to have unearthed every decision, because our objective was to get a general picture rather than a systematic analysis of every case.

We found from two to four cases in each LRRM volume or roughly eight to ten cases a year. Harry Edwards reports here that

---

9. Harris v. Schwerman Trucking Co., 668 F.2d 1204, 109 LRRM 3135 (11th Cir. 1982) (union representatives not held to as strict a standard as a lawyer; to prevail, grievant must show "nothing less than demonstrated reckless disregard"); Grovner v. Georgia Pacific Corp., 625 F.2d 1289, 1290, 105 LRRM 2706, 2708 (5th Cir. 1980) ("arbitration need not follow all the 'niceties' of the federal courts; it need provide only a fundamentally fair hearing"); Rupe v. Spector Freight Systems, 679 F.2d 685, 110 LRRM 3205 (7th Cir. 1982) (doctrine requires "basic diligence"; "egregious" conduct breaches duty. Where performance is "acutely perfunctory" it fails to attain minimum level of acceptable performance); Early v. Eastern Transfer, 699 F.2d 552, 112 LRRM 3381 (1st Cir. 1983) (something worse than absence of forensic skills or lackluster performance required to establish breach; union within range of "acceptable performance";neither negligence nor mistake in judgment violates the duty: nothing less than reckless disregard of employees' rights or grossly deficient conduct is violation); Curtis v. U.T.U., 700 F.2d 457, 112 LRRM 2864 (8th Cir. 1983) ("a union representative is not a lawyer and he cannot be expected to function as one in representing union members"); Dutrisac v. Caterpillar Tractor Co., 113 LRRM 3532 (9th Cir., 1983) (court distinguishes between errors in judgment regarding the merits of a claim and those involving ministerial acts such as timely filing, finding a breach for negligence only in the latter).

While most circuit courts accept the proposition that union representation may at times be so wanting as to be perfunctory, the Seventh Circuit appears to now reject a finding of unfair representation except for intentional misconduct. Dober v. Roadway Express, 707 F.2d 292, 113 LRRM 2594 (7th Cir. 1983).

10. Our examination included volumes 94 to 113 of the LRRM. We studied approximately fifty cases arising during the period covered by these volumes. We occasionally refer to exceptionally illuminating cases decided before this period.

the magnitude of overall fair representation cases has expanded to about eighty a year, so the cases involving completed arbitrations are a sizable proportion of the whole. But like Edwards's statistics, these ten or so cases are but the tip of an iceberg that forms annually. These figures do not include charges filed with the NLRB in which a complaint did not issue, unreported judicial opinions, or litigated cases settled short of a formal opinion; nor do they reflect the volume of complaints that never enter the mainstream of litigation or are worked out informally. It is clear that the volume of claims of unfair representation poses significant institutional burdens in all quarters.

Since the cases deal mostly with individuals who have lost their jobs through discharge or the adverse effect of seniority, there is a natural tendency for them to turn to the courts for relief, especially if the individual thinks the union has let him down. We observed, however, that the individual rarely prevails. We found only two cases that were a square victory for the individual employee.[11] In a handful of cases, the employee survived a union motion to dismiss, but his or her ultimate fate is not reported.[12] This may mean that the grounds for relief are drawn too tightly so that meritorious claims cannot survive. Alternatively, the standards may be so loose and vague that they invite challenge, even though ultimately unsuccessful.

The cases we surveyed also reveal how difficult it is to evaluate the soundness of the decisions. Given the constraints of time, space, and the patience of writers and readers, the opinions cannot lay out the full factual setting. Furthermore, given the natural tendency of a court to write a persuasive opinion, it is difficult for the researcher to question whether the decision was correct.

Finally, an astonishing percentage of cases involve joint committees. The joint committees deal in these cases not just with minor grievances, but with matters of industrial life and death, where jobs

---

11. Milstead v. Teamsters Local 957, 580 F.2d 232, 99 LRRM 2150 (6th Cir. 1978); Del Casal v. Eastern Airlines, 634 F.2d 295, 106 LRRM 2776 (5th Cir. 1981). Del Casal holds that a union that routinely provides counsel in arbitration cannot deny it to a nonmember.

12. Sine v. Teamsters Local 992, 644 F.2d 997, 107 LRRM 2089 (4th Cir. 1981); Novakovich v. McNicholas Transportation Co., 107 LRRM 2857 (N.D. Ohio 1981); McFarland v. Teamsters Local 745, 535 F. Supp. 970, 110 LRRM 3022 (N.D. Texas 1982); Kaftantzis v. D & L Transport Co., 531 F. Supp. 566, 111 LRRM 2028 (N.D. Ill. 1982).

are lost because of discipline or seniority decisions. Their proportion is so great that if they were removed from the body of cases, the problem of fair representation in arbitration might not be worth talking about.[13]

These statistics are weakened by the small sample size. Even so, they point inexorably to a special problem. I have tried to account for the disproportionate number of joint committee cases on alternative grounds. One possible reason is that since joint committees are unique to the trucking industry, they may face special and insoluble problems of meshing seniority lists when terminals are merged. While some of the cases involve such issues, this factor does not account for the others.

Another explanation is suggested by the following reaction of a Teamster joint committee member when a grievant appeared before the committee with his lawyer: "No goddamn lawyers tell the Teamsters how to run their business. Not even Jesus Christ tells the Teamsters how to run their business."[14] If this attitude were prevalent it might account for a more litigious membership, but while this is a nice hypothesis, I doubt it is correct.

Regardless of which of their attributes are correlated with DFR cases, it is probable that joint committees are not suited for the resolution of all issues. While ideal for rapid, informal disposition of routine issues, the system just does not provide enough protection for the individual when his or her job is at stake. Not only are the panel members on a joint committee not individually accountable, but there is too great a danger of collusion if the union views the grievance as unmeritorious or undeserving. A dispute of this signifi-

---

13. Some typical cases in which the court sanctions the joint committee include Ness v. Safeway Stores, Inc., 598 F.2d 558, 101 LRRM 2621 (9th Cir. 1979) (no breach where only two union panel members participated in the decision while all three employer members participated; no showing that this made a difference); Barrentine v. Arkansas-Best Freight System, Inc., 615 F.2d 1194, 103 LRRM 2732 (8th Cir. 1980). Wells v. Southern Airways, Inc., 616 F.2d 107, 104 LRRM 2338 (5th Cir. 1980) (claim that individual union panel member was "institutionally hostile" to the grievant is rejected); Findley v. Jones Motor Freight, 639 F.2d 953, 106 LRRM 2420 (3d Cir. 1981) (no right to challenge makeup of panel); Del Casal v. Eastern Airlines, *supra* note 11 (absent actual showing of bias, joint committee is sufficiently impartial); Early v. Eastern Transfer, *supra* note 9 (union members of joint committee have no duty to deadlock panel, thereby sending case before neutral arbitrator). The National Labor Relations Board has deferred to arbitration decisions issued by joint committees under its Spielberg doctrine. *See,* Denver-Chicago Trucking, 132 NLRB 1416, 48 LRRM 1524 (1961).

14. Budde v. A. & C. Carriers, 97 LRRM 3017 (W.D. Mich. 1978).

cance deserves the attention of a skilled arbitrator, who has the responsibility for the final result and usually must defend his or her decision in a written award.

Six Recipes for Trouble

Six "syndromes" represent the most typical situations in which a union gets into trouble because of the quality of its representation. Each syndrome is a skeletal statement of facts taken from an actual case. I have simplified the facts, and even taken liberties with them, in order to give a more generalized statement of problems to avoid. For each syndrome, I indicate the principal case upon which the pattern is based and in a footnote direct the reader to cases presenting similar situations. I quote the actual test if it illuminates the basis for the court's opinion. The reader is cautioned to read the actual case if he or she wishes to rely upon an exact statement of facts.

What? Where Does It Say That?

An employee needs thirty days of service in a calendar year to attain regular employee status; this in turn entitles him to just-cause protection against discharge. Drivers are routinely assigned to different terminals. Normally, each contract for each separate terminal provides that seniority accumulated at that terminal may not be tacked to seniority at another terminal for purposes of counting days toward regular employee status. But the contract covering terminal Y does not contain the no-tacking provision; whether its omission is inadvertant is not clear.

The grievant is terminated. When he challenges his termination under the just-cause position, the company tells him he lacks regular employee status because his seniority at terminal Y cannot be tacked to his other seniority.

The grievant takes his case before the joint committee and reads a grievance statement. When the company challenges his tacking of seniority, the union representative fails to assert that the no-tacking provision was omitted from the agreement covering terminal Y. The grievance is denied. The union representative testifies at the fair representation trial that he was unaware at the arbitration hearing that this provision was not found in the contract for terminal Y.

This fact pattern is loosely based on *Milstead* v. *Teamsters,* a Sixth

Circuit decision upholding the trial court's refusal to grant a directed verdict in favor of the union and the jury's verdict in the employee's favor.[15] It is the only case in our study in which the individual achieved victory on the merits. The court said, "certainly the duty of fair representation may be breached whenever a union ineptly handles a grievance because it is ignorant of those contract provisions having a direct bearing on the case."[16]

That Argument Is Crazy. Forget It.

The grievant is a long-time employee of a firm that has numerous defense contracts with the U.S. government. In a journal published by dissident union members, the employee writes an article sharply critical of the union, the company, and the permanent impartial arbitrator. The company terminates him. At the arbitration hearing, he is represented by a union attorney who fails to argue that since the company is a defense contractor the First Amendment protects the employee's free speech. The arbitrator denies the grievance.

This is a simplified statement of the notorious *Holodnak* case, in which the Second Circuit found a breach of the duty of fair representation and overturned an arbitration award at least partly because the union lawyer failed to make the above argument, which the court thought critical to the grievant's case.[17] There was also evidence of perfunctory preparation, as well as possible bias by the arbitrator, but the opinion appears to rest most heavily upon the substantive omission just mentioned.

Holodnak was decided earlier than the period we canvassed. But it is such an extreme result, and one no court has squarely repudiated, that it is important to mention it here. On the other hand, no other court has gone so far to find a breach of the duty in a failure to raise a legal argument.[18]

Don't Worry. We've Got Enough to Go On.

The employee, a truck driver, is awakened at 3:30 a.m. by a phone call. Unable to understand the caller, due to static on the wire, he

---

15. 580 F.2d 232, 99 LRRM 2150 (6th Cir. 1978).

16. *Id.* at 235, 99 LRRM at 2153. We have found no other case in which a representative overlooked a critical contract provision. But many cases involve failures to argue contractual or factual positions. A representative sample is collected in note 18.

17. Holodnak v. Avco Corp., 514 F.2d 285, 88 LRRM 2950 (2d Cir. 1975).

18. Many cases deal with the failure to raise arguments suggested by the facts or the contract, but the omission is seldom egregious enough or sufficiently determina-

rolls over and goes back to sleep. Concerned wife, thinking it might have been the dispatcher trying to tell hubby about a run, calls back the dispatcher. "You are right," the dispatcher says. "We did try to call your husband. But since he hung up, he is a voluntary quit." Wife pleads that their phone was broken, but to no avail.

Next morning, the employee calls Ma Bell. A phone technician discovers a corroded wire. He fixes it and restores service. He gives the employee the corroded wire plus an affidavit stating that he found the phone out of service and made the repair.

At the grievance hearing before the joint committee, the union representative presents the grievant, who tells his story, and introduces into evidence the corroded wire and the repair technician's affidavit. He does not call either the wife or repairman as a witness.

The only evidence against the grievant is testimony that the grievant called the dispatcher on the phone and threatened to "get him." The grievant admits this, but asserts that he meant he would get him in court. The joint committee denies the grievance.

This is a simplified version of *Findley* v. *Jones Motor Freight*.[19] Despite a jury verdict for the grievant, the Third Circuit held that the union did not breach its duty of fair representation. The court wrote,

> The standard to be applied to union advocacy in grievance proceedings must be governed by the climate in which it functions. The perimeters of the minimally acceptable conduct cannot be too lax, or there will not be an appropriate safeguard for the union member whose important contractual rights are entrusted to and dependent upon the union's efforts in his behalf. On the other hand, to hold lay union representatives to the demanding tests applied to a trained trial lawyer would defeat the

---

tive of the outcome in arbitration to constitute a breach of the duty. Some representative examples include Novakovich v. McNicholas Transportation Co., *supra* note 12 (union failed to question whether discharge was voluntary quit or refusal to accept a job assignment and failed to make sufficient claim for damages); Kaftantzis v. D & L Transport Co., *supra* note 12 (allegation of union's failure to raise certain points creates triable issue); Newbern v. Vienna Sausage Mfg. Co., 108 LRRM 2252 (C.D. Calif. 1981) (failure to call certain witnesses, to let grievant testify on his own behalf, and to advance an argument suggested by the grievant does not amount to breach of the duty); Rupe v. Spector Freight Systems, *supra* note 9 (total failure to investigate would breach duty); Early v. Eastern Transfer, *supra* note 10 (failure to make certain arguments not a violation if judgment has been exercised; court suggests different result if union simply were unaware of argument); Spielman v. Anchor Motor Freight, Inc., 551 F. Supp. 817, 112 LRRM 3426 (S.D. N.Y. 1982) (employer must show not only error but that it affected the award); Findley v. Jones Motor Freight, *supra* note 13.

19. 639 F.2d 953, 106 LRRM 2420 (3d Cir. 1981).

aims of informality and speedy resolution contemplated by labor-management grievance agreements. . . . The conduct of the union . . . was, at the least, adequate and within the realm of "acceptable performance" contemplated by Hines. . . . Even if we were to adopt the standard of mere negligence . . . the conduct of the union would pass muster. Moreover, even if certain actions of the union were arguably negligent, there has been no showing that they tainted the committee's decision.[20]

You Didn't Get a Notice?

The employee, a twenty-seven-year veteran truck driver, smashes his truck into a parked truck, killing the other driver. He is discharged for recklessness. While he is in the hospital recuperating, the employee's union investigates, visiting the site of the accident, inspecting the vehicles, and reading the police accident report. Without discussing the matter with the employee, the union schedules his case before the joint committee. The employee, still in the hospital, is unable to attend the hearing.

At the hearing, the union reads into the record the fact that it notified the grievant of the hearing; it offers no explanation why the grievant could not attend. The union merely argues that the grievant has better than twenty years seniority and is in his fifties. The joint committee denies the grievance.

In the case this scenario is drawn from, *McFarland v. Teamsters,* the district court rejected most of the employee's arguments of inadequate representation, asserting that enough was done for the grievant and that his basic dissatisfaction is with the outcome of the case.[21] The court, however, refused to grant the union's motion to dismiss, finding a triable issue of fact with respect to the union going ahead without the employee and failing to adequately explain his absence to the joint committee.[22]

---

20. *Id.* at 958, 960–61, 106 LRRM at 2422–23, 2424. Cases in which the union failed to pursue lines of attack the grievant thought would be helpful or presented what the grievant claimed was an inadequate case include Sine v. Teamsters Local 992, *supra* note 12; McFarland v. Teamsters Local 745, *supra* note 12; Harris v. Schwerman Trucking Co., *supra* note 9; Schlepper v. Ford Motor Co., 107 LRRM 2500 (D. Minn. 1980) (failure of union to argue mitigation not a violation; grievant has no right to dictate strategy).

21. 535 F. Supp. 970, 110 LRRM 3022 (N.D. Tex. 1982).

22. A similar problem is raised when the grievant claims the union failed to meet with him to prepare the case. *See, e.g.,* Newbern v. Vienna Sausage Mfg. Co., *supra* note 18.

Equal Justice for All

Workers A and B fight on the job. In arbitration, the union decides not to suggest that either worker instigated the fight. Union takes a neutral position as between the two workers and urges that neither be discharged. Apparently concluding that A instigated the fight, arbitrator sustains B's grievance but denies A's grievance.

In *Johnson* v. *Postal Workers,* from which this summary is taken, the district court found no violation of the duty of fair representation.[23] The court said a requirement that the union provide separate defense teams for each employee would be costly, without precedent, and "extraordinary."[24] The court concluded that the union paid as much attention to A's case as to B's, asserted each employee's position evenhandedly, and had a reasoned basis for its tactical decision not to try to apportion blame.[25]

Equal Justice for None

Company A is absorbed by company B. While the contracts covering both companies provide for a method of merging seniority lists in such cases, the procedure allows for exceptions by agreement of the parties. The union agrees with the company to such an exception, but later, when the company claims hardship, agrees to go back to the union contractual provision. The company A employees and the company B employees both claim seniority rights at company B.

The union takes a position of neutrality with respect to both groups. It states at the arbitration hearing,

> The union's posture here today will not be to align itself on the merits with either [position] . . . but to assist the arbitrator and to assist the representatives of each of the groups of men in placing before you, the Arbitrator, all of the relevant facts, all of the background, all of the

---

23. 102 LRRM 3089 (D.D.C. 1979).

24. *Id.* at 3091.

25. The problem of representing or reconciling divergent interests was recognized by the Court in its early decision in Humphrey v. Moore, 375 U.S. 335, 55 LRRM 2031 (1964), a case involving competing seniority claims of groups of employees. The Court held that the union's decision to take a good-faith position in favor of one group of employees and contrary to the interests of other employees it represents did not violate its duty. More recent decisions upholding such choices include Walters v. Roadway Express, 622 F.2d 162, 96 LRRM 2006 (5th Cir. 1976); Wallace v. A.T.&T. Co., 460 F. Supp. 755, 105 LRRM 2681 (E.D. N.Y. 1978); Rupe v. Spector Freight Systems, *supra* note 9 (union took debatable position with respect to a group of employees, but contract is sufficiently ambiguous to support union's position); Fox v. Mitchell Transport, 506 F. Supp. 1346, 112 LRRM 2262 (D. Md. 1981) (permissible for union to also represent other employees with seniority claims adverse to grievant).

documents to assist each of the representative groups of employees in fashioning their arguments before you and their statements of position before you, to keep the employer on the straight and narrow in terms of presentation of its version of the facts and its arguments with respect to them.[26]

The arbitrator fashions a merged seniority list that offends all the parties. They are unsuccessful, however, in setting it aside on any basis of error in the award itself. The former company A employees contend in addition that the union violated its duty towards them by ineffectually presenting their position.

The district court finds the union represented the company A employees fairly. It "faced the task of representing the adverse interests of two sets of employees. Unable to resolve for itself which position should prevail," it represented both.[27]

Some Propositions

If we examine in detail the roots of the doctrines exposed in these garden variety cases, several propositions emerge.

First, the courts draw very delicate lines. On the one hand, since arbitral finality is at stake, the courts tend to insulate the arbitral process from scrutiny. Thus the courts will tolerate even fairly serious errors of judgment, carelessness, and mistakes. On the other hand, the courts demand a minimal level of union competence. The six recipes give examples of these tenuous verbal distinctions. Further attempts at formulation are found in footnote 9.

Second, it is even harder to apply a standard, once it has been formulated. It is difficult for a reviewing court, particularly if there is no transcript of the arbitration hearing, to recreate the exact situation faced by the union representative. The arbitration award does not usually reveal the preparation and tactical choices of the advocate, nor provide a very useful chronicle of his performance at the hearing. And a joint committee's decision provides even less illumination, if any. Even if the factual finding is secure, it is virtually impossible to tell whether the representative's mistake or omission

---

26. Crusco v. Fisher & Bro., Inc., 458 F. Supp. 413, 417, 99 LRRM 2764, 2767 (S.D. N.Y. 1978).

27. *Id.* at 423, 99 LRRM at 2771. Compare the earlier case of Kesner v. NLRB, 532 F.2d 1169, 92 LRRM 2137 (7th Cir. 1976), in which the union presented the grievant's seniority claim to the abitration panel, but in effect asserted it had no merit. The court wrote "when one's own representative . . . proclaims a lack of merit, it is indeed likely to be a coup de grace to the claim."

made a difference. Furthermore, many decisions rest on judgment. While a Monday morning quarterback can easily second-guess a judgment, a decision made before the representative knew how it would affect the outcome is relatively unassailable.

Third, for the grievant the standard for deciding whether the union represented him fairly can be captured in two words: I lost. Under the rule of arbitral finality, the membrane that insulates an arbitration from judicial review is quite thick. Naturally, the individual seeks to pierce it at its only vulnerable point, through the fair representation doctrine. Given the open-endedness of the reviewing courts' standards, however, the doctrine threatens to cause a rupture rather than provide a window of review.

This leads back to my initial hypothesis: Removal of the *perfunctory* branch of the *Vaca* test in cases involving completed arbitrations would eliminate this vacillating standard and discourage challenges. The more narrow and rigid test of bad faith or discriminatory or arbitrary treatment could be met only by a showing that the union was hostile to the individual or intentionally provided inferior representation.

There is a sound conceptual basis to apply this stricter test of review for cases that have gone to arbitration. The fair representation standard has its genesis in cases in which the union refused to take a case to arbitration. The seminal use of the term perfunctory appeared in the *Maddox* decision, in which an individual brought a direct action seeking to enforce his contractual rights against the employer under section 301.[28] While the court held that the individual was required to exhaust the agreed upon contractual remedy of arbitration, it left open the case in which the union "refuses to press or only perfunctorily presses the individual's claim."[29] *Vaca* amplified *Maddox* by holding that the exhaustion route was satisfied and suit on the contract barred even if the union refused to proceed to arbitration, so long as its decision was fair.[30]

Vaca gives the union the ultimate discretion to block the individual's contract claim if there is a reasoned basis for the union's decision. A decision arrived at honestly—for example, that the grievance is of doubtful merit and limited importance—satisfies this standard. A bad faith or discriminatory decision has no such rea-

---

28. Republic Steel Corp. v. Maddox, 379 U.S. 650, 58 LRRM 2193 (1965).
29. *Id.* at 652, 58 LRRM at 2194.
30. 386 U.S. 171, 64 LRRM 2369 (1967).

soned basis, nor does a decision that is the product of slapdash investigation and haphazard analysis. A decision reached in such a perfunctory manner is no decision at all. Since it has no rational basis, it may not serve to deprive the individual of his contractual rights.

But the cases we are concerned with involve a different configuration of interests. The union has aligned itself with the individual, agreeing to pursue rather than oppose his contractual rights. Since it does not purport to block his contractual rights, it need not justify its position on the basis of rational, overriding institutional interests. If the union represents the individual poorly—even arbitrarily or perfunctorily—it has nevertheless sided with him and need not have its alignment tested by standards of rationality. Further, since the individual actually arrives before the arbitrator there is a good likelihood that his claim will be heard on the merits, despite weak representation. As long as the union treats the individual no worse than any other employee, the individual's only recourse should be the political one of ousting the union so that he will be better represented in any future grievances.

It is anomalous to allow an award to be overturned because of perfunctory representation. If an arbitrator ignores a contract provision that favors the grievant—even one brought to his attention by the union—his award cannot be overturned no matter how blatant the error.[31] But when the error can be traced to the union, as in *Milstead*, the award may be set aside. As I indicated earlier, the only time the Court squarely faced the issue of the union's duty in arbitration, it did not define those elements that constitute unfair representation. So the way is open to establish a different standard.

I now wish to assert the contrary view—and, on reflection, the correct one—of the standard of fair representation in arbitration. Let me first address the theoretical issues.

The four-branch standard of fair representation that has evolved since *Maddox* has not distinguished between prearbitration and postarbitration cases. The seminal *Maddox* language quoted earlier regarding the union pressing the claim "perfunctorily" seems on its face and in the context of the case to refer to the way the claim is presented in arbitration. And in *Hines,* a completed arbitration case,

---

31. United Steelworkers v. Enterprise Wheel & Car Corp., 363 U.S. 593, 46 LRRM 2423 (1960) ("It is the arbitrator's construction which was bargained for; . . . the courts have no business overruling him because their interpretation of the contract is different from his." *Id.* at 599, 46 LRRM at 2426).

the court reiterated the arbitrary and perfunctory branches of the test of *Vaca*, without drawing any clear distinction between cases that do or do not go to arbitration.

The underlying rationale of *Vaca* is that the individual's contractual rights should be extinguished only for a reasoned group interest. There is a collective interest in a speedy, final method of dispute resolution through arbitration that entails a bar to further recourse in most cases. But perfunctory representation is conduct so wanting that it is the equivalent of no representation at all. It connotes not merely error, but total abdication of responsibility to present the case. Such representation forfeits the claim that a rational group interest in finality overrides the individual's rights under the contract.

Finally, the distinction between prearbitration and postarbitration dereliction is not clear. Returning to the *Milstead* example, is there a real difference between the union refusing to go to arbitration because it fails to note the critical contract provision and failing to raise the provision for the same reason in arbitration? Why should the union be absolved of its dereliction just because it works its mischief during arbitration rather than before arbitration?

These theoretical grounds aside, there are practical reasons to retain the perfunctory standard. Most important, it is simply too difficult to show bad faith and discriminatory treatment.[32] The union is unlikely to admit it, and it is wrong to infer it simply from the fact that the individual is out of favor. Both *Hines* and *Holodnak* rest on shaky inferences that the poor representation stemmed from the grievant's disfavor. It seems preferable to make the court focus directly on the quality of representation rather than approach it in a backhanded way by treating it as evidence of hostility or bad faith.

Further, if unions were excused from perfunctory representation, they would have an easy wasy of disposing of grievances. For example, rather than refuse to take a dissident union member's case to arbitration and risk a suit under *Vaca*, the union would be tempted to proceed to arbitration and do a bad job.

---

32. Few of the cases we studied even dealt with this aspect of the *Vaca* test, looking instead at allegations of arbitrary or perfunctory representation. Challenges of bad faith or hostile representation were usually rejected decisively, *e.g.*, Rupe v. Spector Freight Systems, *supra* note 9; Early v. Eastern Transfer, *supra* note 9 (even if hostility shown, must demonstrate its effect on outcome of arbitration); Hines v. Anchor Motor Freight, *supra* note 4.

A third reason to retain the perfunctory standard is grounded in larger issues of policy. Given a choice of standards, we should adopt one that fosters the greatest care by the union. The issues at stake in arbitration are important, especially when the individual's job is involved. The perfunctory standard is an additional assurance that these cases will be presented and resolved properly. This is especially important because of the public nature of some of the issues resolved in arbitration.

Antidotes

While I agree that perfunctory union conduct in arbitration should violate the duty of fair representation, I do not think this should be a very demanding standard. The courts agree, for they rarely find the union's behavior wanting under this test.

There is a way to minimize the disruption of the arbitration process engendered by even a lenient standard of review. Unions should prepare for and conduct their arbitrations in better than perfunctory fashion. Most of the union conduct addressed in the cases is egregious and easily avoided. The cases suggest some formulas for avoiding fair representation litigation.

Prepare Carefully
A union should consult with the grievant early in the grievance process. A professional union staff person usually becomes involved at the second or third step of the grievance, when the grievance has usually been committed to writing and often answered in writing. This is the time for the representative to meet with the grievant. He should explore with the grievant the various theories that might apply to the case and should discuss with the grievant the evidence that might support these theories. If further evidence might be helpful, the union and the individual should reach some understanding as to responsibility for pursuing these leads; there is no reason for the grievant not to be assigned the task of gathering evidence. I assume that any competent union representative keeps a grievance file. He should enter a note of the conference and a general outline of the points covered and the division of responsibilities assumed.

While all this occurs before arbitration, the most egregious breaches in the reported cases occur in the investigative stage: the failure to investigate in *Hines,* the investigation without the grievant's participation in *McFarland,* and the omission to argue the critical contract provision in *Milstead.* Inadequate preparation in the early grievance stages can infect the arbitration.

To preclude another surefire invitation of trouble, notify the grievant of the hearing. If the grievant does not appear at the hearing, it is probably cheaper and less trouble in the long run to postpone the hearing and try to notify the grievant. If there is legitimate reason the grievant cannot attend, as in *McFarland,* the union owes it to him not to arbitrate in his absence. To proceed without even an explanation is to signal the arbitrator that the grievant does not feel strongly about the merits of his own case.[33]

The importance of the final preparation stage was also pointed up in our survey. For example, while not dispositive in *Holodnak,* the court was disturbed by brief, last-minute consultation between attorney and grievant. Given union budgets and time constraints, it may be impracticable for an attorney or international representative to meet with the grievant until the morning of the hearing or the night before. Even so, he ought to allow sufficient time for a final consultation at which strategy is discussed and testimony reviewed. If this is the only meeting between advocate and grievant, there should be preliminary preparation by the local representative, such as the business agent, and correspondence with the advocate.[34]

Base Judgment on Adequate Investigation and Reasoned Consideration

A more difficult area of review involves judgments about general strategies and specific tactics. Examples include the decision in *Johnson* not to allocate blame between the two fighters and in *Findley* not to call the phone technician and the grievant's wife as witnesses. To the extent that judgments may differ, they will usually be allowed to stand. But the judgment must be based on some consideration of the

---

33. Other cases of failure to notify the grievant include Crusco v. Fisher & Bro. Inc., *supra* note 28; Budde v. A & C Carriers, Inc., *supra* note 15. This problem is especially troublesome where the union must choose between divergent interests, as in both Crusco and Budde. Both those cases suggest that the union must notify both sets of employees of the pending arbitration; *see also,* Larry v. Penn Trucking, 112 LRRM 2949 (E.D. Pa. 1982) for this proposition. *See also,* Sine v. Teamsters Local 992, *supra* note 13. This problem is discussed subsequently in the text of this article.

34. Holodnak v. Avco Corp., *supra* note 17. *See also,* Newbern v. Vienna Sausage Mfg. Co., *supra* note 18; Findley v. Jones Motor Freight, *supra* note 13.

evidence and some rational articulation of strategy. It must not be the product of lazy preparation or the means of hurting a disfavored group.

Whatever the choices, it makes good sense for the union representatives to record them in notes or a memo to the file, or even a letter to the grievant. At the very least, the decisions should be discussed with the grievant before the hearing.

The More Obvious the Point, the Greater the Obligation to Take a Correct Position on the Law

The hardest cases involve the failure to argue or pursue obvious legal theories. Some of these issues arise under the contract, and some involve external law.

Conduct that is better than perfunctory requires a minimal level of competence. The key is in the language of *Hines,* which looks to a standard of ordinary or average representation. A court should not insist on the level of skill of the ideal lawyer; the cases properly shrink from such a standard.

A minimal, core standard of competence requires familiarity with the contract. If nothing else, the representative ought to know the contract he administers. The total failure to point to a contract provision right on point, as in *Milstead,* is fatal. When the individual agrees to entrust his contract right to a representative he is entitled to expect that person to present the obvious contract provisions. This is a corollary of Clyde Summers's position that a union may not refuse to take to arbitration a grievance that rests on a clear contractual provision; he would not excuse such a failure simply because it is inadvertent.

Contractual arguments that are not so obvious are another matter. Advocates have different levels of skill and imagination, and if a potential reading of a contract clause is overlooked, the grievant must chalk that up to the luck of the draw. If we take seriously the position of many courts, including the Supreme Court, that the process cannot be error-free, we must accept this result. But if the interpretation of a provision has already been fixed, or even suggested, by a prior arbitration award or is foreshadowed by negotiating history or past practice, it may be the representative's business to know this and make the appropriate presentation.

Other principles of labor arbitration are so settled that it may be inexcusable not to raise them. For example, in all but cases of serious

wrongdoing, the employer must impose progressive discipline—
moving from lesser to greater penalties—before discharging the
employee.[35] An advocate who does not understand this concept or
fails to pursue it provides only perfunctory representation. So does
an advocate who fails to put forth a satisfactory prior work record in
mitigation of discipline.

Legal issues that originate outside the basic rules of labor arbitration raise a more difficult problem. *Holodnak* is a prime example.
The court faulted the grievant's representative, an attorney, urging
that because of government contracts the First Amendment protected the employee's speech. While a lawyer might perhaps be expected to make such an argument, I think it is beyond the ken of the
average nonlawyer union representative.

Suppose a union attempts to challenge a written test as insufficiently job-related to overcome seniority in promotions. The union
fails to investigate whether the test has a disproportionate effect on
black employees and therefore should be eliminated under a contract provision that prohibits discrimination on account of race. This
too is a subtle enough approach that failure to pursue it is not perfunctory representation.[36]

It is asking too much for the doctrine of fair representation to
require a union representative to be familar with the exploding body
of external law that impinges upon arbitration. For example, in discharge cases, the representative could be responsible for understanding the First Amendment, the rehabilitation act, OSHA, and
ERISA (the pension reform act), to name only a few. Of course, certain doctrines of external law eventually make their way into the arbitration literature, for example, recent developments calling for rehabilitation rather than discipline of employees with drinking and
drug problems.[37] As these doctrines become part of the body of arbitration law, it may be appropriate to expect representatives to master them. But the fair representation doctrine should not require expertise at the frontiers or fringes of arbitration law.

---

35. Elkouri and Elkouri, How Arbitration Works 630–32 (3d ed. BNA 1973).

36. This example is suggested by the Detroit Edison litigation, in which the union
challenged a test under both traditional contract grounds and under Title VII. The
Title VII argument was raised in the courts but not in arbitration. Detroit Edison Co.
v. NLRB, 440 U.S. 301, 305 n.4, 100 LRRM 2728, 2729 n.4 (1979).

37. T. S. Denenberg and R. V. Denenberg, Alcohol and Drugs: Issues in the
Workplace (BNA 1983).

Exercise Extreme Care in Representing Disparate Interests

We have seen two examples in which the union either represents all interests with equal vigor, as in the fighting case, or takes a position of virtual abstinence as in the seniority case. Neutrality is acceptable only if the grievance warrants neutrality. If, on the other hand, an investigation of the fighting case reveals that employee A is the instigator and employee B the victim, then the union may have a duty to pursue only employee B's case.

Wisely, the courts have not foisted *per se* rules upon unions in these cases. There is no obligation to *always* represent the senior employee in a promotion dispute or the alleged victim in a sexual harassment case or to provide equal representation for both sets of interests. Rather, the courts take a case-by-case approach and insist only that the union make a thorough investigation and consider fairly the competing interests. The decision to align itself with one or the other faction is usually upheld if it rests on reason. If the decision rests on political strength, it is often invalidated; while this is a commendable theoretical approach, it ignores the reality that the dominant group interest is often that which serves the greatest numbers in the group.[38]

This suggests that the union's responsibility for fair representation of divergent interests is tested primarily in the investigation and preparation stages. This is not entirely satisfactory, for it means that contractual rights are created and extinguished with none of the minimal safeguards and review that attach in arbitration. Furthermore, some issues arise at the arbitration hearing. For example, if the union aligns itself with one set of interests, must it give notice to those adversely affected?[39] May the unrepresented employees present their own case? Should they be allowed their own representative? Should the union provide or pay for separate representation?

Even though a union is not required to represent rival interests, it may be well advised in certain cases to devise mechanisms for these divergent claims to be brought before the arbitrator, for example, by

---

38. *See,* Barton Brands, Ltd. v. NLRB, 529 F.2d 793, 91 LRRM 2241 (7th Cir. 1973); NLRB v. General Truck Drivers, IBT Local 315, 545 F.2d 1173, 93 LRRM 2747 (9th Cir. 1976). *Compare,* Rupe v. Spector Freight Systems, *supra* note 9, which suggests that, at least where contract language is ambiguous, the union may take the position that favors the largest group interest.

39. At least one court has held that the union must give notice to the employee with interests adverse to those of the represented employee, Larry v. Penn Trucking, *supra* note 33.

allowing separate representation. Given the widely diverse situations in which rival claims may clash, responsibility may ultimately fall upon the arbitrator to sort them out and to ensure their protection.

The Arbitrator's Role

Let us move to the arbitration table and consider the arbitrator's role in dealing with fair representation.

Arbitration must be viewed in the context of a fair representation doctrine that makes it difficult for a union to reject those cases it thinks should not be taken to arbitration. While there are no hard data on this phenomenon, I think the other authors would agree that the fair representation doctrine forces unions to take cases to arbitration that they otherwise would drop. Because of the *Bowen* decision, the union faces potentially heavy liability for a wrongful failure to take a case to arbitration: it bears the responsibility for back pay from the time the case should have been taken to arbitration until the grievant is finally made whole.[40] In a discharge case, this can add up to several years of back pay. While participants suggested various devices to shift some of this liability to the employer, *Bowen* remains a powerful incentive to take a case to arbitration. The implications are twofold.

First, take the case of the union that honestly concludes that a grievance should not be taken to arbitration, for example because the grievance is of doubtful merit and would place an undue burden on the union treasury without yielding a proportionate benefit to the membership as a whole. If it arrives at this conclusion after careful investigation and on a reasoned basis, its decision ought to withstand litigation. But the risks of fair representation litigation and the costs and energies expended can be great even if the individual does not prevail in a lawsuit. How much easier and less expensive it is to allow the case to go to arbitration. The representative can make a show of presenting the case, and if the grievant does not prevail, nothing is lost.

If union representation in arbitration is insulated from effective judicial review, then unions have a very easy out for avoiding their

---

40. Bowen v. U.S. Postal Service, 103 S. Ct. 588, 112 LRRM 2281 (1983). In his dissent in Bowen, Justice White predicted that the holding would drive unions to take unmeritorious cases to arbitration. *Id.* at 605, 112 LRRM at 2293.

fair representation obligations in processing grievances. Unless we hold unions to better than perfunctory representation in arbitration, this course of least resistance is too appealing. Not only is effective representation of individuals sacrificed if union performance is not scrutinized, but the arbitration process is flooded with cases that should not be heard.

Second, take the worst case, in which a union is hostile to the grievant, for example, because he opposed the incumbent leadership in the last election. Union officials know that if they refuse to take the case to arbitration, the union is vulnerable to a fair representation suit because of the strong inference that it was motivated by bad faith and not by the merits of the case. To avoid this possibility, the union appears to align itself with the individual and takes his case to arbitration. There, by doing an inept job, it can undermine his grievance. Unless there is a meaningful standard of review, the arbitration process may become the dumping ground for cases of hostile, discriminatory, or bad-faith representation. A standard that condemns perfunctory representation would better enable courts to police these cases.

Although a union's conduct in arbitration is subject to judicial review under this standard, the cases discussed earlier show how difficult it is for an individual to prevail in an unfair representation claim in arbitration. This places a special burden on the arbitrator. I do not suggest that the arbitrator is responsible to police the union's performance to make sure it fulfills its duty of fair representation. The arbitrator, however, presides over a process that is designed to be insulated from judicial review and virtually self-sufficient and self-enforcing.[41] This limited judicial oversight transfers some of the responsibility for fairness to the institution itself.[42] An arbitrator should not allow the trappings of regularity—a hearing and a persuasive written award—to mask a situation in which representation has been inadequate.

---

41. The definitive cases continue to be the Steelworkers Triology, decided in 1960: United Steelworkers v. American Manufacturing Co., 363 U.S. 564, 46 LRRM 2414 (1960); Steelworkers v. Warrior & Gulf Naviagation Co., 363 U.S. 574, 46 LRRM 2416 (1960); and United Steelworkers v. Enterprise Wheel and Car Corp., 363 U.S. 593, 46 LRRM 2423 (1960). Their vitality is reaffirmed in W. R. Grace and Co. v. Rubber Workers, Local Union 759, 103 S. Ct. 2177, 113 LRRM 2461 (1983).

42. For a perceptive, in-depth discussion of this proposition, *see* Gross and Bordoni, *Reflections on the Arbitrator's Responsibility to Provide a Full and Fair Hearing: How to Bite the Hand that Feeds You*, 29 Syr. L. Rev. 877 (1978).

But how can an arbitrator safeguard against unfair representation without inappropriately intruding into the process? Practitioners are emphatic in warning arbitrators not to interfere with the
parties' presentations, for example, by asking gratuitous questions
or pursuing lines of investigation not raised by the parties. There
are practical dangers of such intervention. For example, the arbitrator might wonder why the union has not brought out the grievant's
work history in mitigation of discharge. If he probes this area, the
arbitrator may unearth some adverse employment history the employer overlooked and simply harm the grievant's case. On the other
hand, the arbitrator may want to explore whether there is a past
practice that supports the grievant's position. What if the union does
not raise this because it has agreed to abandon reliance on the practice in exchange for concessions at the bargaining table? It may not
be legitimate for the union to ignore past practices in these circumstances.[43]

The arbitrator cannot be sure why a line of inquiry is not pursued and so should be wary of jumping in. But if he is concerned, he
should call the representatives together during recess. If the arbitrator is satisfied that there are sound reasons for leaving the area
alone, then he should let it rest. But if the arbitrator believes that the
omission unfairly disadvantages the grievant and serves no acceptable institutional purpose, then he may have an additional responsibility. He should advise the parties that unless they pursue the line
of investigation, he will. The arbitrator's intervention need not be
solely on the basis of inadequate representation. Rather, as a result
of his consultation with the representatives, he has discovered that
he lacks sufficient information to make an informed award. He asks
additional questions to enable him to decide the case correctly.

The approach is delicate, and intervention may cost the arbitrator future acceptability. Further, intervention should not be used
simply to shore up a weak advocate. But where an arbitrator concludes with reasonable certainty that inadequate representation may
deprive an individual of his contractual rights, then he has a duty to
take corrective measures. Otherwise, the isolation and impartiality

---

43. Rupe v. Spector Freight Systems, *supra* note 9, suggests it is permissible for a
union to construe an ambiguous contract provision in accordance with the interests of
the larger groups it represents.

of his office gives an erroneous message to a reviewing court that the individual has received adequate representation.

I believe arbitrators need institutional support for such a position. The Code of Professional Responsibility for Arbitrators makes a beginning in this direction, but does not go far enough.[44] In dealing with consent awards, it directs the arbitrator to see that the award is "proper, fair, sound and lawful" before adopting it. The amplifying statement requires some arbitral activism:

> Before complying with such a request [for a consent award] an arbitrator must be certain that he or she understands the suggested settlement adequately in order to appraise its terms. If it appears that pertinent facts or circumstances may not have been disclosed, the arbitrator should take the initiative to assure that all significant aspects of the case are fully understood. To this end, the arbitrator may request additional specific information and may question witnesses at a hearing.[45]

These safeguards are presumably designed to make sure that individual interests are not sacrificed in a consent decree. But the directive of initiative and requesting additional information is just as appropriate in a litigated case, for there is the same possibility of sacrifice of individual rights as in a consent decree. The quoted provisions ought to be treated as a pervasive code of arbitral responsibility and not limited to consent situations.

In the same vein, the code states in the section on hearing conduct in an explanatory comment that "an arbitrator may . . . question the parties' representatives or witnesses, when necessary or advisable, to obtain additional or pertinent information; and request that the parties submit additional evidence, either at the hearing or by subsequent filing."[46] This deserves to be elevated to the text of the code.

The arbitrator can also play a significant role in reconciling divergent interests in arbitration. In a seniority case, for example, the union usually advances the claim of a senior employee. The arbitrator may well ask who represents the interests of the junior employee. The arbitrator may be satisfied that since the employer selected the junior employee, the employer will adequately put forth his case.

---

44. Code of Professional Responsibility for Arbitrators of Labor-Management Disputes of the National Academy of Arbitrators, American Arbitration Association and Federal Mediation and Conciliation Service (1974).

45. *Id.* at ¶65.

46. *Id.* at §5.

But the arbitrator may suggest that the junior employee be permitted to attend and, at least in conference with counsel and the arbitrator, indicate whether there are other areas to pursue.[47]

Suppose an employee challenges a break in his seniority service when he takes disability leave. If the arbitrator decides to give the employee seniority credit for that time, the grievant may displace another employee when he returns. While the arbitrator may not require the attendance of employees potentially affected by his decision, he should at least be aware of their interests to avoid untoward consequences that may create further problems under the contract. He should be receptive to requests for participation by other parties.

But normally an arbitrator does not have the power to impose multiple-party litigation in arbitration. The contract is between the employer and the union, and the third party has no standing to intervene. An arbitrator has an inherent power to obtain additional information, at least through questioning of witnesses called by the parties. To use this power to compel testimony of additional witnesses is a delicate matter. Further, the arbitrator should be loath to allow additional parties to intervene without consent of the contractual parties. Not only does this complicate the hearing, but it enables a third party to advocate contractual positions that do not reflect the intentions or agreement of the contracting parties.

But the arbitrator can suggest third-party participation. In my experience as an arbitrator, the parties have no objection to allowing an individual grievant to participate with his own attorney. This occurred when the individual attorney represented the grievant in a related criminal matter and was familiar with the case; when the union did not approve of the grievant's conduct but was content to give him his day in court; and when the grievant had interests at odds with the rest of the membership. In the last case, the employee was discharged for using drugs on the job. Since the evidence was

---

47. In seeking to persuade counsel for the union and employer to allow a junior employee to participate, the arbitrator should remind them of cases like Belanger v. Matteson, 346 A.2d 124, 91 LRRM 2003 (R.I. S. Ct. 1975), *cert. denied*, 424 U.S. 968, 96 Sup. Ct. 1466 (1976), in which the union represented the senior employee in a promotion case. The court held the union violated its duty to the junior employee by failing to investigate his claim and weigh his entitlement against that of the senior employee. *See also*, Larry v. Penn Trucking, *supra* note 33, which requires the union to give notice of an arbitration to an employee with interests adverse to those of the employee represented by the union.

circumstantial, his vindication in arbitration might suggest that some other employee used the drugs. The union faced a potential conflict of interest in representing the grievant.

The presence of a third-party advocate need not telegraph to the arbitrator that the union does not support the grievant. Such a message might tempt the arbitrator to resolve the case against the grievant, since neither party who may select him in the future wants the grievant to win. I hope that no arbitrator is vulnerable to such a consideration. But even if his pragmatic bent is strong, the arbitrator should recognize that separate representation may mean only that the grievant has confidence in his own attorney and does not reflect the merits of the grievant's claim or the union's institutional support of it.

It may be appropriate for the arbitrator to suggest third-party arrangements to the parties to certain cases.[48] This might have been preferable in the fighting case and was an alternative in the seniority merger case. Judges are commonly called up to consider the adequacy of class representatives to deal with divergent interests, and arbitrators could exercise an analogous power.[49] Attorneys should be receptive to such suggestions, recognizing the direction under the ABA Code of Professional Responsibility not to accept employment that involves conflicting interests.[50] Again, the arbitrator can do no more than suggest, for he lacks the power to impose third-party representation. But if the arbitrator cannot persuade the parties to correct an inherent conflict of interest, he may have to ameliorate this by a more active role in the arbitration process.

In several cases before me, I have suspected the union took the case to arbitration only because it thought this preferable to defending against a fair representation lawsuit. In one or two cases, my suspicions were later confirmed. But in all these cases, I found the representation aggressive and competent. I think this was due less to the fear of litigation than a professional commitment to do a competent

---

48. See the procedure imposed by the arbitrator and approved by the court in Hotel Employees v. Michaelson's Food Service, 545 F.2d 1248, 94 LRRM 2014 (9th Cir. 1976). The arbitrator's award is found at 61 LA 1195 (1973).

49. *See, Comment, Developments in the Law—Class Actions,* 89 Harv. L. Rev. 1319, 1592–97 (1976).

50. American Bar Association Code of Professional Responsibility (1970) Canon 5, "A lawyer should exercise independent professional judgment on behalf of a client."

job. It is easy for an attorney to recognize this obligation and to explain to the union that under his code of professional responsibility he must represent the grievant zealously even if the union is not behind the case.[51]

I would like to see a similar code developed for all representatives in arbitration, lawyers or nonlawyers. It should be developed by practitioners who regularly participate in arbitration. It should capture the notion that the advocate owes his primary allegiance to the grievant, although he may recognize some overriding group interests, for example, by not advocating a contractual interpretation that goes against the understanding reached at the bargaining table. It should oblige the advocate to disclose any potential conflicts of interest. The code might set forth some minimal standards of meeting, notification, and preparation for arbitration as well. I believe that an advocate who means to do well by the grievant needs such a code to help him withstand pressure if the union wishes him to do less than an adequate job or if it simply fails to give him the time or resources to do a proper job.

How far should the arbitrator should go in ensuring an adequate basis of review by the courts? Where the parties know or suspect that the case is one that might end up in the courts, it might be to everyone's advantage to make a transcript, despite the added costs and time. Absent a transcript, the arbitrator should write a thorough decision, setting out the evidence in detail. For example, in the fighting case, the arbitrator should indicate what was said on behalf of each of the participants in the fight. This is a good device for pushing the union into doing a better job. If the arbitrator is concerned, he may tell the parties at a conference that he intends to spell out in detail the contentions and evidence advanced by the union.

It is not the arbitrator's responsibility to decide whether a union has represented an individual fairly. The arbitrator should not make such a pronouncement in his award, nor should he engage in the unseemly charade of asking the grievant if he feels he was adequately represented and recording the answer in the award.[52] On the other hand, a careful, detailed arbitration award will put the re-

---

51. *Id.*, Canon 7.

52. This occurs quite often in the reported cases, *e.g.*, Liotta v. National Forge Company, 473 F. Supp. 1139, 102 LRRM 2348, (W.D. Pa. 1979); Spielman v. Anchor Motor Freight, Inc., *supra* note 18; Findley v. Jones Motor Freight, *supra* note 13; Early v. Eastern Transfer, *supra* note 9.

viewing court much closer to the actual representation and in a better position to assess its adequacy.

The Impact of External Law

We tend to think of labor arbitration as a means of private dispute resolution. The rights vindicated by the system are created privately by collective bargaining. But as statutory regulation of the workplace multiplies, labor arbitration takes on an increasingly public nature. Boiler plate contract provisions stating that the employer will not discriminate and will provide a safe and healthy workplace are now laden with content from public law, such as Title VII and the Occupational Safety and Health Act. Various other statutes also affect the terms and conditions of employment normally dealt with in the collective agreement. These cover age discrimination, wages and hours, pension reform, handicapped individuals, and protection under the National Labor Relations Act. Pressure for new legislation protecting against plant closures, and judicial developments cutting back on the employment-at-will doctrine make inroads upon the central position of labor arbitration in protecting employee rights.[53]

Unions must decide how expansive a role to take in vindicating employee rights created by these statutes. Both unions and employers must determine whether arbitration presents a more promising forum for resolving such disputes. If labor arbitration becomes freighted with public issues, we must consider whether existing legal doctrines are adequate to the new tasks, for example, whether unions have sufficient access to information about toxic substances

---

53. The closest we have come on a national level to a bill giving some protection to workers in the event of plant closing is H.R. 2847, the National Employment Priorities Act, approved by the House Education and Labor Subcommittee on Labor-Management Relations in October 1983. The bill was given little chance of passage but was hailed as an important first step. No. 195 Daily Labor Report p. 1 (BNA, 10/6/83). There is some legislation regarding plant closings at the state level. A good example of the employment-at-will issue is suggested in Harris v. Schwerman Trucking, *supra* note 9, in which a driver was discharged for refusing to make a delivery at a toxic waste site. His discharge was upheld by a joint committee and survived attack under a fair representation challenge. But it raises the more universal issue of whether our legal system should tolerate the discipline or discharge of employees who attempt to vindicate public interests such as health and safety. There are numerous excellent articles on the employment-at-will doctrine. A good recent compilation is *Report of Committee on Labor and Employment Law*, 36 Record of the Ass'n of Bar of City of New York 170.

to deal adequately with health and safety and whether the Steel-workers Trilogy provides adequate judicial review where public is-sues are involved.[54]

I assume that unions and employers will find it desirable to re-solve their disputes through arbitration even though they involve public issues. For example, an employee who is discharged because of a handicap may want to pursue the matter as a just-cause arbitra-tion before taking statutory routes for relief; or the parties may de-cide to resolve a safety matter before an arbitrator rather than work through the Occupational Safety and Health Administration.

This raises new fair representation issues for unions. Is it worth undertaking representation in new and difficult areas, given the risk that the representation will be found inadequate under the duty of fair representation? But can a union afford not to provide services in these emerging areas of concern? Although there is little solid au-thority on point, if a union chooses to represent an employee outside the grievance-arbitration process, for example, in an unemployment compensation hearing, it should not owe a duty of fair representa-tion to the employee, because the duty stems only from the powers derived as exclusive representative under the contract. Why should a union undertake greater liability by bringing the matter up in arbi-tration?

One answer is that if the outside matter has an effect upon con-tract rights, for example, an unemployment hearing decision intro-duced in evidence at the arbitration, the duty of fair representation may attach in the other forum as well. But even if the duty of fair representation does not apply outside the strict boundaries of the contract, the union undoubtedly owes some obligation of care under accepted theories of contract and fiduciary responsibility. Surely if the union's lawyer takes an unemployment compensation case, he owes his client minimal standards of effective representation. While there is little authority on this point, a similar obligation may be im-posed upon a lay representative. Indeed, it may well be that the doc-trine of fair representation actually insulates the union's conduct by imposing a less strict standard than in another forum. In a line of cases involving alleged breaches by the union of its duty to provide

---

54. *Compare*, Minnesota Mining & Manufacturing Co., 261 NLRB No. 2, 109 LRRM 1345 (1982), *aff'd*, 113 LRRM 3163 (D.C. Cir. 1983) with 29 CFR § 1910.20 and New York Labor Law §§ 875–880 (McKinney 1983).

a safe workplace, unions have used fair representation as a shield against liability.[55] Thus, the union may incur no greater liability by proceeding in arbitration than in a public forum.

Having chosen to vindicate a public right through arbitration, may the grievant relitigate the matter in another forum? Resolution of public issues in private forums creates a dilemma: if the process fails to adequately protect the grievant's rights, should he not have the chance to redress them in a more appropriate forum? But does not this give the individual the undesirable opportunity to present the same case twice? This is an issue of much larger concern, which we will be hearing more of in coming years.[56] Fair representation is a small aspect of this problem.

The legal system has devised several schemes for handling arbitration awards that fail to adequately deal with public issues entrusted to arbitration. We have not directly modified the standards of judicial review; *Enterprise Wheel* still provides very limited grounds for reversal of an award, even if it involves public issues.[57] The only exception is public sector arbitration awards, in which some courts, for example in New York State, will overturn an award that goes against a rather elastic notion of public policy.[58] In general, however, the courts have dealt with the problem indirectly, letting the award stand but allowing the individual in appropriate cases to litigate again in another forum. There are two models for such indirect review.

In one, under the National Labor Relations Act, the NLRB will defer to an arbitration award in which the arbitrator had before him the facts necessary to resolve the statutory issue, so long as the arbitration result is not repugnant to the act and the proceedings are fair

---

55. *E.g.*, House v. Mine Safety Appliances Co., 417 F. Supp. 939, 92 LRRM 3688 (D. Idaho 1976); Mahoney v. Chicago Pneumatic Tool Co., 111 LRRM 2839 (W.D. Mich. 1982). *Cf.*, Dunbar v. Steelworkers, 602 P2d 21, 103 LRRM 2434 (Idaho Sup. Ct. 1979). *See*, Morris, The Developing Labor Law 1559–60 (2d ed. BNA Books, 1983).

56. In 1984, the Supreme Court had the opportunity to consider the issue in the context of the effect of an arbitration award holding the employee was discharged for just cause upon a section 1983 suit by the employee contending he was discharged for exercising his right of free speech. McDonald v. City of West Branch, Docket No. 83-219.

57. *Supra* note 31.

58. *See*, Dover Union Free School v. Dover Wingdale Teachers Ass'n, 61 N.Y.2d 913, 474 N.Y.S.2d 716 (1984).

and regular. If the Board defers, the matter is ended; if the Board proceeds, the case is tried de novo.[59]

The Board has vacillated on the question of just how clearly the statutory issue must be decided in arbitration to be entitled to deferral, but I do not consider that issue here.[60] Rather, I am concerned with whether the Board properly considers the adequacy of the union's representation in determining whether the proceedings are fair and regular. One example will suffice: a shop steward is discharged for talking back to his foreman. The union brings the case to arbitration and appeals for leniency based on the employee's long work history. The grievance is denied; the man remains fired. Should the grievant be allowed to proceed before the NLRB on the theory that as a shop steward he was entitled to be treated as an equal with his foreman and to engage in aggressive advocacy?[61] I do not think the Board can decide this issue unless it knows whether the union decided to raise the statutory issue and whether it was competent to do so. In the cases I have looked at, the Board has paid little or no attention to the quality of the union's representation in arbitration.[62]

---

59. The seminal Board case on deferral is Speilberg Mfg. Co., 112 NLRB 1080, 36 LRRM 1152 (1955). For its modern dress, *see*, Sea-Land Service, Inc., 240 NLRB 1146, 100 LRRM 1406 (1979) and NLRB v. Joseph Magnin Co., 704 F.2d 1457, 113 LRRM 2476 (9th Cir. 1983). When a charge filed with the Board raises issues that could be resolved in arbitration, the Board will not entertain the charge until arbitration has run its course. Collyer Insulated Wire, 192 NLRB 837, 77 LRRM 1931 (1971). But charges of unlawful discharge under section 8(a)(3) will proceed despite the availability of arbitration. General American Transportation Corp., 228 NLRB 808, 94 LRRM 1483 (1977).

As this book went to press, the Board handed down new decisions in this area that alter the doctrines discussed. United Technologies, 268 NLRB No. 83, 115 LRRM 1049 (1984) (Board overrules General American Transportation and defers to arbitration in discharge case); Olin Corp., 268 NLRB No. 86, 115 LRRM 1056 (1984) (reviews and revises deferral standards under Spielberg).

60. *See, e.g.,* Suburban Motor Freight, Inc., 247 NLRB 146, 103 LRRM 1113 (1980), Bay Shipbuilding Co., 251 NLRB 809, 105 LRRM 1376 (1980), and Atlantic Steel, 245 NLRB 814, 102 LRRM 1247 (1979). This too is affected by the recent Board decisions mentioned in the previous note.

61. Board cases allowing a union representative some latitude to advocate a position without fear of discipline are discussed in Atlantic Steel Company, *supra* note 60. Of course if the individual files a section 8(a)(3) charge before the arbitration award is issued, these problems do not arise. *See,* General American Transportation Corp., *supra* note 59. *But see,* the new cases cited in note 59.

62. *See, e.g.,* Hawaiian Hauling Services, Ltd., 219 NLRB 765, 90 LRRM 1011 (1975); Clara Barton Terrace Convalescent Center, 225 NLRB 1028, 92 LRRM 1621 (1976); Ad Art, Inc., 238 NLRB 1124, 99 LRRM 1626 (1978). *Compare,* Atlantic Steel,

The other model allows the individual a second bite at the apple, but gives the arbitration award appropriate weight in the new statutory forum. The doctrine set forth in *Alexander v. Gardner-Denver* held that the issues before an arbitrator are different from those in a Title VII case, and a determination in arbitration does not preclude a trial de novo of the Title VII issues in court.[63] The same approach has now been applied to wage-hour cases under the Supreme Court's *Barrentine* decision,[64] and lower courts have done the same with OSHA cases.[65] Thus, the arbitration world is gradually becoming *Gardner-Denver*ized.

I endorse the premise that an individual's statutory rights should not be automatically foreclosed by an attempt to vindicate a parallel set of rights in arbitration. But it is wasteful to litigate the exact same issue twice. For example, suppose the sleepy truck driver in the *Findley* case had been black. If the case had been presented to an impartial arbitrator, rather than a joint committee, should not a finding that the driver was discharged for just cause dispose of his Title VII claim as well? What is it about this garden variety discharge case that makes us uneasy about accepting an arbitrator's decision? Do we really believe that the quality of the decision is better in a judicial proceeding under Title VII? While theoretical pronouncements are made about the individual's right to have a Title VII claim adjudicated by a court, we are hard put to explain why this is necessary as a matter of fairness. If the arbitration award is put before the court, can we not confidently give it weight, especially where the court has the opportunity to review the award in light of the contentions of counsel?

The *Gardner-Denver* Court addressed this issue in a footnote, holding that the weight to be given to the arbitration award must be

---

supra note 60, at 820 n.14, 102 LRRM 1247, 1249 (1979), in which the union's refusal to allow the grievant to hire an attorney of his choosing was thought by the administrative law judge to be a "serious procedural irregularity," yet was not held a basis to refuse to defer.

63. 415 U.S. 36, 7 FEP Cases 81 (1974).

64. Barrentine v. Arkansas-Best Freight System, Inc., 450 U.S. 728 (1981).

65. *E.g.*, Marshall v. N.L. Industries, Inc., 618 F.2d 1220, 8 OSHC 1166 (7th Cir. 1980). *But compare*, Mahan v. Reynolds Metal Co., August 18, 1983 (E.D. Ark. 1983) holding that an employee cannot relitigate a pension dispute under ERISA after losing the claim in arbitration. *But see*, Santiago Amaro v. Continental Can Co., DLR No. 25 (Feb. 7, 1984), following the Gardner-Denver approach in a pension dispute.

determined on a case-by-case basis. Factors include "the degree of procedural fairness" in the arbitration, and "the special competence of particular arbitrators." The Court stated that "where an arbitral determination gives full consideration to an employee's Title VII rights, a court may properly accord it great weight."[66] I have examined the post-*Gardner-Denver* cases in which footnote 21 is applied. The cases are scarce, but in the ten or so I found, hardly any attention was paid to the adequacy of the union's representation and of its competence to deal with the Title VII issue.[67] Yet this is at least as important a factor as the arbitrator's competence. To return to the truck driver example, suppose a thorough investigation would have revealed that black drivers are disciplined more severely than white employees for comparable offenses and that a disproportionate number of black employees are discharged. This would be a promising approach under Title VII. Title VII should not be foreclosed where the union had neither the idea, nor perhaps even the competence, to pursue such a theory in arbitration.

Gardner-Denver mentioned the union's duty of fair representation. In a footnote it expressed its concern that a union might submerge a member's claim of racial discrimination because it is not in harmony with the union's institutional interests. And, said the Court, "a breach of the union's duty of fair representation may prove difficult to establish."[68]

The same analysis was applied in *Barrentine,* where an individual lost an overtime claim in arbitration. The individual first tried to overturn that award for lack of fair representation, but failed. Then he brought a separate action under the wage-hour act. Again the court mentioned fair representation, saying "even if the employee's claim were meritorious, his union might, without breaching the duty of fair representation, reasonably and in good faith decide not to support the claim vigorously in arbitration."[69] This is a disturbing recognition that the representation doctrine cannot be counted

---

66. 415 U.S. at 60 n.21.

67. *See, e.g.,* Burroughs v. Marathon Oil Co., 446 F. Supp. 633, 17 FEP Cases 612 (E.D.Mich. 1978); Kornbluh v. Stearns & Foster Co., Inc., 14 FEP Cases 847, 73 FRD 307 (D.C. Ohio 1976); Washington v. Johns-Mannville Products Corp., 17 FEP Cases 606 (D.C. Calif. 1978); Green v. U.S. Steel Corp., 481 F. Supp. 295, 20 FEP Cases 1248 (E.D. Pa. 1979); *compare,* Becton v. Consolidated Freightways, 490 F. Supp. 464 (E.D. Mich. 1980), *rev'd,* 687 F. 2d 140, 29 FEP Cases 1078 (6th Cir. 1982).

68. 415 U.S. at 58.

69. *Supra* note 64, at 742.

upon to keep unions to a minimally acceptable level of representation. Chief Justice Burger, in dissent, would have blocked the individual's recourse to a wage-hour suit. He concluded that there is no
danger of the union failing to vindicate a member's interests because
of the "abundant" availability of the duty of fair representation doctrine.[70]

The majority and the dissent cannot be talking about the same
duty of fair representation; but that is not the point. The real concern is not with cases in which the union deliberately holds something back, for proper policing of the fair representation doctrine
would prevent such a result. The hard, determinitive issue, not
touched upon by the Supreme Court or the lower courts, is whether
the union has the competence or the ability to raise the statutory
claim in arbitration. In a world of increasing opportunity to resolve
issues in multiple forums and to establish private systems of dispute
resolution, we need to develop a more sophisticated handle for determining the adequacy of union representation. We need more, not
less, scrutiny of the quality of union representation.

Is this greater degree of scrutiny required back in the garden
variety of cases, where public issues are not involved? Perhaps not.
But it is useful, in anticipating the future direction of arbitration,
to focus on the competence of unions in dealing with increasingly
complex issues. A doctrine that condemns perfunctory representation provides an incentive for unions to provide quality representation. In the long run, therefore, I think we are better off to subject
unions to this standard. The end product of more competent unions
is worth the institutional price.

---

70. *Id.*, at 750–51.

The NLRB and the Duty

John C. Truesdale

It is now well settled that a union violates section 8(b)(1)(A) of the National Labor Relations Act (NLRA) by failing to represent fairly all employees in the bargaining unit. Although the union's legal duty is clear, the parameters of this duty remain confusing and unclear. This confusion is confounded by the fact that state and federal courts continue to have concurrent jurisdiction with the National Labor Relations Board and to apply their own standards. Also, the duty of fair representation has been described using vague and imprecise phrases. The absence of clear standards and the extremely broad approach taken by some courts may operate to affect adversely national labor policy in several important ways. First, unions wishing to avoid a potential duty of fair representation charge may take a cautious approach and process most, if not all grievances to arbitration. Although arbitrators may benefit from this tactic, such an approach is a severe drain on both management and union resources, as well as a disincentive to pursue a fair settlement before arbitration. Second, employees with no more than a vague notion that they have been treated unfairly may believe that they should file a charge with the Board, which, if they retain private counsel, will become a monetarily and perhaps emotionally expensive proposition.

Although the concept of the duty of fair representation has been a part of labor law for almost forty years, beginning in 1944 with *Steele* v. *Louisville & Nashville Railroad*,[1] it was not until 1962, in

---

1. 323 U.S. 192, 15 LRRM 708 (1944).

Miranda Fuel Company, Inc.,[2] that the Board first enunciated the doctrine that a breach of the duty of fair representation constituted an unfair labor practice. In that case, the Board found that section 7 of the NLRA conferred upon employees the right to be free from unfair, irrelevant, and invidious treatment by their exclusive collective bargaining representative in matters affecting their employment. Thus, it found the union involved breached its duty of fair representation in violation of section 8(b)(1)(A) of the act when it caused an employee's reduction in seniority for considerations that were irrelevant, invidious, or unfair. The Board characterized the union's conduct as "arbitrary conduct."[3] In *Teamsters Local 692 (Great Western Unifreight System),*[4] the Board cited with seeming approval the dictionary definition of "arbitrary" as ". . . done capriciously or at pleasure; without adequate determining principle; not founded in the nature of things; not rational; not done or acting according to reason. . . ."

A union's duty of fair representation requires it to serve the interests of all the employees it represents fairly and in good faith and without hostile discrimination based on unfair, arbitrary, irrelevant, or invidious considerations.[5] In the performance of this duty, however, the effective administration of a contract requires that a union be afforded broad discretion in deciding what grievances to pursue and the manner in which they should be handled.[6] On these points, I think we can all agree.

Under the NLRA as interpreted by the Board, a union is permitted a wide range of discretion in deciding whether and how to pursue a grievance, so long as its determination is not colored by considerations that bear on union membership or are otherwise arbitrary, perfunctory, or in bad faith. Misconduct ordinarily cannot be inferred from a union's simple refusal to institute grievance ac-

---

2. 140 NLRB 181, 51 LRRM 1584 (1962), *enf. denied,* 326 F.2d 172, 54 LRRM 2715 (2d Cir. 1963).

3. *Id.* at 185, 51 LRRM at 1587.

4. 209 NLRB 446, 447, 85 LRRM 1385, 1386 (1974).

5. Vaca v. Sipes, 386 U.S. 171, 64 LRRM 2369 (1967); Glass Bottle Blowers Local 106 (Owens-Illinois), 240 NLRB 324, 100 LRRM 1294 (1979).

6. Vaca v. Sipes, *supra* note 5, at 191–92, 64 LRRM at 2377; Ford Motor Co. v. Huffman, 345 U.S. 330, 338, 31 LRRM 2548, 2551 (1953); Teamsters, Local 705 (Associated Transport, Inc.), 209 NLRB 292, 86 LRRM 1119 (1974), *aff'd sub nom.* Kesner v. NLRB, 532 F.2d 1169, 92 LRRM 2137 (7th Cir. 1975), *cert. denied,* 429 U.S. 983, 93 LRRM 2843 (1976).

tion.[7] If, however, a union undertakes to process a grievance but decides to abandon the grievance short of arbitration, the finding of a violation turns not on the merit of the grievance but rather on whether the union's disposition of the grievance was perfunctory or motivated by ill will or other invidious considerations.[8] In instances of negligence or poor judgment, Board decisions support the principle that something more than mere negligence is required for union action or inaction to be considered arbitrary and, therefore, a breach of the duty of fair representation in violation of section 8(b)(1)(A). In the Board's view, the mere fact that a union is inept, negligent, unwise, insensitive, or ineffectual will not, standing alone, establish a breach of the duty of fair representation. The Board's narrow definition of the scope of the obligation, however, has not met with unanimous approval. Some courts, particularly the Ninth Circuit, hold the union to a higher standard than does the Board.

Overview of Board Decisions

A survey of the Board's decisions shows that the forms of representation to which the duty applies include, among other things, operation of the hiring hall referral system, operation of the seniority system, presentation of grievances, representation of the employees at an interview with management, and informing employees of rights and obligations under the contract.[9]

---

7. Vaca v. Sipes, *supra* note 5.

8. Glass Bottle Blowers, Local 106 (Owens-Illinois), *supra* note 5, at 324, 100 LRRM at 1294.

9. On hiring hall referral system, *see, e.g.,* Boilermakers Local Lodge No. 40 (Envirotech Corp.), 266 NLRB No. 86, 112 LRRM 1390 (1983); Operating Engineers Local 406 (Ford, Bacon and Davis Construction Corp.), 262 NLRB No. 6, 110 LRRM 1258 (1982); Iron Workers, Local 433 (RPM Erectors, Inc.), 266 NLRB No. 36, 112 LRRM 1311 (1983); Journeymen Pipe Fitters, Local 392 (Kaiser Engineers, Inc.), 252 NLRB No. 44, 105 LRRM 1426 (1980), *enf. denied,* 712 F.2d 225, 113 LRRM 3500 (6th Cir. 1983). On seniority system, *see,* Stage Employees, Local 695 (Twentieth Century-Fox Film Corp.), 261 NLRB 590, 110 LRRM 1078 (1982). On grievance presentation, Food and Commercial Workers, Local 324 (Fed Mart Stores, Inc.), 261 NLRB 1086, 110 LRRM 1234 (1982); Furniture Workers, Local 1010 (Leggett & Platt, Inc.), 261 NLRB 524, 110 LRRM 1093 (1982); Lea Industries, 261 NLRB 1136, 110 LRRM 1221 (1982). On management interviews, *see,* Clothing and Textile Workers Union, Local 148 T (Leshner Corp.), 259 NLRB 1120, 109 LRRM 1087 (1982). On informing employees, Operating Engineers, Local 406 (Ford, Bacon and Davis Construction Corp.), *supra;* Law Enforcement & Security Officers, Local 40B (South Jersey Detective Agency), 260 NLRB 419, 109 LRRM 1162 (1982).

Since the Board cannot act on a case until the general counsel has issued a complaint, instructions to the field issued in 1979 by General Counsel John Irving concerning a union's duty of fair representation are informative. A look at Board decisions that have narrowly defined the scope of a union's duty indicates, thus far at least, that the Board has seemed to agree with these guidelines.

The guidelines divided the duty of fair representation issues into four categories: improper motives or fraud; arbitrary conduct; gross negligence; and a union's conduct after it has decided to grieve on behalf of the employee. Instead of using the various word tests espoused by the courts, the guidelines categorize, by fact pattern, the various circumstances in which the duty of fair representation fairly can be said to have been breached. Regional directors of the NLRB were advised to dismiss charges in situations where the union's conduct did not fall within one of those categories. It was stressed, and indeed the Board's decisions have held, that "the mere fact that the union is inept, negligent, unwise, insensitive, or ineffectual, will not, standing alone, establish a breach of the duty."

It is clear that a union breaches its duty of fair representation if its actions are attributable to improper motives or fraud. Both require intentional misconduct. With respect to improper motives, there are some cases in which the union's conduct is based on section 7 activities of the employees. For example, if the union refuses to process a grievance because of the employee's efforts to bring in another union, intraunion political activities, or nonmembership in the union, such refusal violates the act. In *Southern New York Area Local, American Postal Workers Union,* Chairman John Miller and Members Jenkins and Hunter found the union to have violated section 8(b) (1)(A) by refusing to process a grievance of a part-time career employee because the grievant was not a member of the union.[10] In so holding, the Board noted that the grievance concerned a violation of the national agreement between the employer and the union and was not clearly frivolous.

Similarly, in *Steelworkers Local 15167 (Memphis Folding Chairs, Inc.),* Members Fanning, Jenkins, and Zimmerman found a violation of the duty when the union steward refused to sign and process the grievance of a discharged employee because of a personal confrontation she had had with the grievant.[11] The local president and the

---

10. 266 NLRB No. 57, 112 LRRM 1384 (1983).
11. 258 NLRB 484, 108 LRRM 1132 (1981).

chief steward also failed to process the grievance. The Board found that the union's failure to process the grievance was not due to mere negligence or to a determination that the grievance lacked merit but rather to the personal confrontation. Since the union is "subject always to complete good faith and honesty of purpose in the exercise of its discretion," the union may not refuse to represent a bargaining unit employee because of personal hostility toward that employee.[12] Accordingly, a violation was found.

In *Henry J. Kaiser Co.,* the same panel found the union to have violated section 8(b)(1)(A) by its unlawful failure to accept and process a grievance on behalf of a discharged worker who was a "traveler," a member of another local of the same international.[13] The facts indicated that the union steward refused, without investigation, to give a grievance form to the discharged employee. After the employee filed an unfair labor practice charge, the union's business manager ostensibly investigated the grievance and decided not to pursue it. The Board, however, held that this was in retaliation for the grievant's filing the charge, and the union gave the case "merely a minimal effort, perfunctory at best."[14] This case is also of interest for its discussion of the appropriate remedy. The Board found the union liable for back pay from the date of the employee's discharge until either the union secured consideration of his grievance by Kaiser and thereafter pursued it with good faith and due diligence, or until the employee was reinstated by Kaiser or obtained substantially equivalent employment. The Board specifically declined to make the back pay award conditional on the merits of the grievance.

In *Lea Industries,* Chairman Van de Water and Members Jenkins and Hunter decided that the union violated the act by failing to file a unit employee's grievance and misleading her to believe, to her detriment, that the union was pursuing her grievance, when the reason for the failure to file was her nonmembership in and open opposition to the union.[15]

If no bad faith motivation is shown, however, the union, as the

---

12. Ford Motor Co. v. Huffman, *supra* note 6, at 338, 31 LRRM at 2551. *See also,* Glass Bottle Blowers, Local 106 (Owens-Illinois, Inc.), *supra* note 5.

13. 259 NLRB 1, 108 LRRM 1230 (1981).

14. *Id.* at 9.

15. *Supra* note 9. *See also,* Local 299 International Brotherhood of Teamsters (McLean Trucking Co.), 270 NLRB No. 188 (1984).

exclusive bargaining agent, is free to decide how it wants to pursue a grievance. For example, in *Clothing and Textile Workers Local 148T (Leshner Corp.)*, Members Fanning, Jenkins, and Zimmerman found no violation of the duty of fair representation when the union refused to accept the employer's offer to reinstate one of two discharged employees because the offer was conditioned on not rehiring the other employee.[16] The employer then declined to reinstate either employee. In so holding, the Board noted that the union acted in good faith in an attempt to achieve reinstatement of both employees. Furthermore, the union's refusal to invoke arbitration was not violative because there was no evidence that its decision was based on animosity, irrelevant considerations, or discrimination to the employee who would have been reinstated.

The union can, of course, refuse to process a grievance if, after making a good-faith evaluation of the merits of the grievance, it determines the grievance is nonmeritorious or frivolous. It cannot, however, refuse or fail to process it for an arbitrary or invidious reason, or "without reason, merely at the whim of someone exercising union authority."[17] In *Food and Commercial Workers Union Local 324 (Fed Mart Stores, Inc.)*, Members Jenkins and Zimmerman, with Member Fanning dissenting, found a breach of the duty of fair representation when the union processed a grievance in a perfunctory and arbitrary manner by failing to insist on reinstatement and back pay for an employee who was discharged for theft but later acquitted of the crime.[18] The facts showed that the union indicated to the employee that first it would seek sick and vacation pay for her and later go after reinstatement and back pay, but then it closed the grievance file after obtaining only sick and vacation pay. The union also violated section 8(b)(1)(A), the Board said, by misinforming the employee about the manner in which it would process her grievance. In finding a violation, the Board stressed that the union's conduct did not entail mere negligence or fall within the purview of permissible discretion in grievance handling, since it specifically committed itself to seeking the full remedy of reinstatement and back pay but told the employer without justification that it would not push for reinstatement. Members Jenkins and Zimmerman also found that the

---

16. *Supra* note 9.

17. Teamsters, Local 315 (Rhodes & Jamieson, Ltd.), 217 NLRB 616, 89 LRRM 1049 (1975), *enf'd*, 545 F.2d 1173, 93 LRRM 2747 (9th Cir. 1976).

18. *Supra* note 9.

union engaged in unlawful arbitrary conduct by failing to pursue its commitment in more than a perfunctory manner.

Fanning's dissent is instructive in positing the countervailing arguments for not finding a violation:

> Whether the Union here had a firm intention to secure reinstatement and backpay . . . as well as the vacation and sick pay it secured for her as "terminated," is, I believe, not significant. A union is entitled to exercise its discretion in processing grievances for the unit as a whole. This includes assessing the action urged by one employee in the context of future actions anticipated for other employees. It is a grave mistake, I believe, to hold a union responsible for failure to proceed with an action on behalf of an employee that, at the time, has no chance of success and would tend only to make more difficult the future processing of grievances on behalf of the unit.[19]

In determining whether the union's conduct is arbitrary and thus in violation of the duty of fair representation, the Board contemplates whether there is any basis on which the union's conduct can be explained. Thus, the union would violate section 8(b)(1)(A) if it refused to process a grievance without any inquiry or with such a perfunctory or cursory inquiry that it is tantamount to no inquiry at all. For example, in *Beverly Manor Convalescent Center*, the Board said that the failure to inquire into the stated reason for a discharge and the willingness to evaluate the worth of an employee solely through the employer's evaluation is more than mere negligence or ineptitude and amounted to perfunctory grievance handling so unreasonable as to be arbitrary.[20] In *Furniture Workers Local 1010 (Leggett & Platt, Inc.)*, Chairman Van de Water and Members Fanning and Zimmerman held that the union's failure to process the discharge grievance to arbitration was unreasonable and arbitrary in a case in which the union officer admitted that he saw the employee's name on a petition protesting a new labor agreement and considered him a troublemaker.[21] As a result, the union officer failed to investigate the grievance seriously and accepted the employer's word that the employee had excessive absence and tardiness, and the grievance meeting was merely a display for the chief shop steward and the employee.

It must be emphasized, however, that the union's inquiry into the facts concerning the grievance need not be as exhaustive as that

---

19. *Id.* at 1088.
20. 229 NLRB 692, 95 LRRM 1156 (1977).
21. *Supra* note 9.

which might be done by an attorney or skilled investigator. As the Board said in *Beverly Manor,* the nature of the relation between the union and employee is more nearly that of a legislator to a constituent.[22] Further, the mere fact that the union's investigation reaches a conclusion that is later shown to be erroneous does not establish a violation. Similarly, if a contract provision supports an employee under one interpretation and the union reasonably gives the contract another interpretation, the fact that the union's interpretation may be "wrong" does not establish a violation.[23] So long as the union makes some inquiry into the facts or the union's contract interpretation has some basis in reason, the union's refusal to process the grievance will not be considered arbitrary.

The Board is clear in its position that mere negligence will not establish breach of the duty of fair representation. Sometimes, however, Board decisions in this area are difficult to sort out. In the 1974 case *Teamsters, Local 692 (Great Western Unifreight System),* Chairman Edward Miller and Members Fanning and Penello found that a union's negligent failure to file a grievance in a reasonable and timely fashion was not a breach of the duty of fair representation.[24] "It is clear," the Board said, "that negligent action or nonaction by a union by itself will not be considered to be arbitrary, irrelevant, invidious or unfair so as to constitute a breach of the duty of fair representation violative of the Act. Something more is required."[25]

In *Crown Zellerbach Corporation,* Chairman Dotson and Members Jenkins and Hunter noted with approval the administrative law judge's conclusion, citing *Great Western Unifreight System,* that the union's negligent failure even to think about the effect of a bonus computation on unreinstated strikers was insufficient, standing alone, to find a breach of the duty of fair representation.[26]

The often-cited *Great Western Unifreight System* case was relied on again by the administrative law judge whose decision was adopted without comment by Members Jenkins, Zimmerman, and Hunter in *Union of Security Personnel.*[27] In this case, the union failed to file a

---

22. *Supra* note 20.
23. Washington-Baltimore Newspaper Guild, Local 35 (CWA), 239 NLRB 1321, 100 LRRM 1179 (1979).
24. *Supra* note 4.
25. *Id.*
26. 266 NLRB No. 207, 113 LRRM 1121 (August 5, 1983).
27. 267 NLRB No. 155, 114 LRRM 1161 (1983).

grievance after a union official indicated that he would file a grievance and take it to arbitration. There was no evidence of hostile motivation. The union thereafter simply failed to investigate the inci-
dent, and the record contained no evidence of the reason for its
nonaction. The judge found that the union's nonaction amounted to
a willful failure to pursue the grievance and was therefore "perfunctory." The difference between this case and *Great Western Unifreight,*
then, might be that here the union said that it would "get this case
into arbitration" but did not, whereas in *Unifreight,* no misinforma-
tion was apparent.

The same panel again turned to *Great Western Unifreight System,*
in *Teamsters Local 282 (Transit-Mix Concrete Corp.).*[28] *Transit-Mix* involved the familiar question of how to merge seniority lists when one
company takes over another. Colonial Sand and Stone Company
had been purchased by Transit-Mix Concrete Corp. Colonial's drivers were end-tailed, were told at a meeting that they should "shape"
at Transit-Mix's facility the next morning, that those not hired then
would be placed on indefinite layoff, would maintain their seniority
indefinitely, and should not shape again until recalled by registered
letter. Subsequently, however, an arbitrator ruled that an employee
must shape or contact Transit-Mix at least once a year to maintain
his seniority. The union told the stewards at Transit-Mix to get the
word out; they announced the award at the "shape-up" the following morning. No other effort was made to communicate the terms of
the arbitration award to the laid-off Colonial drivers. The Board
found that something more than mere negligence was involved. It
found that the union had an affirmative obligation, in the circumstances of this case, to communicate the terms of the arbitration
award to the laid-off Colonial drivers, because it was contrary to information on which they were relying. Failure to do so, the Board
said, was not mere negligence but due to an affirmative decision not
to deviate from the union's normal practice. Because the union set
forth no rational basis for this affirmative decision, the Board found
that the union's action was arbitrary and a breach of the duty of fair
representation.

The *Transit-Mix* and *Union of Security Personnel* cases are interesting applications of an earlier Board decison finding that a union's

---

28. 267 NLRB No. 187, 114 LRRM 1148 (1983), *enf'd.,* 740 F.2d 141 (2d Cir.,
July 19, 1984).

duty of fair representation imposes on it a duty not purposely to keep employees uninformed or misinformed concerning their grievances.[29] In a 1984 case, *Office and Professional Employees Local 2*,[30] Chairman Dotson and Members Zimmerman and Dennis reviewed at some length *Great Western Unifreight System* and its holding that "something more than mere negligence" is required before a breach of the duty can be found. The Board said that "something more" is not susceptible to precise definition; the totality of circumstances in each case must be examined and evaluated. Examining in this case the union's negligent failure to file a grievance on behalf of a terminated employee, the Board did not find the discrimination, hostility, or willful deception that had marked the "something more" in other cases and dismissed the complaint.

Guidelines from the Courts

Courts are far from unanimous in their interpretations of the duty of fair representation and, in some circuits, have more broadly defined the scope of the union's duty. Because the Board does not have exclusive jurisdiction in this area, a review of court cases must accompany any discussion of Board precedent. Indeed, the Board's jurisdiction in this area has never been specifically passed on by the Supreme Court. In *Vaca*, the Court assumed, without deciding, that a breach of the duty of fair representation would constitute an unfair labor practice, but rejected the argument that the doctrine of federal preemption gave the Board exclusive jurisdiction over such cases.[31] It is generally accepted that the Board shares jurisdiction with both federal and state courts. As you might expect, this diversity of forums has contributed to the general confusion over the duty, a confusion the guidelines from the Supreme Court have not relieved.

Thus, the Court has spoken of representing employees "without hostile discrimination, fairly, impartially, and in good faith"; of a requirement of "complete good faith and honesty of purpose in the exercise of [the union's] discretion"; of finding no breach unless

---

29. Auto Workers Local 17 (Falcon Industries, Inc.), 261 NLRB 527 (1980).

30. Office and Professional Employees International Union, Local No. 2, AFL-CIO, 268 NLRB No. 207 (1984).

31. *Supra* note 5.

there is "substantial evidence of fraud, deceitful action or dishonest conduct," conduct that is "arbitrary, discriminatory, or in bad faith," or union conduct consisting of "arbitrarily ignor[ing] a meritorious grievance or process[ing] it in a perfunctory fashion."[32]

On the other hand, the Court has also stated that

> union discretion is essential to the proper functioning of the collective-bargaining system. Union supervision of employee complaints promotes settlements, avoids processing of frivolous claims, and strengthens the employer's confidence in the union. [citation omitted] Without these screening and settlement procedures . . . the costs of private dispute resolution could ultimately render the system impracticable.[33]

The vague and, what some perceive as, contradictory standards employed by the Supreme Court have left us in quite understandable confusion, as each forum must parse the Court's words in its own fashion. Courts have not consistently agreed on identification of the essential elements of the duty. The Third, Seventh, and Tenth Circuits suggest that the breach of duty occurs only if there is bad faith or hostile discrimination by the union.[34]

In a recent case in the Seventh Circuit, *Dober* v. *Roadway Express, Inc.*, the Court held that its standard regarding the duty of fair representation is "intentional misconduct."[35] Thus, a "union breaches its duty to fairly represent a worker if it deliberately and unjustifiably refuses to represent that worker in processing a grievance." "Negligence," however, "even when gross, does not violate the duty of fair representation." In so holding, the Seventh Circuit reasoned,

> It would be unrealistic to require workers "grieving" on a part-time basis to come up to some judicially devised standard of competent representation akin to that required of lawyers on pain of being found to have committed professional malpractice. The adoption of such a standard in fair representation cases would simply encourage the filing of trivial cases such as this, cases that prevent not only federal judges, but unions and employers from getting on with more important matters. There is no need for us to assume such a burden in order to protect workers who

---

32. Respectively, Steele v. Louisville & Nashville Railroad, *supra* note 1, at 204, 15 LRRM at 712; Ford Motor Co. v. Huffman, *supra* note 6, at 338, 31 LRRM 2548; Humphrey v. Moore, 375 U.S. 335, 348, 55 LRRM 2031, 2037 (1964); and Vaca v. Sipes, *supra* note 5, at 190, 191, 64 LRRM at 2376, 2377.

33. IBEW v. Foust, 442 U.S. 42, 101 LRRM 2365 (1979).

34. Reid v. Automobile Workers, Local 1093, 479 F.2d 517, 83 LRRM 2406 (10th Cir. 1973), *cert. denied*, 414 U.S. 1076 (1973); Medlin v. Boeing Vertol Co., 620 F.2d 957, 104 LRRM 2247 (3d Cir. 1980).

35. 707 F.2d 292, 295, 113 LRRM 2595, 2597 (7th Cir. 1983).

have meritorious grievances. They do not need our protection against representation that is inept but not invidious. If a local union does an incompetent job of grieving, its members can vote in new officers who will do a better job or they can vote in another union . . . (U)nion democracy no more guarantees a minority against oppression by the majority than political democracy does.[36]

The Ninth Circuit, however, holds the union to a much higher standard of representation. In *Dutrisac* v. *Caterpillar Tractor Company,* the court of appeals rejected the union's argument that it should not be held liable for unforeseeable acts of negligence by union's stewards and business agents.[37] Instead, the court held that the union breached its duty by inadvertently filing a request for arbitration two weeks late, even though a court ultimately rejected the employee's claim that he was unlawfully discharged by the employer and there was no ill will toward the grievant. The Court reasoned that "[U]nions are not powerless to make their agents observe the contractual time limits more carefully . . . keeping track of deadlines is a mechanical function that depends on establishing a tickler system and diligence in using it, not on special training." Recognizing that the decision widens the potential liability of unions, the Ninth Circuit limits its holding that union negligence may violate the act to cases "in which the individual interest at stake is strong and the union's failure to perform a ministerial act completely extinguishes the employee's right to pursue his claim." Although the discharge was upheld, the union was ordered to pay $2,000 in damages for legal costs incurred by the grievant.

The Sixth Circuit does not require a showing of bad faith, but holds that mere negligence or mistaken judgment is insufficient to establish a breach of the union's duty.[38] In *Poole* v. *Budd,* the Sixth Circuit observed that a union's conduct may be sufficiently arbitrary to establish a breach of its duty to fairly represent its members when it handles a grievance in a "perfunctory" manner, with caprice or without a rational explanation to the employee. The Court held in *Poole,* however, that the union did not breach its duty when it failed to take a discharged employee's grievance to arbitration after it investigated the grievance and processed it through several stages.

---

36. *Id.* at 294, 113 LRRM 2596.
37. 113 LRRM 3532 (9th Cir. 1983).
38. Poole v. Budd Co., 706 F.2d 181, 113 LRRM 2493 (6th Cir. 1983).

Gross mistake or inaction, however, which has no rational explanation, may constitute a breach of the duty in the Sixth Circuit.[39] In *Milstead* v. *Teamsters, Local 957,* the union representative was found to have handled the grievance in a perfunctory manner when, in its presentation of the grievance before a joint committee, it was unaware of a critical fact in support of the grievant's claim.[40]

The ambiguity in the case law in this area leaves both unions and employers in a quandary and exposes both to potential liabilities. The Supreme Court has held that an employer who relies on an arbitration decision, a settlement, or a decision by the union not to process a grievance at all is liable to the wrongfully discharged employee even if the employer relied in good faith on the union's handling of the case.[41] The Court held in *Vaca* v. *Sipes,*

> The governing principle . . . is to apportion liability between the employer and the union according to the damage caused by the fault of each. Thus, damages attributable solely to the employer's breach of contract should not be charged to the Union, but increases if any in those damages caused by the union's refusal to process the grievance should not be charged to the employer.[42]

Recently in *Bowen* v. *U.S. Postal Service,* the Supreme Court reiterated the "governing principle" of *Vaca* and held that a union that had breached its duty of fair representation by refusing to arbitrate a discharged employee's "apparently meritorious grievance" is primarily liable for that part of the employee's damages caused by the union's default.[43] Even though both the employer and the union caused damage suffered by the employee, the union was held responsible for the increase, and as between two wrongdoers, should bear its portion of the damages. The Supreme Court noted that this apportionment of damages "will provide an additional incentive for the union to process its members' claims where warranted. This is wholly consistent with the union's interest. It is a duty owed to its

---

39. *See, e.g.,* Williams v. Teamsters, Local 984, 625 F.2d 138, 105 LRRM 2030 (6th Cir. 1980) (per curiam) (union's conduct arbitrary, apparently because no rational explanation for its refusal to process grievance); Milstead v. Teamsters, Local 957, 580 F.2d 232, 235, 99 LRRM 2150, 2153 (6th Cir. 1978) (inept handling of grievance due to gross ignorance of contract may be breach of duty of fair representation).
40. *Supra* note 39.
41. Hines v. Anchor Motor Freight, Inc., 424 U.S. 554, 91 LRRM 2481 (1976); Vaca v. Sipes, *supra* note 5.
42. Vaca v. Sipes, *supra* note 5, at 197–98, 64 LRRM at 2379–80.
43. 103 S. Ct. 588, 112 LRRM 2281 (1983).

members, as well as consistent with the union's commitment to the employer under the arbitration clause."[44]

Employers and unions sometimes find themselves in a no-win situation. In *Washington-Baltimore Newspaper Guild, Local 35 (CWA)*, there were two bidders for a single position. The junior bidder was awarded the promotion; and the senior bidder grieved.[45] The union did not attempt to compare the qualifications of the bidders. It was unclear under the contract whether the clause governing promotions called for the most qualified person to be promoted, with seniority to be applicable only if overall qualifications were relatively equal; or, rather, whether it called for the most senior person to be promoted as long as both bidders were at least minimally qualified. There was evidence that the union considered the contract as incorporating the latter interpretation. For this reason, the Board concluded that the union had no reason to weigh the relative qualifications of the bidders, because the union determined that, under *its* interpretation of the contract, the most senior qualified bidder should have received the promotion.

The interesting thing about this case, however, is the position in which the union and the employer found themselves. Simultaneously with the proceedings before the Board, the grievance was being processed through the contractual procedures. Presumably the Board's decision did not render moot the arbitration proceedings, because the validity of the union's contract interpretation remained to be determined. And, because of the Board's eventual decision that the union had not breached its duty of fair representation, the validity of the resolution at the arbitration stage would not be subject to challenge before the Board.

But, while the case was pending before the Board, the union and employer faced the following alternatives: First, they could settle the grievance. If they settled in favor of the grievant, and the Board subsequently found that the union had not fairly represented the other employee (the one who originally received the promotion), the employer, the union, or both might be liable for back pay to the original recipient of the promotion. If they settled adversely to the grievant, the union remained subject to a possible charge alleging a breach of its duty of fair representation to the grievant, in that it

---

44. *Id.* at 598, 112 LRRM at 2287.
45. *Supra* note 23.

abandoned the grievance without having engaged in a comparison of the qualifications of the two bidders. In either event, there could be no certainty about any settlement until procedures outside the contractual grievance procedure had concluded. Second, the parties could process the grievance to arbitration. No matter which way the arbitrator ruled, the losing bidder could file a charge with the Board or initiate a court suit seeking to establish that the union had in some way breached its duty of fair representation, on the same grounds as a challenge of a settlement. This, in turn, raises the risk that the arbitration might have to be heard again, or that the employer or union, or both, might be liable to the losing bidder for damages.

The Hobson's choice faced by the parties to proceedings of this nature is hardly conducive to peaceful labor relations. Rather than inflict this uncertainty on employers, unions, and employees, Board decisions indicate that so long as the union acts fairly, without invidious discrimination, and with some rational basis for what might otherwise seem to be arbitrary conduct, it is inappropriate for the Board to ask whether the union also acted with the utmost effectiveness or skill. In retrospect, in the atmosphere of a courtroom or Board hearing room, experienced lawyers might well conclude that particular cases were ineptly handled. But shop stewards, often elected from among rank-and-file employees for qualities other than their ability to parse out the phrases of a contract or court decision, are held to a less stringent standard in making on-the-spot judgments in furtherance of the collective bargaining agreement. Asking anything more could undermine the bargaining relationship between unions and employers.

Time for a Midcourse Correction?

James E. Jones, Jr.

Although this chapter's title is phrased as a question, it is the conclusion of this essay that congressional action is needed to correct the substantive and procedural disarray that is the current law of the union's duty of fair representation. It contends that Congress, after sufficient study, should provide statutory guidance regarding the nature of the union's duty of fair representation under the National Labor Relations Act and should mandate that the National Labor Relations Board's jurisdiction over such matters is exclusive and preempts the field. To ensure that individuals will not be subject to denial of access to the Board by the general counsel's unreviewable authority to issue complaints in unfair labor practice cases, it suggests that, like Title VII of the Civil Rights Act of 1964, the complaining party, in DFR cases only, be provided the right to present his case to the National Labor Relations Board by his own representative, despite the general counsel's conclusion that no complaint should be issued. Such an approach would provide for the concerns expressed by the Supreme Court in previous cases that the plaintiffs in such matters have access to justice, while at the same time ensuring that the law regarding the duty of fair representation would be developed in an orderly and uniform fashion consistent with the major policy dictates of the National Labor Relations Act.

No suggestion is made regarding the Railway Labor Act, because under that act any substantive violations of the rights of employees in the nature of unfair labor practices must be vindicated in the courts. If pressed, however, the author would conclude that little justification, save history, exists for maintaining the Railway Labor Act as a separate entity restricted to the dying railroad industry and the sputtering airline industry. Those industries could easily be made subject to the National Labor Relations Act without needless duplication in a separate structure. To the extent that special expertise is necessary, such expertise could be provided by expanding the National Labor Relations Board.

Such an approach would harmonize our labor laws, provide a more rational process of judicial review, and contribute to judicial efficiency by substantially reducing the proliferation of duty of fair representation cases that have increasingly burdened the courts since the mid-1960s.[1]

It may also be possible for the Supreme Court to correct, or substantially relieve, the conditions that it has largely created during the last twenty years. That, however, would require it to overrule a substantial number of prior cases, particularly *Vaca* v. *Sipes*[2] and its progeny. I do not believe this Court yet has the humility for such a course of action, though a case for it can easily be made:

1. *Vaca* was a five-four decision, and only two members of that majority remain on the Court today;

2. The major premises upon which it rested, if valid then, are not valid now;

3. The Supreme Court, itself, has substantially rejected the state action—constitutional theory upon which the DFR was originally based,[3] except in DFR cases in which, beginning with *Humphrey* v. *Moore*,[4] the theory has been expanded beyond recognition and without any congressional input.

The Court has not always been concerned for the plight of the poor plaintiffs of whom it was so solicitous in *Vaca*. Even if its concerns were valid, that is a congressional problem (See, e.g., *Guss*,

---

1. *See* Appendix A and Appendix B, for compilations of DFR case loads and commentary.

2. 386 U.S. 171, 64 LRRM 2369 (1967).

3. Steele v. Louisville & Nashville Railroad, 323 U.S. 192, 15 LRRM 708 (1944); Wallace Corp. v. Labor Board, 323 U.S. 248, 15 LRRM 697 (1944); Bolling v. Sharp, 347 U.S. 497 (1954). *See also*, Moose Lodge, No. 107 v. Irvis, 407 U.S. 163 (1971); NAACP v. FPC, 425 U.S. 662, 96 S. Ct. 1806, 48 L.Ed. 2d 284 (1976). *See also*, Handy Andy, Inc., 228 NLRB 44, 94 LRRM 1354 (1977).

4. 375 U.S. 335, 15 LRRM 2031 (1964).

Fairlawn, and *Garmon* and the famous "no-man's land"[5]). Moreover, DFR plaintiffs could be required *by the Court* to exhaust available administrative remedies (i.e., file unfair labor practice charges and see if complaints would issue) before resorting to Court intervention. If the Court would also articulate some meaningful DFR standards, coupled with DFR-NLRB exhaustion requirements, it could close the floodgates and provide more uniformity, without endorsing wholesale preemption of DFR–unfair labor practice cases.

The labor-management community does not have another twenty years to wait for court enlightenment, however. Congress is the faster—and more reliable—vehicle for the changes that are needed.

Background

The union's duty of fair representation, a judicial invention mothered by constitutional necessity, has developed to a point far exceeding its original purpose and justification. In the thirty-seven years of the life of this concept, Congress has never considered the desirability of an independent cause of action for breach of the duty of fair representation or the consistency of judicial concepts creating and interpreting the duty with our major labor relations law. The Supreme Court has taken the classic view that Congress, by its inaction, has ratified the Court's interpretations.[6]

The duty of fair representation is not specifically mentioned in either the Railway Labor Act or the National Labor Relations Act. It has been implied by the Supreme Court as a statutory obligation deriving from section 2 of the Railway Labor Act and section 9(a) of the National Labor Relations Act.[7] In its decision in which it originated the duty, the Supreme Court, in order to avoid constitutional questions regarding the exclusive authority of unions under the law, held that the union's power must be exercised without hostile or invidious discrimination, fairly, impartially, and in good faith on be-

---

5. Guss v. Utah Labor Bd., 352 U.S. 817, 39 LRRM 2567 (1957); Amalgamated Meat Cutters v. Fairlawn, 353 U.S. 20, 39 LRRM 2571 (1957); San Diego Bldg. Trades Council v. Garmon, 353 U.S. 26, 39 LRRM 2574 (1957).

6. *Cf.,* Vaca v. Sipes, *supra* note 2.

7. Respectively, 45 U.S.C. § 152 and 29 U.S.C. § 159(a).

half of all employees represented by the union.[8] *Steele* was a Railway Labor Act case that involved a collective bargaining agreement between the union and the railroad that denigrated the seniority rights of black employees, who were by union constitution and practice excluded from membership because of race, while by law they were in the class or craft exclusively represented by the labor organization.

On the same day, in a much-ignored case arising under the Wagner Act, the Supreme Court held that a certified union owed its constituents a similar duty.[9] It noted that the duties of a bargaining agent selected under the terms of the Wagner Act extend beyond the mere representation of the interest of its own group members. By its selection as bargaining representative, it has become the agent of all employees, charged with the responsibility of representing their interests fairly and impartially. The *Wallace* case did not involve racial inequity but rather an attempt by collective bargaining agreement to exclude from employment, those individuals who had supported a rival union. In 1944 there were no union unfair labor practices set forth in the law, and a closed shop, generally speaking, was entirely legal. The NLRB, however, found that the employer, by acquiescing in the union's demand, had committed unfair labor practices, and the Supreme Court sustained the Board's determination. Without the union's breach of its duty of fair representation, it would be difficult to find that the employer had violated the law.

These first formulations of the unions' duty concentrated on intentional acts, motivated by hostile or discriminatory purposes, against individuals for either racial reasons or reasons infringing freedom of association or freedom of choice. Although the concept was not restricted to invidious or hostile discrimination rooted in race, the overwhelming majority of cases considered by the courts between 1944 and 1964 involved racial discrimination. In theory,

---

8. It is worth noting as background that *Steele* v. *Louisville* arose in the state court of Alabama. There was no serious question raised regarding the state's jurisdiction, and the Supreme Court there determined that the statute contemplated resort to the usual judicial remedies of an injunction and damages when appropriate for breach of the duty imposed. It also determined there was no available administrative remedy under the Railway Labor Act, and consequently the individuals were entitled to seek relief in the courts. On the same day as *Steele,* the Court determined in *Tunstall* v. *Brotherhood of Locomotive Firemen and Enginemen* (323 U.S. 210, 15 LRRM 715 (1944)) that federal courts had jurisdiction to entertain a nondiversity suit in which the employees sought injunctive relief and damages on the same theory as in *Steele*. Steele v. Louisville & Nashville Railroad, *supra* note 3.

9. Wallace Corporation v. Labor Board, *supra* note 3.

the doctrine was available for the vindication of the rights of racial minorities, but it was ineffective in providing real relief.[10]

While it was clear that a union owed employees it represented a duty of fairness and good faith, the Supreme Court early established that unions are not barred from making agreements that may have unfavorable effects on some members of the bargaining unit. Differences within groups are the norm, and complete satisfaction of all persons represented by such an organization would be rare indeed. The Supreme Court, therefore, recognized that a union must be allowed "a wide range of reasonableness in the exercise of its judgment on behalf of the unit which it represents, subject always to complete good faith and honesty of purpose."[11] Even in these early cases, the courts had substantial flexibility in interpreting terms like "fairly, impartially, and in good faith," which were balanced by the equally flexible concept of "wide range of reasonableness." Crude as these standards have proven to be in more recent cases, they were sufficient to deal with egregious conduct of labor organizations when there was clear evidence of hostility.[12]

Subsequent cases have become preoccupied with the difference between the duty of the union in the negotiation of a contract and its duty in the administration of contracts. No such distinction was made in the earlier cases as both *Steele* and *Wallace* involved both the negotiation process and the administration of collective bargaining agreements.[13]

Although the *Wallace* case applied the duty of fair representation to Wagner Act unions in 1944, the issue was back before the Supreme Court in *Syres* v. *Oil Workers International Union*.[14] In *Syres* the Supreme Court made it clear beyond peradventure that the duty of fair representation applied to unions under the Taft-Hartley Act. By 1957 the court had to declare specifically that the duty covered

10. *See* Neil M. Herring, *The Fair Representation Doctrine: An Effective Weapon against Racial Discrimination?*, 24 Md. L. Rev. 113 (1964).

11. Ford Motor Co. v. Huffman, 345 U.S. 330, 31 LRRM 2548 (1953).

12. The Supreme Court went so far as to hold that, under the Railway Labor Act, a union owed a duty to persons not only outside of the bargaining unit but represented by other unions. It held the union was under a duty not to use its power to cause an employer to discriminate against such persons on the basis of race. Railroad Trainmen v. Howard, 343 U.S. 768, 9 FEP Cases 414 (1952).

13. So too did Ford Motor Co. v. Huffman, *supra* note 11, and Railway Trainmen v. Howard, *supra* note 12.

14. 223 F.2d 739, 36 LRRM 2290 (5th Cir. 1955), *rev'd and rem'd per curiam,* 350 U.S. 892, 9 FEP Cases 430 (1955).

the administration of collective bargaining agreements as well as the negotiation of them.[15]

It is not until *Graham* v. *Brotherhood of Locomotive Firemen and Enginemen,* that the specific issue of the applicability of the Norris-LaGuardia Act to federal court injunctive relief in DFR cases was raised and disposed of.[16] The Court held that the act did not deprive federal courts of jurisdiction to enforce employee rights to nondiscriminatory representation by their union through the injunction.

Probably the limited number of such cases entertained during the early period (1944–64) was more a function of the slender financial resources of the plaintiffs than anything else. Since these cases were predominantly civil rights cases and since a union had to be present under one of the laws in order for there to be any leverage for litigation, it would be surprising indeed if in the first twenty years there had been a great deal of litigation of this type.

Most *nonracial* discriminatory or arbitrary treatment by a union after 1947, when Congress amended the National Labor Relations Act to provide specific unfair labor practices for union conduct, was likely to be an unfair labor practice.[17] Consequently, except for racial discrimination, not explicitly addressed in the Taft-Hartley Act, there was little cause for other plaintiffs to resort to the tortured duty of fair representation theory to vindicate protected rights. At least as early as *Ford* v. *Huffman,* preemption of duty of fair representation issues by the National Labor Relations Act was argued; but it was belatedly made a part of that case and got no resolution from the Supreme Court.[18] Although preemption has lurked in the in-

---

15. Conley v. Gibson, 355 U.S. 41, 9 FEP Cases 439 (1957).

16. 338 U.S. 232, 9 FEP Cases 399 (1949).

17. As the Supreme Court has belatedly recognized, "even if not all breaches of the duty are unfair labor practices, however, the family resemblance is undeniable, and indeed there is substantial overlap. Many fair representation claims . . . include allegations of discrimination based on membership status or dissident views, which would be unfair labor practices under 8(a)(1) or (2). Aside from these clear cases, duty of fair representation claims are allegations of unfair, arbitrary, or discriminatory treatment of workers by unions—as are virtually all unfair labor practice charges made by workers against unions. . . . Similarly, it may be the case that alleged violations by an employer of a collective bargaining agreement will also amount to unfair labor practices." DelCostello v. Teamsters, 103 S. Ct. 2281, 113 LRRM 2737 (1983), in the slip copy that quotation appears accompanying footnote 22 in the Court's decision.

18. *Supra* note 11, 345 U.S. at 332 n. 4, 31 LRRM 2549 n. 4.

terstices of labor law since *Hill* v. *Florida*,[19] it did not come to full fruition as a problem for duty of fair representation until after the National Labor Relations Board concluded that breach of the duty was an unfair labor practice.[20] The full development of preemption of matters arguably subject to the National Labor Relations Act awaited *San Diego Building Trades Council* v. *Garmon*,[21] and although the Supreme Court continues to struggle with drawing lines under its preemption concept, exceptions threaten to swallow the rule.

The conceptual difficulties contributing to the problems of the duty of fair representation relate in part to the Supreme Court's determination in *Smith* v. *Evening News* that a suit could be brought for breach of a collective bargaining agreement under section 301 of the Labor-Management Relations Act, even though the alleged violation would also constitute an unfair labor practice.[22] A section 301 action, which is also a major exception to preemption, may be brought in either federal or state courts;[23] however, in either forum federal substantive law must be applied.[24]

The Supreme Court's
"Complex and Necessarily Confusing Guidebook"

One of the best arguments for congressional attention to the duty of fair representation and ultimate amendment of the law to provide the National Labor Relations Board with exclusive primary jurisdiction over DFR matters is the Supreme Court's attempts to deal with the issue in the last twenty years. The Court substantially expanded the scope of DFR and contributed to the proliferation of cases in this area.[25]

In 1964 the Supreme Court decided *Humphrey* v. *Moore*.[26] This case signals a turning point in the duty of fair representation from preoccupation with intentional or malicious injury and with the scope of the duty of fair representation to concern about the nature

---

19. 325 U.S. 538, 16 LRRM 734 (1945).

20. *See*, Miranda Fuel Co., 140 NLRB 181, 51 LRRM 1584 (1962), *enforcement denied*, 326 F.2d 172, 54 LRRM 2715 (2d Cir. 1963).

21. 359 U.S. 236, 43 LRRM 2838 (1959).

22. 371 U.S. 195, 51 LRRM 2646 (1962).

23. Dowd Box Co., Inc., v. Courtney, 368 U.S. 502, 49 LRRM 2619 (1962).

24. Teamsters Local 174 v. Lucas Flour Co., 369 U.S. 95, 49 LRRM 2717 (1962).

25. Vaca v. Sipes, *supra* note 2. (Justice Fortas concurring at 203, 64 LRRM at 2380).

26. *Supra* note 4.

of the process through which the duty is exercised and the quality of the performance of the duty by the labor organization.

By this time the court had already decided the famous trilogy giving deference to the arbitration process.[27] Furthermore, *Republic Steel Corp.* v. *Maddox* required an employee to attempt to exhaust the grievance and arbitration procedures established by collective bargaining agreement before resort to the court for action against the employer for wrongful discharge.[28]

These cases set the stage for *Vaca* v. *Sipes* in which the Supreme Court addresses a multitude of issues, including the relationship between the union's duty of fair representation and the employee's right to enforce the collective bargaining agreement by direct suit against his employer.[29] The Supreme Court there rejected preemption of DFR suits as unfair labor practices and interjected the courts into the subtleties of labor relations with little to guide or restrain them.

Pandora's box was opened with *Humphrey* v. *Moore.* But in *Vaca* the Court propped open the lid and invited the flood of cases in three respects: (1) the confusion of the nature of the cause of action—suggesting the section 301-DFR hybrid case, the section 301 case on the contract alone, and the duty of fair representation case against the union alone without any clarity as to the basis for the causes of action invited multiple law suits and continued earlier confusion regarding the jurisdictional base for such law suits; (2) the expansive language used to describe, without adequate guidelines, the nature of the duty of fair representation action; and (3) rejection of the preemption argument of DFR/ULP cases on dubious grounds.

Before we can understand the utter confusion of *Vaca,* it is necessary to discuss *Humphrey* v. *Moore,* which preceded it by three years. In the twenty years since *Humphrey* (decided Jan. 6, 1964) each Supreme Court contribution to DFR lore has generated further confusion. Justice White writing for the majority, despite Justice Goldberg's efforts to correct the court's view of labor relations, charts a flawed course from which we have yet to recover.

---

27. United Steelworkers v. Warrior & Gulf Navigation Co., 363 U.S. 574, 46 LRRM 2416 (1960); United Steelworkers v. American Mfg. Co., 363 U.S. 564, 46 LRRM 2414 (1960); United Steelworkers v. Enterprise Wheel & Car Corp., 363 U.S. 593, 46 LRRM 2423 (1960).

28. 379 U.S. 650, 58 LRRM 2193 (1965).

29. *Supra* note 2.

The facts in *Humphrey* were not extremely difficult as labor relations problems go and involved a common predicament. Two companies engaged in the transportation of new automobiles from plants in the area were faced with declining business and informed by the manufacturer, Ford Motor Company, that there was only room for one of them. After deliberations, they made arrangements whereby one company would take over the transportation operation of the other. The question precipitating the litigation was, What happens to the employees' seniority as the operations are merged?

The collective bargaining agreement provided in the event that the employer absorbs the business of another carrier or is a party to a merger of lines, the seniority of the employees affected shall be determined by mutual agreement of the parties. Any controversy was to be submitted to the grievance procedure.

Elsewhere in the collective bargaining agreement, it was agreed that all matters pertaining to interpretation, upon request, were to be submitted to the joint conference committee, which after listening to both sides would make a decision. In other words, matters of interpretations were to be decided by mutual agreement, and the employers agreed to be bound by the collective bargaining contract.

There were some differences as to whether the union representative misled the employees and some argument in the court below about a conflict of interest in the union representing employees from both companies. While those are not critical to this discussion, they do evidence the court's willingness to look at various aspects of the union's activities as subject to the duty of fair representation. What is significant in *Humphrey* for this discussion is the Court's characterization of the nature of the action before it. The Court discussed the nature of the action, noting that plaintiff Moore's claim was that the joint committee exceeded its power in making its decision and that therefore the settlement was a nullity and his discharge pursuant thereto a breach of the contract. Second, the plaintiff claimed the decision of the committee was obtained by dishonest union conduct in breach of the duty of fair representation and that a decision so obtained cannot be relied upon as a valid excuse for his discharge under the contract.

The Supreme Court, agreeing with the Kentucky court, concluded that the action was one arising under section 301 of the Labor-Management Relations Act and was controlled by federal law even though brought in a state court. While the Court noted there were different views regarding whether violation of the duty of fair representation was an unfair labor practice, it was not necessary to resolve the issue in this case. Even if it were an unfair labor practice case, the complaint would still allege a violation of the contract and therefore was within the cognizance of federal and state courts. The court characterized the union's position as taken honestly and in good faith and without hostility or arbitrary discrimination. It noted that by choosing to integrate seniority lists based on length of service at either company the union acted upon wholly relevant considerations, not upon capricious or arbitrary factors. The court concluded that the evidence showed no breach of the union's duty of fair representation.

Having already contributed to future confusion by comingling the action against the employer and DFR action against the union as both arising under the contract, the Court utters further mischief by suggesting that if the union had acted on *less than wholly relevant considerations* or upon *arbitrary* or *capricious* factors — terms nowhere defined — it would breach its duty of fair representation. These expansive terms invite lawyers to bring DFR cases seeking to establish union conduct that fits into the inverse of what was found in *Humphrey* v. *Moore* to be nonactionable.

Finally, the Supreme Court directs its attention to the fairness of the hearing and the adequacy of the representation the complaining parties received before the joint conference committee. In directing its attention to that aspect, the Court opens the door to scrutiny of the quality of the union's representation as well as of the fairness of the hearing process. These are two distinct matters: one connoting *due process* concerns, the other connoting a *standard of care* or, as we shall see in later cases, the question of malpractice.[30]

---

30. There is another disturbing aspect to the *Humphrey* case which seems to me even more significant, though it has received scant attention until recently. Justice Goldberg, with whom Justice Brennan joined, concurred in the results of *Humphrey* v. *Moore*, but challenged the determination of the majority that the complaint properly arose under section 301. In his view, the plaintiff's case should have been treated as an individual employee's action for a union's breach of the duty of fair representation derived from the National Labor Relations Act itself. He notes that under the collective bargaining agreement and the language under scrutiny, a mutually acceptable grievance settlement, which is what the joint committee decision was, could not be challenged by an individual employee on the grounds that the parties exceeded their contractual powers in making the settlement. He points out that the arbitration process is determined by what the parties agree to submit to an arbitrator and that in *Humphrey*, the parties were free to resolve the dispute by amending the contract if

We turn now to *Vaca* v. *Sipes*. It tends to escape notice, given the other complexities of that case, that the rationale of *Vaca*, like *Humphrey*, was endorsed by only five members of the Court. Justice Black dissented, and Justice Fortas, joined by Warren and Harlan, concurred only in the results. Of the members who participated in this decision, only Justices Brennan and White remain on the bench. Justice Fortas strongly contended that the principle of preemption should apply to the case, indicating that the facts of *Vaca* virtually paralleled the situations in *Iron Workers* v. *Perko*[31] and *Plumbers Union* v. *Borden*.[32]

One of the many vices of *Vaca* is that it has spurred so much discussion since 1967. I shall spare you another repetition of its facts and note only that the Supreme Court majority agreed with the petitioners that Owens had failed to prove that the union breached its duty of fair representation in the handling of the grievance and that the Supreme Court of Missouri, in rejecting that contention, applied a standard that was inconsistent with federal law. The majority concluded that the Missouri court erred in upholding the verdict solely on the ground that the evidence supported the plaintiff's claim that he had been wrongly discharged. The Court had no quarrel with that aspect of it. The Court, however, stated the statutory duty of fair representation occurs only when a union's conduct toward a member of the collective bargaining unit is arbitrary, discriminatory, or in bad faith. So far on safe ground. The Court then said, "we accept the proposition that a union may not arbitrarily ignore a meritorious grievance or process it in a perfunctory fashion."[33]

---

necessary. Justice Goldberg notes that the settlement of the seniority dispute was deemed by the parties to be an interpretation of their agreement not requiring an amendment. This was part of the *negotiation* process—not arbitration.

   Consequently, the plaintiffs' claim against the union was a cause of action like *Syres* and *Steele* rather than a section 301(a) contract action. The Court has finally clarified the basis for these cases but it has taken sixteen years to recognize Justice Goldberg's point. DelCostello v. Teamsters, 103 S. Ct. 2281 at 2290, 2294 (1983). The rationale of the *Humphrey* v. *Moore* majority was joined in wholeheartedly by only five justices. The disagreements expressed by the others, I submit, strongly argue that even the Supreme Court was ill equipped to deal with the nuances of the duty of fair representation. What could we have expected from the lower courts of Kentucky?

   31. 373 U.S. 701, 53 LRRM 2327 (1963).

   32. 373 U.S. 690, 53 LRRM 2322 (1963); for an interesting discussion of preemption see Bryson, *A Matter of Wooden Logic: Labor Law Preemption and Individual Rights*, 51 Tex. L. Rev. 1037 (1973). This view seemed to have prevailed subsequently in Motor Coach Employees v. Lockridge, 403 U.S. 274, 77 LRRM 2501 (1971).

   33. Vaca, *supra* note 2, at 190, 191.

There we have proliferation of confusion. May a union arbitrarily ignore a nonmeritorious grievance or process it in a perfunctory fashion? May a union ignore a meritorious grievance so long as it does not arbitrarily do so? Should a union be able to process any grievance in a perfunctory fashion? What in God's name is a perfunctory fashion? And by what standard does one evaluate a meritorious grievance? Who ought to be making these judgments? Any judge of any court with jurisdiction of the parties? How could the Court imagine that such a state of chaos would have no adverse effect upon the national labor policy?

The Court would have done all of us a favor had it disposed of *Vaca* with a much shorter opinion on a much narrower basis, or if it could not resist writing its magnum opus, it had done so with a great deal more care and attention to labor-management relations matters.

While the Court dwells on arbitrarily ignoring a meritorious grievance and recognizes that the grievance machinery contemplates that the parties will endeavor in good faith to settle grievances short of arbitration, it seems to think that the settlement process filters out only frivolous grievances. It is the not-so-clear grievance and contract interpretation that provide the grist for the arbitration mill, at least before the chilling effect of the duty of fair representation cases. The realities of the collective bargaining system are such that when the parties make deals they trade things that are of some potential value. If only frivolous grievances were washed out, or if the parties could only settle frivolous grievances except risking duty of fair representation cases, the collective bargaining process would be seriously compromised. The *Vaca* language raises questions of the viability of trading "meritorious grievances." Prudence would suggest any case in which there is a fifty-fifty chance of winning at arbitration must be pressed for fear that the party offended by a settlement would pursue a duty of fair representation claim. How do you assess a fifty-fifty chance of winning in *ad hoc* arbitration? How, under *Vaca*, do we keep the trial court from examining the *merits* of the claim, a task the court says is for the arbitrator? May I suggest, with due respect, *Vaca* is impossible to comply with.

The Case for Preemption by the NLRB

The *Vaca* opinion of Justice Fortas appropriately takes the majority to task for its elaborate discussion of problems the concurring justices dubbed irrelevant. They noted that the case was not an action by an employee against the employer, and thus the extended discussion of the requisites of such an action was unnecessary. The Court argued that the employee could sue his employer under section 301 and that to maintain such an action he would have to show that he had exhausted his remedies under the collective bargaining agreement, or alternatively that he was prevented from doing so because the union had breached its duty to him by failure completely to process his claim. The majority, I agree, needlessly confuses matters in its rambling discussion of the jurisdictional base for the case. It concludes that the employee's suit against the employer is a 301 suit, and even assuming that the breach of the duty by the union is an unfair labor practice, jurisdiction remains in the courts. Then it opines that if to facilitate his case the employee joins the union as a defendant, the situation is not substantially changed. The action is still a 301 suit, and the jurisdiction of the court is not preempted under the *Garmon* principle. Insofar as adjudication of the union's breach of its duty is concerned, the court says the result is no different if the plaintiff sues the employer and the union in separate actions, as it did in this case.

Perhaps the dispute regarding the scope of 301 is a tempest in a teapot, since it may relate only to matters of correct pleading, but it has been a source of confusion among lawyers and lower courts. Unions may breach the duty of fair representation in the process of negotiating collective bargaining agreements or in other failures to represent employees that occur separately from the administration of the contract. If there is no contract issue involved, it is difficult to see how the duty of fair representation can be characterized as a 301 action unless the individual is bringing the action against the union under the union's constitution and bylaws as a contract. The Supreme Court has only recently determined that the union's constitution is a contract for purposes of 301(a) of the LMRA.[34] While that case does not decide the issue of whether an individual can sue the union for breach of the constitution on a contract theory, it would seem to follow, given *Smith* v. *Evening News*. Obviously, the internal procedures of unions are relevant to the collective bargaining process as the court has recognized in *Clayton* v. *UAW*.[35]

---

34. United Association of Journeymen and Apprentices of the Plumbing and Pipe Fitting Industry v. Local 334, 452 U.S. 615, 101 S. Ct. 2546 (1981).

35. 451 U.S. 679, 107 LRRM 2385 (1981).

The majority opinion in *Vaca* makes its case against preemption on the following propositions: (1) the preemption doctrine has never been rigidly applied to cases where it could not be fairly inferred that Congress intended exclusive jurisdiction to lie with the NLRB; (2) Congress itself has carved out exceptions to the Board's exclusive jurisdiction, noting sections 301, 303 and 14(c). It also notes those exceptions represented by *Linn* v. *Plant Guards Workers*[36] regarding matters of merely peripheral concern of the Labor Management Relations Act or touching interests so deeply rooted in local feeling and responsibility that, absent compelling congressional direction, the Court would not infer that Congress had deprived the states of power to act.

I suggest that the duty of fair representation proposition falls into none of the above. I would also argue that the primary justifications for the preemption doctrine, that is, the need to avoid conflicting rules of substantive law in the labor relations area and the desirability of leaving the development of such rules to the Board, which the court asserts is not applicable to cases involving alleged breaches of the union's duty of fair representation, is a truism at the point uttered and not the question before the house. Though the doctrine was indeed judicially developed, that should not have ended the inquiry in *Vaca*. Granted that the Board was somewhat tardy in asserting unfair labor practice jurisdiction over DFR cases, the question is, Now that the Board has done so, should the Court reassess the question of preemption?

Even if we concede the stronger case in 1967 was supportive of leaving DFR jurisdiction with the courts, do the considerations applicable then still apply? The majority argued that the duty of fair representation doctrine serves unique interests, and its argument had a profound effect on the applicability of the preemption rule to that class of cases. The Court then drags out quasi-constitutional justification for the creation of the duty in *Steele* v. *Louisville,* a case grounded in invidious discrimination in a period before the ripening of the constitutional requirement of equal protection-due process of the Fifth Amendment.[37] Three years before *Vaca*, Congress passed the Civil Rights Act of 1964 inclusive of Title VII,[38] which addressed all the issues encompassed in *Steele* and many, many more.

---

36. 383 U.S. 53, 61 LRRM 2345 (1966).

37. *See, e.g.,* Bolling v. Sharp, *supra* note 3, a companion case to Brown v. The Board of Education.

38. 42 U.S.C. § 2000(a) et seq.

The Court pointed out that the NLRB general counsel has unreviewable discretion to refuse to institute an unfair labor practice complaint, and preemption of DFR cases by the NLRB would deprive plaintiffs of the protection of judicial oversight. First, I question the unreviewable discretion of unfair labor practice complaints, particularly if a general counsel regularly refused to issue them in cases involving racial or sex discrimination. Under current law and practice, I would suspect such refusals would quickly result in diminution of the general counsels' so-called unreviewable discretion.

The intensely practical considerations offered by the Court are equally suspect.[39] The Court asserted that the duty of fair representation often requires review of substantive positions taken and policies pursued by the union in its negotiation of a collective bargaining agreement and in its handling of the grievance machinery. These are matters not normally within the Board's unfair labor practice jurisdiction, it opined. It expresses doubt that the Board brings substantially greater expertise to bear on those problems than do the courts.

With due respect, even a bad Board brings substantially more expertise than do the courts and than does the Supreme Court itself, as evidenced by its abortive attempts to handle the duty of fair representation nuances. The record of the untold number of courts in DFR cases is probably substantially worse. Moreover, if the Board does not have the current expertise, and certainly it has more now that it has been up to its ears in DFR, it has the capability of developing the expertise. That capability is totally lacking in the courts and in the Court.[40]

At one point, the Fortes opinion in *Vaca* says, "The Court's difficulty, it seems to me, reflects the basic awkwardness of its position: it is attempting to force into the posture of a contract violation an alleged default of the union which is not a violation of the collective bargaining agreement but a breach of its separate and basic duty fairly to represent all employees in the union. This is an unfair labor practice and should be treated as such." It points out that concern with the subtleties of the union's statutory duty to employees, including those who may not be members, is precisely and especially the kind of judgment that Congress intended to be entrusted to the

---

39. Vaca v. Sipes, *supra* note 2, at 184-86, 64 LRRM at 2373-76.

40. For a note on the NLRB expertise *see*, Fortas's dissent in Vaca v. Sipes, *supra* note 2, at 202 n. 5, 64 LRRM at 2382 n. 5 and cases cited.

Board. "The nuances of union employee and union employer relationship are infinite and consequential, particularly when the issue is
as amorphous as whether the union is guilty of 'arbitrary or bad
faith conduct' which the court states as the standard here applicable.
In all reason and all good judgment this jurisdiction should be left
with the Board."[41]

Probably the strangest case of record on the duty of fair representation is *Motor Coach Employees* v. *Lockridge*.[42] If a demonstration
of the need for Congress to bring order out of chaos in the duty of
fair representation is required, a reading of the three opinions in
Lockridge ought to be persuasive. The Supreme Court, reversing the
Supreme Court of Idaho, concluded that the matter was preempted
by the National Labor Relations Act and that the state court was
without jurisdiction. The state court had entertained the plaintiff's
case in a 301 action in which the employee alleged, among other
things, that the union had acted wrongfully, wantonly, willfully,
and maliciously and without just cause and had violated the constitution and general bylaws of the union. He contended that such laws
constituted a contract between the plaintiff as member and that the
union had breached its duty of fair representation. The facts are
extremely complicated and involve a union shop provision under
which the issue was whether the failure to pay dues for a short time
justified suspension of the individual from membership in the union
and discharge.

There is no question, on the facts, that there could be a breach
of the union's duty of fair representation as well as a violation of the
National Labor Relations Act. What is not clear, however, is how the
majority of the Court concluded that the preemption doctrine applied in this case.[43]

The majority opinion, written by Justice Harlan is persuasive as
to the desirablity of preemption. What is not persuasive, however, is
the attempt to distinguish preempting this case and not other duty
of fair representation-unfair labor practice cases.

What is more perplexing about *Lockridge* is that it sets forth a
standard of breach of the DFR that is different from the one the

---

41. *Supra* note 2, at 202-203, 64 LRRM at 2383.
42. *Supra* note 32.
43. The majority opinion is written by Justice Harlan; Douglas dissents, and
White and the Chief Justice dissent separately. The three opinions together provide
anything but clarity.

court enunciated in *Vaca* v. *Sipes*. The majority asserts that in order to make a case against the union, there must be substantial evidence of fraud, deceit, or dishonest conduct. That would be a return to a pre-*Humphrey-Vaca* era in which bad faith conduct was the norm for DFR cases. If that bad faith standard were to obtain, it would make the argument that the courts be taken out of the DFR area less compelling. It is the post-*Vaca* expansive standard that has created the most difficulty and that threatens uniformity of labor law. Perhaps the case stands for the proposition that some DFR claims are preempted. If so, no post-*Lockridge* Supreme Court case has indicated what they are.[44]

There has been some insistance that bad faith or fraud be proven in order to make out a duty of fair representation breach. The cases that have predominated the reports, however, are those that apply the more expansive standards enunciated in *Humphrey* v. *Moore,* and further explicated in *Vaca* v. *Sipes*. If *Lockridge* lives, perhaps further argument should be made to the court that the *Lockridge* standards should be extended and that the scope of *Vaca* et al. be correspondently restricted. But I see no indication in the Court's substantive cases that it would be receptive to such a plea. It may be that *DelCostello* v. *Teamsters* is a harbinger of things to come.[45]

Negligence and the Duty of Fair Representation

The Supreme Court
Despite the fact that the Supreme Court stated that a distinction between honest, mistaken conduct on the one hand and deliberate and severely hostile and irrational treatment on the other needs to be strictly maintained, in the post-*Lockridge* cases, the Court seems to have approved, at least sub silentio, some form of negligence as a breach of the union's duty of fair representation.

In his overview chapter in *The Duty of Fair Representation,* Ben Aaron raised the question of exactly what types of conduct constitute violation of the duty of fair representation: "on this point, the Supreme Court has spoken with such impenetrable ambiguity that

---

44. *See,* Waggoner v. R. McGray, 607 F.2d 1229, 1233-36, 102 LRRM 2492 (9th Cir. 1979); Baker v. Newspaper & Graphics Communications Union, Local 6, 628 F.2d 156, 162-65, 104 LRRM 2197, 2202-3 (D.C. Cir. 1980).

45. *Supra* note 17.

the federal courts, which bear the brunt of construing the nature and scope of the duty, are understandably in disagreement as to what the law is."[46]

In the chapter Origins of the Concept in the same book, I suggested that the Supreme Court in *Hines* v. *Anchor Motor Freight*[47] contributed to the drift toward negligence. What emerged in the *Hines* case was judicial evaluation of the *manner* in which the union conducted the arbitration. Terms like "arbitrary, capricious, perfunctory" and inquiries into "whether the employer knowingly or negligently relied on false evidence" and whether the employer was implicated in the union's *malfeasance* all bring us closer to considerations of negligence as the standard by which union behavior will be evaluated."[48]

The *Hines* case involved the failure of the union sufficiently to investigate the grievants' claim of innocence. In the duty of fair representation case, their attorney obtained the deposition of a motel clerk that revealed falsification of records for which the employees had been discharged. What the Supreme Court decided was the narrow issue regarding the necessity of implicating the employer in the union's misconduct. But it left untouched the lower court's use of terms like "knowingly and negligently relying on false evidence, malfeasance, and whether the union's conduct was in the range of acceptable performance by a collective bargaining agent." I submit, that these terms invite further application in duty of fair representation cases of these negligence concepts with which courts are more comfortable. Every law student studies torts though not all study labor relations law. Lawyers and courts of general jurisdiction are familiar with concepts of intentional tort and negligence. The remarks of a perceptive observer of labor law about another area of law are equally applicable here: "These ideas are not described here in order to analyze the implications. Rather, they have operated as forces on the minds of those who shape the law. They represent ways of thought that possess a long jurisprudential history and are embed-

---

46. Aaron, *The Duty of Fair Representation: An Overview* in The Duty of Fair Representation 18 (J. T. McKelvey ed., Cornell University, New York State School of Industrial and Labor Relations, 1977).

47. 424 U.S. 554, 91 LRRM 2481 (1976).

48. Jones, *The Origins of the Concept of the Duty of Fair Representation* in The Duty of Fair Representation 41–42 (J. T. McKelvey ed., Cornell University, New York State School of Industrial and Labor Relations, 1977).

ded in the attitudes of lawyers. Once a concept is grasped, it is often applied without conscious awareness of or reference to its genesis. This predisposition is fundamental in understanding the actions taken by administrators, advocates, and judges."[49]

While a majority of the circuit courts have not accepted a mere negligence standard, some form of negligence, although variously described, has crept into the DFR folklore.[50]

In 1979 the Supreme Court had another opportunity to enlighten us on the limits of the duty of fair representation in *International Brotherhood of Electrical Workers* v. *Foust*.[51] What the case clearly decides is that the Railway Labor Act does not permit an employee to recover punitive damages for a union's breach of its duty of fair representation. More significant than the holding of the case, in my judgment, are the matters about which the justices quarrel in their disposition of it. Justice Blackmun, with whom Chief Justice Burger and Justices Rehnquist and Stevens joined, concurring in the results, objects to the majority's adoption of a *"per se* rule that the union's breach of its duty of fair representation can never render it liable for punitive damages no matter how egregious the breach." Blackmun's opinion complains that whatever the merits of the majority's *per se* rule, it was not necessary to propound such a blanket prescription in this particular case for here "the union's conduct betrayed nothing more than negligence, and thus presented an inappropriate occasion for awarding punitive damages under any formula."[52]

The majority opinion quarrels a bit with the concurrence by noting that Blackmun surmises as a matter of law the union's conduct "betrayed nothing more than negligence. . . . This conclusion necessarily assumes that there was insufficient evidence of malice, wanton, or oppressive conduct to justify the jury's punitive damage award. We, however, are unwilling to substitute our judgment for

---

49. Blumrosen, *Strangers in Paradise: Griggs v. Duke Power Co. and the Concept of Employment Discrimination*, 71 Mich. L. Rev. 59, 71 (1972).

50. *See, e.g.*, Wells v. Southern Airways, Inc., 616 F.2d 107, 104 LRRM 2338 (5th Cir. 1980); Alvey v. General Electric Co., 622 F.2d 1279, 104 LRRM 2838 (7th Cir. 1980); Newport News Shipbuilding and Drydock Co. v. NLRB, 631 F.2d 263, 104 LRRM 2630 (4th Cir. 1980); Self v. Drivers, Local 61, 620 F.2d 439, 104 LRRM 2125 (4th Cir. 1980); Williams v. Teamsters Local 984, 625 F.2d 138, 105 LRRM 2030 (6th Cir. 1980); Ruzicka v. General Motors Corp., 523 F.2d 306, 90 LRRM 2497 (6th Cir. 1975); Ruzicka II, 649 F.2d 1207, 107 LRRM 2726 (6th Cir. 1981); Robesky v. Qantas Empire Airways Ltd., 573 F.2d 1082, 98 LRRM 2090 (9th Cir. 1978).

51. 442 U.S. 42, 101 LRRM 2365 (1979).

52. *Id.* at 53, 101 LRRM at 2369 (Blackmun concurring in the results).

that of the jury, district court, and the court of appeals on this essentially evidentiary question."[53]

I think the decision a correct one on punitive damages as a matter of basic labor law. The fact that that issue had to go all the way to the Supreme Court demonstrates, yet again, the danger to uniformity of labor law of permitting all courts to try DFR cases. Remedy is a matter of national concern and conflicting remedies threaten uniformity. I suggest that this exchange, while obviously dicta, encourages lawyers in lower courts to the view that some form of negligence is breach of the duty of fair representation. In fact, nothing in this exchange suggests that even mere negligence is inappropriate for lower courts to consider in evaluating union conduct.

What was characterized in 1976 as a drift toward negligence seems in 1983 to be a well-established fact. The issue now is what form of negligence constitutes breach of the duty of fair representation.[54]

The NLRB

Of at least equal significance to Supreme Court cases for the development of standards of union conduct was the issuance on July 9, 1979, by the general counsel of the National Labor Relations Board of a Memorandum to NLRB Field Offices explaining the Board's policy on the union's duty of fair representation.[55] Because the John Truesdale chapter discusses the current state of the duty of fair representation in Board cases, suffice it to say here that the Board has made a distinction between conduct that is inept, negligent, unwise, and insensitive or ineffectual and conduct that is actionable. It noted, however, that if there is no basis upon which union conduct could be explained, the conduct would be considered arbitrary, an example being when there is a contract or internal union policy that clearly and unambigously supports an employee's

---

53. *Id.* at 46 n.7, 101 LRRM at 2367 n.7.

54. *See, e.g.*, Note, *Determining Standards for a Union's Duty of Fair Representation: The Case for Ordinary Negligence*, 65 Cornell L. Rev. 634 (1980); Note, *IBEW v. Foust: A Hint of Negligence in the DFR*, 32 Hastings L. J. 1041 (1981); Kopp, *The Duty of Fair Representation Revisited*, 5 Employee Relations L. J. 3 (1982); Swedo, *Ruzicka v. General Motors Corp.: Negligence, Exhaustion of Remedies, and Relief in Duty of Fair Representation Cases*, 33 Arb. J. 6 (1978).

55. 101 LRR 224 (7/23/79).

position and the union without explanation refuses to support it.[56] The memo also emphasized that the union was not expected to engage in the kind of exhaustive inquiry that a skilled investigator would, and the mere fact that a union reaches a conclusion later shown to be erroneous would not establish a violation. However, the union is expected to make some inquiry into the facts and its contract interpretation to have some basis in reason.

Mere negligence will not constitute a violation, but a breach would occur where the negligence is so gross as to constitute reckless disregard of the interests of the employee. The memo notes that the First Circuit has held that a union breached its duty by failing to process a grievance in a timely fashion for unexplained reasons.[57] It will be interesting to watch the development by the NLRB of clarity between the standards "arbitrary conduct and gross negligence."[58]

Even the expertise of the Board will be taxed in drawing lines between acceptable and unacceptable conduct. They may well be more "nice than bright." But it seems to be preferable to the current confusing state of affairs to have one expert agency struggling with the problem in the first instance, and to have the courts, under the limited standards of judicial review provided for in the NLRA, assess the Board's decisions.

The Board's position, potentially in conflict with the courts, is that the mere fact that the union is inept, negligent, unwise and insensitive or ineffectual will not standing alone establish a breach of the duty. But in *Milstead* v. *Teamsters Local 957* the district court found the union to have breached its duty of fair representation because of inept handling of the employee's grievance due to apparent ignorance of the provisions in the collective agreement.[59] The Court of Appeals for the Sixth Circuit affirmed. Granted that the

---

56. Arbitrary conduct is that conduct for which there is no basis upon which it can be explained. For example, a union would violate section 8(b)(1)(a) if it refused to process cases without any inquiry, or with such a perfunctory or cursory inquiry that it is tantamount to no inquiry at all. Beverly Manor Convalescent Center, 229 NLRB 692, 95 LRRM 1156 (1977); P&L Ceta Products, 224 NLRB 244, 93 LRRM 1341 (1976). *See also* Teamsters, Local 692 (Great Western Unifreight), 209 NLRB 446, 85 LRRM 1385 (1974).

57. The memo cites Robesky v. Qantas, *supra* note 50, and Ruzicka v. General Motors Co., *supra* note 50.

58. Segarra v. Sea-Land Service Inc., 581 F.2d 291, 99 LRRM 2198 (1st Cir. 1978).

59. 580 F.2d 232, 99 LRRM 2150 (6th Cir. 1978).

court in the *Milstead* case was operating under the rather narrow standard of review governing denial of the union's motion for a directed verdict, the facts of the case are sufficient to demonstrate the potential conflict I wish to underline. The case, as well as *Ruzicka v. General Motors*,[60] in which the union representative negligently failed to process the grievant's case within the time limit, seems to be contrary to the general counsel's view that inept, negligent, and ineffectual conduct is not a breach of the DFR so as to constitute an unfair labor practice. If the Board followed the views expressed in the memorandum, neither the facts of *Ruzicka* nor of *Milstead*, standing alone, would establish breach of the duty of fair representation. On appeal for enforcement to the Sixth Circuit, it is conceivable that the Board's dismissal of the case against the union would be sustained. The standard of review of determinations by the National Labor Relations Board is more limited than the standards of review of cases arising in the district courts. Under the National Labor Relations Act, the Board's findings of fact are not to be tampered with by reviewing courts, if there is substantial evidence on the record considered as a whole.[61] With regard to the law, the court of appeals is not to substitute its judgment for that of the Board's where there is a rational basis and warrant in the law. Of course, the judgment of the Board is subject to judicial review, but if its construction of the NLRA is reasonably defensible, it should not be rejected merely because the courts might prefer another view of the statute.[62]

It seems theoretically possible, therefore, with our current system that the law in a given circuit could look both ways at once.[63]

It is also theoretically possible for plaintiff to pursue at the same time a duty of fair representation case before the National Labor Relations Board and in the district court and to prevail in one forum and to lose in the other. On appeal, both decisions could be sustained by the same reviewing court as different standards of judicial review would obtain. It is undesirable to create by interpretation

---

60. *Supra* note 50.

61. NLRB v. Universal Camera, 340 U.S. 474, 27 LRRM 2373 (1951).

62. Ford Motor Co. v. NLRB, 441 U.S. 488, 497, 101 LRRM 2222, 2225 (1979).

63. *Cf.*, United Brick and Clay Workers v. Deena Artware Inc., 198 F.2d 637, 30 LRRM 2485 (6th Cir. 1952), *cert. denied*, 344 U.S. 897, 31 LRRM 2157 (1952) and NLRB v. Deena Artware, Inc. 198 F.2d 645, 30 LRRM 2479 (6th Cir. 1952), *cert. denied*, 345 U.S. 906, 31 LRRM 2444 (1953). Section 303 creates this problem of potential conflict in the statute. It should not be persuasive authority for the creation of yet another inconsistency in labor law by interpretation.

what Congress created in section 303 with regard to damage actions under the National Labor Relations Act for secondary boycotts. The judgment that secondary boycotts were so bad as to justify damages, where no other unfair labor practice does, warrants the congressional judgment that the potential inconsistency is tolerable. Congress has not explicitly decided anything about the breach of the duty of fair representation.

Another example of the potential conflict arising out of one circuit depending on the forum chosen by the plaintiff is *Hoffman* v. *Lonza, Inc.*[64] The general counsel takes the position that the act is violated as a breach of DFR if the union refuses to process a grievance without any inquiry at all or with such a perfunctory inquiry that it is tantamount to no inquiry or where the union fails to act and offers no explanation. *Lonza* is described as raising the single question of whether a labor union can be sued in the federal court for breach of its duty of fair representation because the union, without explanation, permitted the employee's grievance to be terminated by failing to file a timely notice of intent to carry the grievance to arbitration.[65] While it may be an overstatement of the matter on the facts as described by the Seventh Circuit, the majority, citing *Lockridge*,[66] stated that substantial evidence of discriminatory intent must be shown and that a distinction between honest, mistaken conduct on one hand and deliberate and severely hostile and irrational treatment on the other needs to be strictly maintained.[67]

The dissenting judge asserted that a more appropriate standard is whether the union has been guilty of malfeasance and whether its conduct was within the range of acceptable performance by a collective bargaining agent.[68]

The general counsel will issue a complaint, and the Board will sustain breach of the duty of fair representation where the union's conduct was arbitrary or perfunctory. Under deference to the Board's choice of a rational legal standard and to the inferences drawn from substantial evidence on the record considered as a whole, the Seventh Circuit would be obliged to support the Board. However, on the same set of facts, following its own interpretation

---

64. 658 F.2d 519, 108 LRRM 2311 (7th Cir. 1981).
65. *Id.* at 520, 108 LRRM at 2312.
66. 403 U.S. at 301.
67. 658 F.2d at 522, 108 LRRM at 2314.
68. *Id.* at 524, 108 LRRM at 2316.

of the law in *Hoffman* v. *Lonza, Inc.*, it would decide against the plaintiff on appeal from a district court case, and there is the possibility that, given the current state of affairs, the Supreme Court would support both judgments.[69]

Confusion in the Lower Courts

Two cases from the spring of 1981 demonstrate the utter chaos of the duty of fair representation in American courts today. In *Anderson* v. *Paper Workers Union*[70] the Eighth Circuit concluded that the doctrine of the duty of fair representation extended to alleged facts that the union had misrepresented during contract ratification meetings by stating that a special security fund which guaranteed the contractually negotiated severance pay existed and would be available in the event of the employer's bankruptcy. Testimony established that the assurances were made despite the knowledge of the union representative that no such fund existed. The company went bankrupt, and the employees received only a portion of the severance pay due them. When the employees sued the union alleging that the misrepresentations violated the duty of fair representation, a jury awarded them severance pay and punitive damages against the union along with attorneys fees. The court of appeals agreed that the doctrine extended to the alleged misrepresentations during contract ratification meetings. But it concluded that the union did not breach its duty of fair representation because the evidence failed to demonstrate any causal link between the misrepresentations and the employees' injuries arising from the employers' failure to pay the full amounts of the severance pay.

Obviously, after *International Brotherhood of Electrical Workers* v. *Foust*,[71] punitive damages will not lie. The court concluded on the testimony, however, contrary to the district court's judgments, that the plaintiffs had not proven that "but for" the misrepresentation they would have obtained the severance pay to which they claimed entitlement. The court points out that even had they known the truth they may not have been successful in forcing the company to

---

69. Compare, Baldini v. UAW, Local 1095, 581 F.2d 145, 99 LRRM 2535 (7th Cir. 1978) with Hoffman v. Lonza, *supra* note 64. *See also,* Miller v. Gateway Transportation Co., Inc., 616 F.2d 272, 277 n.11, 103 LRRM 2591, 2594 n.11 (7th Cir. 1980), where the Seventh Circuit declares the DFR may be breached without scienter on the part of the union.

70. 641 F.2d 574, 106 LRRM 2513 (8th Cir. 1981).

71. *Supra* note 51.

undertake additional obligations even with the strike, and whether the employees would have struck was speculative. It concluded that the union could not be liable absent a showing that but for the misrepresentations the severance pay would have been paid. It noted that its determination that misrepresentation in the negotiation process would support a cause of action is consistent with decisions which found breach of the DFR where the union failed to inform members of decisions not to arbitrate grievances.

It also recognized that the mere fact that the allegations related to union misconduct in the internal processes of the union did not remove the matter from the scope of the duty of fair representation. Control over admission to union membership, it noted, was held subject to the duty of fair representation in *Wallace Corporation* v. *Labor Board*.[72] The jury apparently found and the district court concluded that the employees relied upon the misrepresentations and were injured by the failure to receive the severance pay. But that did not establish a causal link between such reliance and the injury.

Deciding a case with similar facts only two months later, on May 4, 1981, the Fifth Circuit in *Christopher* v. *Safeway Stores, Inc.*, came to the opposite conclusion regarding the breach of the duty of fair representation and sustained relief to the injured employees.[73] This case has an added dimension in that the plaintiffs also brought their action pursuant to section 411(a)(1) of the Labor-Management Reporting and Disclosure Act of 1959 (the Landrum-Griffin Act).[74]

In this case the union had failed to present to the membership a mandatory matter of union business under its constitution and by-laws. The evidence below established that the union submitted its new contract proposals for approval and presented the membership with a single sheet that purported to list the changes. There was no reference on the change sheet to any changes in the seniority system. The plaintiffs are two individual members who, because of the changes, were laid off from their jobs. Had the preexisting seniority system been in effect they would have had enough seniority to withstand layoffs. The plaintiff sued the company and the union seeking reinstatement; lost wages; compensatory and punitive damages; and a declaration of the invalidity of the seniority system, injunctive relief, and attorneys fees. In addition to the charge of violation of the

---

72. 323 U.S. 248 (1944).
73. 644 F.2d 467, 107 LRRM 2554 (5th Cir. 1981).
74. 29 U.S.C. § 401 et seq.

Landrum-Griffin Act, they claimed that the company breached the collective bargaining agreement by terminating their employment and that the union violated its duty of fair representation by refusing to arbitrate their grievance against the company.

The court below found that the company had not breached the contract by its termination and the union *had not* violated its duty of fair representation by declining to arbitrate the issue. On appeal, the Sixth Circuit affirmed, concluding that the district court correctly viewed the matter and that the company had correctly interpreted and applied the terms of the collective bargaining agreement. Moreover, the union was justified in refusing to press for arbitration of the complaints.

The court below, however, found that the union violated section 411(a)(1) of LMRDA, but that such a violation was not coterminus with the finding that the union violated its duty of fair representation. It noted that the two inquiries are separate, albeit frequently related, and ruled as a matter of law that the failure of the union to submit the proposed change to the members violated the Landrum-Griffin Act. It awarded damages for lost wages but declined to assess any other damages. The court of appeals sustained this determination.

Perhaps both these cases demonstrate the confusion among lawyers as much as differences in perceptions among the various courts. In the *Anderson* case, the union representative clearly lied to the members. In the *Christopher* case, the deception was one of omission, but the distinction is without difference with regard to obligations of the union to inform the membership. In *Christopher*, the plaintiffs got lost wages and their attorneys got fees, albeit under a different law. The causal link is just as speculative in both cases. Moreover, it seems clear in both cases that the complaining parties are injured, at least to the extent that their rights have been infringed, by the union's clear breach of its duty to deal fairly and honestly with the members. The question then is, What should the remedy be?

On the case argued in *Christopher*, the court was correct in concluding that the plaintiffs had not made out breach of the collective bargaining agreement. But this suggests a limitation in the advocacy. The issue which should have been vigorously argued was that the collective bargaining agreement was *void* as it had been obtained through fraud. It seems to me that if the finality of the arbitration process is subject to attack because of taint in the procedure by the union's failure in its duty of fair representation, an adverse clause in the collective bargaining agreement would be subject to revocation because of the same kind of breach in the process. If union misconduct does not shield the finality of the arbitration process, then it should follow that union misconduct should not sanctify provisions in a collective bargaining agreement that adversely affects the plaintiffs.

Does this sound novel or revolutionary? It should not, if we recall the circumstances of *Steele* v. *Louisville Nashville Railroad* and of *Wallace Corporation*. Both involved attacks upon collective bargaining agreements by the plaintiffs. The plaintiff's quest for relief in *Steele* was not unlike those of the individuals in *Christopher*. In the *Christopher* case, however, under a different theory, the parties got substantial relief, and probably more important, their lawyers were paid under a substantial benefits rationale.[75] The *Wallace Corporation* relief was even more grave as it was raised before the National Labor Relations Board and resulted in disestablishment of the offending union, even though there were no union unfair labor practices in existence at that time.

The other point of contrast is the overlap between section 411(a)(1) of the Landrum-Griffin Act and the concept of breach of the duty of fair representation. As neither of those statutes purports to preempt, an action may be brought under both. Moreover, the duty of fair representation is broader as it may be brought by non-members, of a union, which is not the case under the bill of rights provision of the Landrum-Griffin Act.

Finally the two cases are interesting in that one raises the causal issue and the "but for" analysis and defeats recovery, while the other, on comparable facts, does not discuss those issues at all. Given the litigation that the duty of fair representation spawns, it should come as no surprise if future cases of like kind dwell upon the causal link issue and "but for" analysis.[76]

In *Graf* v. *Elgin, Joliet and East Railroad*, additional evidence of confusion in the lower courts abounds.[77] This is a Railway Labor Act case in which the majority for the Seventh Circuit sets out to clarify the duty of fair representation standard in that circuit. Judge

---

75. *See*, Hall v. Coal, 412 U.S. 1, 83 LRRM 2177 (1973).

76. In the two years since these cases were decided they have not been followed.

77. 697 F.2d 771, 112 LRRM 2462 (7th Cir. 1983).

Posner says: "The standard is as follows. Union has a duty to represent every worker in the bargaining unit fairly but it breaches the duty only if it deliberately and unjustifiably refuses to represent the worker. Negligence, even gross negligence—a much criticized standard— . . . is not enough; and, obviously, intentional conduct may not be inferred from negligence, whether simple or gross. Although extreme recklessness is so close to intentional wrongdoing that the law treats it as the same thing, . . . we need not worry about that refinement in this case."[78] The court goes on to point out that the DFR standard in the Seventh Circuit is a narrow one especially under Railway Labor Act cases, and the proper standard cannot be determined by parcing ambiguous dicta.

In *Findley* v. *Jones Motor Freight,* the Third Circuit Court of Appeals, reversing a lower court decision and a jury determination that the union was guilty of a breach of the duty of fair representation, gives yet another illustration of the difficulty in giving meaning to duty of fair representation standards.[79] The court repeats most of the platitudes which have now become familiar and adds yet another to our concerns. It notes that "proof of arbitrary or bad faith union conduct in deciding not to proceed with the grievance is necessary to establish lack of compliance with the fair representation. . . . But once the grievance mechanisms have been utilized, . . . the issue here is whether the union's representation in the grievance proceedings was within the 'range of acceptable performance,' and if not, whether it tainted the adverse arbitral decision."[80]

At the same time, after reviewing evidence of numerous allegations of failures on the part of the union in the process, the court asserts that proof that the union may have acted negligently or exercised poor judgment is not enough to support a claim of unfair representation.[81] It reiterated that in order to state a claim for breach of the DFR it was essential that the plaintiffs allege a bad faith motive on the part of the union. What constitutes bad faith in a given case, of course, depends upon the circumstances.[82] While

---

78. *Id.* at 778, 112 LRRM at 2467.

79. 639 F.2d 953, 106 LRRM 2420 (3d Cir. 1981).

80. *Id.* at 958, 106 LRRM at 2422.

81. Citing itself in Bazarte v. UTU, 429 F.2d 868, 872, 75 LRRM 2017, 2019 (3d Cir. 1970).

82. Medlin v. Boeing Vertol Co., 620 F.2d 957, 961, 104 LRRM 2247, 2250 (3d Cir. 1980).

lapses were in evidence, and "certain acts or omissions by a union may in a proper case support a finding that the grievance was processed in a perfunctory manner,"[83] in this case the union's presentation of the grievance could not be so characterized. The conduct of the union was at least adequate and within the realm of acceptable performance as contemplated by *Hines*. The court closes with the statement that even if it were to adopt the standard of mere negligence, the conduct of the union in this case would pass muster. Moreover, it continues, even if certain actions of the union were arguably negligent, there has been no showing that they tainted the committee's decision.[84]

I submit that this decision looks both ways at once. It denies that mere negligence or exercise of poor judgment are enough to support a claim of breach of the duty of fair representation, while at the same time asserting that the union's conduct in the grievance procedure is subject to evaluation to determine if it is within the "range of acceptable performance." It further demonstrates schizophrenia by citing the two commentators for contrary propositions, one for the rejection of the negligence standard and the other for the proposition that the perfunctory standard is in fact enabling the courts to impose some minimum duty of care, a negligence concept.

The Third Circuit persists in asserting that a showing of actual bad faith or arbitrary conduct is required to make out a DFR case.[85] It cites with approval *Ruzicka I* and *Ruzicka II,* in which the Sixth Circuit undertakes to determine what degree of negligence amounts to the requisite arbitrariness.[86] This circuit, too, has indicated that certain acts or omissions by a union may in a proper case support a finding that the grievance was prosecuted in a perfunctory manner. I submit this ambivalence is precisely what encourages duty of fair representation litigation, and as has been noted elsewhere, the Supreme Court has done nothing to discourage it.[87]

---

83. Ely v. Hall's Motor Transit Co., 590 F.2d 62, 66 n.10, 100 LRRM 2206, 2208 n.10 (3d Cir. 1978).

84. Hines v. Anchor Motor Freight, Inc., *supra* note 47.

85. Riley v. Letter Carriers, Local No. 380, 668 F.2d 224, 109 LRRM 2772 (3d Cir. 1981).

86. Ruzicka I, 523 F.2d 306, 90 LRRM 2497 (6th Cir. 1975); Ruzicka II, 649 F.2d 1207, 107 LRRM 2726 (6th Cir. 1981).

87. *See,* Hines v. Anchor Motor Freight, *supra* note 47, and IBEW v. Foust, *supra* note 51.

Next on my list of confused cases is *Harris* v. *Schwerman Trucking Co.*[88] In *Harris* the Eleventh Circuit Court of Appeals asserts that neither ineptness nor ineffectiveness is an appropriate standard by which to conclude the grievance was processed in a perfunctory manner. A union is allowed considerable latitude in its representation of employees, and the grievance and arbitration process is not conducted in a judicial forum. Union representatives are not held to strict standards of trial advocacy. The court then advises us that the cases are uniform in holding that neither negligence nor mistaken judgment is sufficient to support a claim that the union acted in an arbitrary and perfunctory manner, citing among other cases: *Finley* v. *Jones Motor Freight, Ruzicka* v. *General Motors Corp.,* (this is *Ruzicka II*) and *Robeski* v. *Qantas Empire Airways Ltd.*

Both *Jones* and *Ruzicka II* recognize a negligence standard, although, perhaps, *gross* negligence rather than *mere* negligence. Moreover, what is difficult about this standard is that one court's *mere* is another court's *gross.* The Court says nothing less than a demonstration that the union acted with reckless disregard for the employees rights or was grossly deficient in its conduct will suffice to establish a DFR claim. In this context, the Court believes that the claim that a union acted perfunctory requires a demonstration that it ignored the grievance, inexplicably failed to take some required step, or gave the grievance merely cursory attention. This, I submit, is a negligence standard. Is it any wonder that the duty of fair representation cases proliferate?

It is the propensity of the courts to decry negligence on one hand while at the same time speaking of reckless disregard for the employees rights and gross deficiency in conduct on the other that is most confusing. Lawyers are quite properly perceiving that these are labels with the elasticity of an old-fashioned garter. They can be stretched over a multiplicity of factual situations, and if the judge and the jury are persuaded that the union's conduct was unfair, it is quite likely that the decision of breach of the duty of fair representation will be forthcoming with labels appropriate to fit the legal standard.

There is another patently erroneous proposition that floats through the cases, and it is that a breach of the union's duty of fair representation depends upon the union ignoring a meritorious

---

88. 668 F.2d 1204, 109 LRRM 3135 (11th Cir. 1982).

grievance or processing it in a perfunctory manner. That proposition must necessarily be plainly wrong. It seems to me in situations in which there is hostility or discriminatory motive, the union breaches the duty whether or not the grievance was a good or a bad grievance. Once it decides to grieve even a bad case, it must do so adequately.[89] It is quite likely that because breach of the DFR is a shield to an action against the employer for wrongful discharge under section 301, it is true, as a practical matter, that a meritorious grievance is essential. But the overgenerous assertion that there must be a meritorious grievance or there is no DFR breach possible is plainly wrong. The union can be sued in a separate suit. The question of what would be remedy for such union misconduct is a separate one.

The Late "Blooming" Problem of the Statute of Limitations

The Strange Case of United Parcel Service, Inc. v. Mitchell

The DFR has been around for almost forty years as a cause of action in both federal and state courts, under both the Railway Labor Act and the National Labor Relations Act.[90] It is only in recent years that the choice of an appropriate statute of limitations in DFR cases has become a cause célèbre or at least received the attention of the Supreme Court. The problem should have been anticipated[91] and resolved in a manner that would have limited the waste of legal resources that has accompanied the recent treatment of the issue in

---

89. Kesner v. NLRB, 532 F.2d 1169, 92 LRRM 2137 (7th Cir. 1977). *See also, e.g.,* United Steelworkers v. NLRB, 692 F.2d 1052, 1057, 111 LRRM 3125, 3128 (7th Cir. 1982) where the court says "while a union must be allowed considerable discretion in deciding which grievances to present and how to present them, it may not ignore a meritorious grievance. . . . (citations omitted). Consistent with that principle, courts have rejected any claim for lost earnings against the union which has allegedly breached its duty where the claimant fails to show that its claim against the employer had merit." *See also* Kesner v. NLRB, *supra;* Newport News Ship Building v. NLRB, *supra* note 50; Wyatt v. Interstate & Ocean Transport Co., 623 F.2d 888, 104 LRRM 2408 (4th Cir. 1980); Self v. Drivers, *supra* note 50.

90. *See,* Steele v. Louisville & Nashville Railroad, *supra* note 3; Tunstall v. Brotherhood of Locomotive Firemen and Engineermen, 323 U.S. 210, 15 LRRM 715 (1944). Wallace Corp. v. Labor Board, *supra* note 3; Ford Motor Co. v. Hoffman, *supra* note 11 at 337, 31 LRRM at 2550-52.

91. *See, e.g.,* a comparable problem and note, *Legislation: Limitation of Actions under Section 16(b) of the Fair Labor Standards Act,* 45 Colum. L. Rev. 444 (1945).

the courts. The Supreme Court's treatment of the issue in *United Parcel Service Inc.* v. *Mitchell*[92] and in *DelCostello* v. *Teamsters*[93] and the utter chaos that reigned in the courts below in the intervening two years is yet another illustration of the dire need for Congress to act. Even *DelCostello* has left us with a host of problems that will lead to further clutter in the courts below. And while the later case may provide a single statute of limitations in certain kinds of future cases under the National Labor Relations Act, it does not address the issue of the appropriate statute of limitations under the Railway Labor Act.

In *United Parcel Service, Inc.* v. *Mitchell*,[94] the Supreme Court specifically decided which state statute of limitations should apply to an employee's action against his employer under section 301(a) of the Labor Management Relations Act, and *Hines* v. *Anchor Motor Freight Inc.*[95] What the court concluded was, given the *choices presented in that case* and the undesirability of suspending the grievance process for long periods of time, the district court properly chose the ninety-day period for an action to vacate an arbitration award rather than the six-year statute of limitations provided in New York law for breach of contract.

The inability of a majority of the Court to agree on a rationale is troubling enough, but even more troubling is the question of why the Court granted certiorari to a case of such limited value in the first place. The employee was fired for a dishonest act, which he denied, and requested that his union file a grievance contesting his discharge. The collective bargaining agreement provided a grievance procedure culminating in arbitration. The arbitration committee upheld the discharge decision, which was binding on all parties. Seventeen months later, the grievant filed his complaint in the U.S. district court against the union and his employer under section 301 of the Labor Management Relations Act. He charged the union had breached the DFR and that the company fired him for a stated reason which it knew to be false. Both defendants moved for summary judgment on the ground that the action was barred by the New York's ninety-day statute of limitations for actions to vacate arbitration awards. The district court accepted the defendants' argument,

---

92. 451 U.S. 56, 101 S. Ct. 1559, 107 LRRM 2001 (1981).
93. *Supra* note 17.
94. 101 S. Ct. 1559, 1561 (1981).
95. Respectively, 29 U.S.C. § 185(a) (1976); 424 U.S. 554 (1976).

and the grievant appealed to the Second Circuit, which reversed. That court held that the district court should have applied the state's six-year limitation period for breach of contract actions. It reasoned that the cause of action was analogous to a breach of contract action because the issues were whether the collective bargaining agreement had been breached and whether the union had contributed by its failure in the DFR. The Supreme Court granted certiorari.

One has to turn to Justice Stevens's dissent to ferret out the narrowness of the issue. He points out that the union did not petition for review of the court of appeals' decision.[96] He also noted that the employer had not taken a position with respect to which statute of limitations governed the respondent's claim against the union, but rather vigorously denied that the question was present in the case at all.

Justice Stewart, concurring in the judgment, would have decided that neither of the state statutes should have been used in this case but rather section 10(b) of the National Labor Relations Act, which provides for the filing of unfair labor practice claims within six months. Stewart contended that this was a much more appropriate choice and the Court was not bound to use a state statute of limitations at all.

Mr. Stevens, concurring in part and dissenting in part, agreed that it was appropriate to characterize the suit against the employer as an action to set aside an arbitration award. He argued vigorously, though, that the employee's claim against his union was properly characterized as a malpractice claim and that there is no conceptual reason why that claim should not survive even if the employer is able to rely on a shorter statute.[97]

Having made his point about the malpractice statute, he argued that it was inappropriate in this case to address this matter since the union did not seek review. He then attacks Stewart's proposal as strained and asserts that the six-month limitation period upon which Justice Stewart relies was added to section 10(b) in 1947. *Six years later,* the Court decided *Ford Motor Co.* v. *Huffman* the first in a series of cases recognizing that the National Labor Relations Act imposes a duty of fair representation upon unions.[98] Stewart's proposal suggests that Congress intended that section 10(b) of the National La-

---

96. 451 U.S. at 71, 101 S. Ct. at 1568, 107 LRRM at 2007.
97. *Id.* at 74, 101 S. Ct. at 1569-70, 107 LRRM at 2007.
98. *Id.* at 76 n.9, 101 S. Ct. 1571 n.9, 107 LRRM at 2008 n.9.

bor Relations Act be applied to a cause of action that the Supreme Court had not yet divined when section 10(b) was enacted. In this exchange, both Mr. Stewart and Mr. Stevens are clearly wrong.[99] While it may not be of presiding significance, this historical error demonstrates yet again why these matters ought not be pressed upon the courts but should be commended to the tender care of the agency solely concerned with matters of like kind.

The Supreme Court itself applied the duty of fair representation to Wagner Act unions on the same day it decided *Steele* v. *Louisville* under the Railway Labor Act.[100] Although *Wallace Corporation* v. *The National Labor Relations Board* involved employer unfair labor practices, such unfair labor practices would not have been sustained by the Court without it concluding that the union had breached the duty implicit in the Wagner Act. There were no union unfair labor practices in 1944.[101] They were not added until 1947, as was section 301, which is now relied upon by the courts for a cause of action against the employer. It is worth noting that while the duty of fair representation was imposed upon the union in *Steele*, the style of the case and the defendants in the law suit were both the union and the railroads. It is not until recently that the Court has started to separate duty of fair representation causes of action with such precision and confusion.

An explanation has been tendered that the reason for the citation to *Huffman* is that it is the first case in which the Court recognized the duty outside the context of an unfair labor practice proceeding. If that reason is valid, then *Huffman* is still not the right case to cite. *Trailmobile Co.* v. *Whirls*[102] recognizes the applicability of the duty of fair representation to unions under the Wagner Act, and it is a case on facts and statutes very similar to the action in *Huffman*.

It is clear that the Supreme Court recognized the applicability of the duty of fair representation to unions under the Wagner Act substantially before 1953,[103] The Court had indeed "divined" a

---

99. The uncorrected error has been picked up by a lower court with the confidence that a Supreme Court citation supplies. *See,* Hall v. Printing and Graphic Arts Union, Local 3, 696 F.2d 494, 499, 112 LRRM 2151, 2154-55 (7th Cir. 1982).

100. *Supra* note 3.

101. *Supra* note 3.

102. 331 U.S. 40, 19 LRRM 2531, 2535 (1947).

103. *Supra* note 3; 331 U.S. 40, 44-49, 19 LRRM 2531, 2535-38. *See also,* Justice Jackson dissenting, *id.* at 68-69, 19 LRRM at 2540-44. *See also,* Communication Ass'n v. Douds, 339 U.S. 382, 401-2, 26 LRRM 2084, 2091 (1950); Colgate-Palmolive Peet

duty of fair representation cause of action when the six months limitation in section 10(b) of the National Labor Relations Act was enacted. The error goes undetected by the majority even after Stewart won the day on the statute of limitations issue.[104]

Post-Mitchell Conflicts in the Circuits

United Parcel Service v. *Mitchell* was decided April 20, 1981. Since then, a host of lower courts faced and resolved DFR statute of limitations issues in the light of *Mitchell*.[105] It may be necessary for some future purpose to determine the status of the application of *Mitchell* in the circuits and to categorize them in majority and minority views. I have not attempted such an analysis in this piece but rather have selected cases to illustrate the conflicts in post-*Mitchell* application.

Some of the courts below have strictly applied their understanding of *Mitchell* and held that section 301–DFR actions are subject to state statutes of limitations relating to the law regarding vacation of an arbitration award.[106] In one of these cases, *Stevens*, the Seventh Circuit applies the *Mitchell* rule even though the state statute of limi-

---

Co. v. NLRB, 338 U.S. 355, 364, 25 LRRM 2095, 2099 (1949). Although *Colgate* is an unfair labor practice case, its facts arose before 1947 when there were no union unfair labor practices in the law. *See also,* Hunt v. Crumboach, 325 U.S. 821, 16 LRRM 808 (1945). "Those cases [Steele, Tunstall, Wallace] stand for the proposition that a bargaining agent owes a duty not to discriminate unfairly against any of the group it purports to represent." *Id.* at 825-26, 16 LRRM at 810.

104. *See,* DelCostello v. Teamsters, *supra* note 17.

105. To determine the applicability of Mitchell since its issuance in April 1981 and the DelCostello decision of June 1983, a LEXIS search was made using the Supreme Court, Law Week, and U.S. Report citations and the key words "United Parcel and statute within five limitations." It yielded for the Supreme Court, 2 cases (DelCostello and Mitchell); for all circuits, 30 cases; for district courts, 134 cases; for all higher state courts, 1 case; and for all reported state court cases, 1 case. These are 167 cases that might never have been litigated, or at least the extra effort devoted to the statute of limitations issues would not have been litigated. There are fewer NLRA cases than 167 as, no doubt, some of these cases involved the Railway Labor Act, and it is not clear that either Mitchell or DelCostello controls those cases.

For all DFR cases between Mitchell and DelCostello, using the following search request: fair! w/5 represent! w/5 duty and union and date aft 4/30/81 and date 5/1/83, LEXIS provided the following: Supreme Court, 2; circuit, 121; district, 292; highest state courts, 12; and all reported state courts, 44—for a total of 471.

106. *See, e.g.,* McNutt and AirCo Indus. Gases Division, 687 F.2d 539, 111 LRRM 2212 (1st Cir. 1982) Massachusetts statute of limitations; Stevens v. Gateway Transportation Co., 696 F.2d 50, 112 LRRM 2177 (7th Cir. 1982), Illinois statute; Williams v. United Airlines, et al., 553 F. Supp. 862, 113 LRRM 2025 (N.D. Cal. 1982); Sunquist v. American Hoist and Derrick, Inc., 553 F. Supp. 924 (D. Minn. 1982); Fedor v. Hygrade Food Products Corp., 533 F. Supp. 269, 111 LRRM 2259 (E.D. Pa. 1982).

tations excluded collective bargaining.[107] Other courts apply the most analogous rule of *Mitchell* but do not adopt the statute of limitations for vacation of an arbitration award. Because labor disputes are specifically excluded from the state statute in *Badon* v. *General Motors Corp.*,[108] where the grievance had never been arbitrated, the Sixth Circuit adopted section 10(b) of the NLRA. In *Badon*, the court rejected the argument that the union's failure to appeal a case to arbitration justified a different approach;[109] the point in the grievance process that the union breaches the duty of fair representation is irrelevant. In *Edwards* v. *Sea Land Service, Inc.*,[110] the Fifth Circuit applied *Mitchell* but adopted the Texas four-year catchall statute because, like in *Badon*, the state arbitration statute expressly excluded collective bargaining from coverage.

In *Assad* v. *Mount Sinai Hospital*,[111] the Second Circuit concludes that *Mitchell* was not controlling where the case was never arbitrated and rejected New York's ninety-day statute of limitation in favor of section 10(b) of the NLRA for the employee's section 301 count. The court concluded, however, that *Mitchell* did not decide whether the statute of limitations therein was applicable to the union, and the court choose New York's three-year malpractice statute of limitation for the duty of fair representation action.[112]

Some lower courts have adopted a federal standard but have chosen the one-year statute of limitation in the Federal Arbitration Act.[113] There is even argument regarding the desirability of uni-

---

107. *Supra*, 696 F.2d at 504, 112 LRRM at 2179.

108. 679 F.2d 93, 110 LRRM 2562 (6th Cir. 1982).

109. *See also* Bigbie v. Teamsters, Local 42, 530 F. Supp. 402, 111 LRRM 2658 (N.D. Ill. 1981).

110. 678 F.2d 1277, 110 LRRM 3029 (5th Cir. 1982).

111. 703 F.2d 36, 112 LRRM 3116 (2d Cir. 1983).

112. *Accord*, Christianson v. Pioneer Sand and Gravel, 681 F.2d 577, 110 LRRM 3132 (9th Cir. 1982). For other illustrations of the havoc of Mitchell, *see*, Lawson v. Teamsters, Local 100, 698 F.2d 250, 112 LRRM 2553 (6th Cir. 1983); *see also*, Hall v. Printing and Graphic Arts Union, Local 3, *supra* note 97; and Hand v. Chemical Workers, 681 F.2d 1308, 111 LRRM 2038 (11th Cir. 1982), Washington v. Northland Marine Co. Inc., 681 F.2d 582, 110 LRRM 3044 (9th Cir. 1982). *Compare* San Diego County District Council v. G. L. Corry, Inc., 685 F.2d 1137, 111 LRRM 2222 (9th Cir. 1982) with SEIU, Local No. 36 v. Office Center Services, Inc., 670 F.2d 404, 109 LRRM 2552 (3d Cir. 1982).

113. Derwin v. General Dynamics Co., 551 F. Supp. 1128 (D. Mass. 1982); Lumber Production and Industrial Workers, Local 3303 v. Champion International Corp., 486 F. Supp. 812, 105 LRRM 3501 (D. Mont. 1980); *but see*, SEIU v. Office Center Services, *supra* note 112, and Edwards v. Sea-Land Service Inc., *supra* note 110 rejecting the Federal Arbitration Act as inapplicable.

formity of statute of limitations in such cases as a matter of national policy.[114]

The Supreme Court did not decide whether *Mitchell* was retroactive, and the circuits are in disagreement on this issue also.[115]

In June 1983, the Supreme Court decided *DelCostello* v. *International Brotherhood of Teamsters et al.,* and *Steelworkers* v. *Flowers.*[116] In both cases the issue was what statute of limitation is applicable in an employee suit against an employer and a union in a section 301–DFR case. In both cases, the grievance was processed through arbitration and the decision went against the employee. In both, the employee sued the employer and the union alleging breach of the collective bargaining agreement and the DFR by the union for "representing him in a discriminatory, arbitrary and perfunctory manner" or that "preparation, investigation and handling of respondents' grievances were so inept and careless as to be arbitrary and capricious."[117]

The Supreme Court reviews and explains its prior holdings. The majority states that "the issue presented is what statute of limitation to apply to such suits. In *United Parcel Service Inc.* v. *Mitchell,* . . . we held that a similar suit was governed by a state statute of limitations for vacation of an arbitration award, rather than by a state statute for an action on the contract. We left two points open, however. *First,* our holdings are limited to the employee's claim against the employer; we did not address what state statute should govern the claim against the union. *Second,* we expressly limited our consideration to a choice between two state statutes of limitations, we did not address the contention that we should instead borrow a federal statute of limitations, namely section 10(b) of the National Labor Relations Act."[118] The Court explains that it did not address the section 10(b) issues in *Mitchell,* despite Justice Stewart's concurring judgment that would have reached the issue and applied section 10(b), because the petition for certiorari did not present the issue and the

---

114. *Compare* San Diego County District Council v. Corry, *supra* note 112, with SEIU v. Office Service Center, *supra* note 112.

115. *Compare,* Lawson v. Teamsters, Local 100, *supra* note 112, and Davidson v. Roadway Express Inc., 650 F.2d 902, 107 LRRM 2741 (7th Cir. 1981) (Mitchell retroactive) with Singer v. Flying Tiger Line, Inc., 652 F.2d 1349, 108 LRRM 2392 (9th Cir. 1981) (Mitchell not retroactive). *But see* Carpenters, Local 1020 v. FMC Corp., 658 F.2d 1285, 1289-90, 108 LRRM 2761, 2766 (9th Cir. 1981).

116. *Supra* note 17.

117. DelCostello v. Teamsters, 103 S. Ct. at 2286, 113 LRRM at 2739.

118. *Id.* at 2285, 113 LRRM at 2737-38.

parties did not contend in the Supreme Court or below that a federal statute of limitations should have been used.

The majority adopted Justice Stewart's *Mitchell* rationale as its own in *DelCostello*. It concluded that state limitations for vacating arbitration awards fail to provide an aggrieved employee with a satisfactory opportunity to vindicate his rights under section 301 and the fair representation doctrine.[119] While the majority recognizes that Justice Stevens's suggestion that borrowing the state statute of limitations for legal malpractice would be more analogous to a DFR claim against the union, it rejects that approach because ". . . it suffers from objections peculiar to the realities of labor relations and litigation. It also has the unfortunate effect of establishing different limitation periods for the two halves of the section 301/Fair Representation Suit."[120]

The Court concluded that the federal statute of limitations in section 10(b) is more apt than any of the suggested state law parallels.

The Court noted that it had twice declined to decide the correctness of the Board's position on breach of the DFR as an unfair labor practice, and it does not address the question in this case. It opined that even if not all breaches of the duty of fair representation are unfair labor practice, the family resemblance is undeniable and indeed there is substantial overlap. While many fair representation cases include such allegations as discrimination in membership status and against dissident views, which would be unfair labor practices under 8(a)(1) or (2), aside from those clear cases, DFR claims are allegations of unfair, arbitrary, or discriminatory treatment of workers by union as are virtually all unfair labor practices charged against unions. Significantly, the Court says, "Similiarly, it may be the case that alleged violations by an employer of a collective bargaining agreement will also amount to an unfair labor practice."[121]

Finally, the Court quotes Justice Goldberg's caution in *Humphrey v. Moore* that, "In this Court's fashioning of a federal law of collective bargaining, it is of the utmost importance that the law reflect the realities of industrial life and the nature of the collective bargaining process. We should not assume that doctrines evolved in other con-

---

119. *Id.* at 2291, 113 LRRM at 2742.

120. *Id.* at 2292, 113 LRRM at 2743.

121. *Id.* at 2294, 113 LRRM at 2744 (citing Gorman's text on labor law, pp. 729-34).

texts will be equally well adapted to the collective bargaining process."[122]

It seems that the court's majority is becoming increasingly, though belatedly, aware that the realities of labor-management relations have not been served by its prior treatment of the duty of fair representation.

The Court's handling of the statute of limitations issue is a startling illustration of why Congress should give this entire area to an expert body and limit the courts' involvement. Why grant certiorari in a case like *Mitchell* if its disposition was to be so limited? Conservation of judicial energy would have dictated a denial of certiorari in that case if it were inappropriate to consider all of the issues including, as Justice Stewart urged, the possibility of accepting section 10(b) of the NLRA as the appropriate (uniform) statute of limitations.

As the Supreme Court did not decide the retroactivity question in *Mitchell,* it is likely that more litigation on the statute of limitations question will be filed. It does not seem unreasonable to anticipate that some of those cases that were disposed of by the application of the *Mitchell* rule will be brought to some court with the argument that they should be decided on the basis of *DelCostello.* If that surmise is correct, we will get further utilization of increasingly scarce judicial resources, as well as lawyers' time and plaintiffs' money.

Statute of Limitations under the Railway Labor Act

Although frequently the courts have borrowed concepts from either the Railway Labor Act or the National Labor Relations Act in applying the duty of fair representation, there would be no basis at all, it seems to me, to use the *DelCostello* rule in a Railway Labor Act case.[123]

In *Singer* v. *Flying Tiger Line Inc.,* the Ninth Circuit applied the California three-year statute of limitation in an action against the

---

122. *Id.* (citing Humphrey v. Moore, 375 U.S. 335 (1964)).

123. *See* Graf v. Elgin, Joliet and East Railroad, 112 LRRM 2462 (7th Cir. 1983) for an illustration of the struggle with the jurisdictional base for fair representation suit under the Railway Labor Act. The court goes back and forth between duty of fair representation cases under both statutes. *See also,* Andrews v. Louisville and Nashville Railroad Co., 406 U.S. 320, 80 LRRM 2240 (1972). The Supreme Court, in a case requiring exhaustion of administrative remedies before the National Railroad Adjustment Board where an employee sought to sue his employer for wrongful discharge, invokes Taft-Hartley Act from Textile Workers v. Lincoln Mills to Republic v. Mad-

union in a breach of its duty of fair representation and its four-year statute in an action against an employee for violation of contract, rather than the states' one-hundred-day limitation period for actions to vacate an arbitration award.[124] While the court recognized that this was a Railway Labor Act case, it said, "In the future, as *Mitchell* requires, when the action is commenced after an unfavorable arbitral decision we shall treat suits against a union for breach of the duty of fair representation and against an employer for breach of the collective bargaining agreement under this type of limitation statute." California has a one-hundred-day statute of limitations for actions to vacate an arbitration award. What will the Ninth Circuit do now, continue to apply *Mitchell* to Railway Labor Act cases or reach over and strain to apply *DelCostello?*

What it could do is to read the Railway Labor Act more closely. The court stated that "the Railway Labor Act does not contain a statute of limitations and it is therefore necessary to look to relevant state law.[125] The fact of the matter is the Railway Labor Act provides: "All actions at law based upon the provisions of this section shall be begun within two years from the time the cause of action accrues under the award of the division of the adjustment board, and not hereafter."[126] Section 153 sets out the provisions establishing the powers of duties, divisions, hearings and awards, and judicial review of the National Railroad Adjustment Board. The NRAB has jurisdiction over "minor" disputes, which is shorthand under that act for arbitration. It would seem that section 153(r) of Title 45 would be even more appropriate for the issues of the duty of fair representation-breach of the collective bargaining agreement under the Railway Labor Act than is section 10(b) for the National Labor Relations Act. The fact that no comparable provision appears in subchapter 2 of Title 45, section 181 through 188, making parts of the Railway Labor Act applicable to carriers by air, should be of no substantial impediment to applying a single rule to both the railway and the airline industry. It would be odd to have a two-year statute of limita-

---

dox. *See also,* Czosek v. O'Mara, 397 U.S. 25, 73 LRRM 2481 (1970) (where the court applies the Vaca rule in a Railway Labor Act case). In Bowen v. United States Postal Service, 103 S. Ct. 588, 112 LRRM 2281 (1983), the Supreme Court refers to the rule as the Vaca-Czosek rule. *Id.* at 602, 112 LRRM at 2287–88.

124. 108 LRRM 2392 (9th Cir. 1981).

125. *Id.* (citing UAW v. Hoosier Cardinal Corp., 383 U.S. 696, 61 LRRM 2545 (1966), a Taft-Hartley Act case).

126. In 45 U.S.C. § 153 (r) 1976 edition.

tions in cases for railroads and airlines and their unions and a six-month statute of limitations for others. That is, however, not nearly as odd as having these two separate labor laws. Since Railway Labor Act enforcement has been committed to litigation in the courts from the beginning, with the comparable unfair labor practice sections being subject to criminal penalties, leaving DFR where it is is not as destructive as in the situation under the NLRA.[127]

It is easy to predict further litigation regarding the applicable statute of limitations in duty of fair representation cases subject to the Railway Labor Act.

Apportionment of Damages—More Trouble on the Horizon

It is worth noting, but only briefly, that *Bowen* v. *United States Postal Service* grapples with the problem of apportionment of damages between a union and employers in a duty of fair representation case.[128] The court concluded that where the employee's damages caused by the employer's unlawful discharge were increased by the union's breach of its duty of fair representation, apportionment between the employer and union was required.

Bowen is an interesting case and has to be a frightening one for labor organizations. The district court, with the aid of the jury to which it gave a series of questions to be answered as a special verdict, entered judgment holding that the U.S. Postal Service had discharged the grievant without just cause and that the union had handled his "apparently meritorious grievance . . . in an arbitrary and perfunctory manner. . . ." It also concluded that in doing so, both the union and the employer had acted "in reckless and callous disregard of the grievant's rights." It concluded that had the union arbitrated the grievance, the employee would have been reinstated. It seems that the Supreme Court majority in *Bowen* accepts the

127. 45 U.S.C. § 152 (10th) provides for fines for not less than $1,000 or more than $20,000 or imprisonment for not more than six months or both fine and imprisonment for violation of § 152 (3rd, 4th, 5th, 7th or 8th), which are style misdemeanors. It's also interesting to note that under 152 (11th) state right-to-work laws do not apply to union security agreements under this act.

128. 103 S. Ct. at 599 n. 19, 112 LRRM at 2288 n.19. *See also* Dutrisac v. Caterpillar Tractor Co., 113 LRRM 3532 (9th Cir. 1983), which has adopted the callous and reckless standard for an unintentional mistake in time of filing for arbitration.

"reckless and callous disregard of rights" standard as a breach of the union's duty of fair representation.

There is vigorous dissent pointing out that the trial court has to determine a hypothetical date on which an arbitrator would have issued an award had the union taken the matter to arbitration. The trial court also has to determine the merits of the arbitration, although in the case at hand the court referred to it as an "apparently meritorious grievance."[129]

It seems to me contrary to the spirit, if not the letter, of the Steelworkers Trilogy and national labor policy, that present law DFR puts in the court—*any court with jurisdiction of the parties*—the tasks of determining whether there was a meritorious grievance, when it would have been arbitrated, and what the outcome would have been. The court then tries the issue of breach of collective bargaining agreement. All these judgments necessarily include what the arbitrator would have determined. Under any view of the obligations of the trial court in the section 301–DFR case, or even in just a section 301 case in which the DFR issue is being tried only as a matter of the employer's defense, the court must get into matters that sound labor policy should commit to the exclusive primary jurisdiction of the National Labor Relations Board.

I shudder to suggest yet another problem in the vices of *Vaca.* If the choice of an employee is to sue only the employer under section 301, is the union's breach of the duty of fair representation part of the employee's burden upon which he must plead and prove? Or is it in the nature of an affirmative defense on which the burden is the employer's to plead and prove by preponderance of the evidence? I know of no cases raising these points and certainly of none in the Supreme Court. If we leave the duty of fair representation where it is, however, I predict this will be a future issue.

Recommendations

I do not believe we need to accept that the guidebook on DFR has to be "complex and necessarily confusing." Complex, maybe, but not as much as under the present multijurisdictional system. "Necessarily

---

129. 470 F. Supp. 1127, 1129, 103 LRRM 2366, 2368 (W.D. Va. 1979).

confusing"—not anymore than ordinary unfair labor practices under the National Labor Relations Act.

Justice Jackson said prophetically thirty years ago, "a multiplicity of tribunals and a diversity of procedures are quite as apt to produce conflicting adjudications as are different rules of substantive law."[130] No clearer evidence of the desirability of exclusive primary jurisdiction in the National Labor Relations Board exist today than the DFR morass which this piece has demonstrated. It is literally impossible for a lawyer to advise a client with any certainty on the DFR obligation, even if looking only at a specific local jurisdiction. Any issue is likely to find its way to the Supreme Court, and even its rulings are unreliable.[131]

A number of young scholars recently have suggested theories to bring order to DFR law.[132] They could prove useful if the Supreme Court adopted them in a sufficient number of cases. However, the labor-management community should not have to wait another twenty years while a multiplicity of scholars compete for the attention of the Supreme Court. Moreover, the adoption of a theory, no matter how good, will not solve the problems illustrated in this essay. We would still have untold numbers of courts addressing DFR issues, and their several applications of new theory are likely to be as gross as their applications of *Vaca*.

The last DFR proposed draft did not get sufficient support, I understand, and the issue is considered unlikely to attract much attention in the near term.[133] The reason I would not have endorsed the draft I have seen is that it left the matter in the hands of the court—any court. It would have been a bit better than our present chaos, as the DFR standards would have been written into the National Labor Relations Act—action or inaction that is "arbitrary, discriminatory and in bad faith would be a violation, simple negligence would not constitute breach." The inference is strong that other

---

130. Garner v. Teamsters, Local 776, 346 U.S. 485, 490-91, 33 LRRM 2218, 2221 (1953).

131. *Compare* United Parcel Service, Inc. v. Mitchell, *supra* note 90 with DelCostello v. Teamsters, *supra* note 17.

132. Vandervelde, *A Fair Process Model for the Union's Fair Representation Duty*, 67 Minn. L. Rev. 1079 (1983); Cheit, *Competing Models of Fair Representation: The Perfunctory Processing Case*, 24 B. C. L. Rev. 1 (1982).

133. DFR draft #8, 11/2/81, "The Stabilization of Collective Bargaining Relationships Act," copy on file, University of Wisconsin Law School.

than simple negligence would be actionable, and both the degree of negligence and the content of *arbitrary* would still be up for grabs.

I propose that the DFR issue be given primarily to the National Labor Relations Board to the exclusion of other tribunals. Even a bad Board is better than a multiplicity of courts. Moreover, it is the responsibility of the Board to develop the necessary expertise to administer its law. Courts, as institutions, are ill suited to the development of expertise in a multiplicity of narrow areas. That is the reason for the creation of expert agencies and concepts of judicial deference. If the Board is insufficient, we should amend the law to correct the deficiencies. If the members nominated are insufficiently expert, Congress should refuse to confirm them. Indeed, standards of professionalism for Board members could be written into the statute.[134]

But overhauling the NLRA is not the burden of this piece; only suggesting corrections for major DFR problems. Appendix C is a proposed amendment to the NLRA that would substantially eliminate the current mess. It is a short proposal to amend section 8(a) by making it an unfair labor practice for an employer to discharge or otherwise discriminate against an employee in breach of the collective bargaining agreement.[135]

Section 8(b) is amended by making breach of the duty of fair representation by a union an unfair labor practice. The proposal incorporates the good faith standard as well as the reckless or callous disregard of rights standard.[136]

Section 301 of the NLRA is amended to ensure that courts do not have jurisdiction of these unfair labor practices, except on judicial review under section 10 of the NLRA. Violations of other provisions of the NLRA may not be construed to be breach of the duty of fair representation. Restricting the unfair labor practice to employer breach of the collective bargaining agreement which injures employ-

---

134. For instance, a requirement that they be professional neutrals in labor-management disputes settlement with five to ten years experience would eliminate advocates from both sides.

135. The Wisconsin law has had breach of the collective bargaining agreement as an unfair labor practice for many years without any substantial problems in its administration. Wis. Stats. 111.06(f).

136. This seems to be the likely consensus standard that is emerging in the federal courts and that seems to have been accepted by the National Labor Relations Board.

ees would leave section 301 applicable to enforcement of institutional obligations of contract between unions and employers and between labor organizations under current law.

The Supreme Court, in its *Vaca* decision, expressed concern for the poor plaintiffs and offered as a reason for rejecting preemption that the general counsel to the board had unreviewable discretion to issue unfair labor practice complaints. Without DFR jurisdiction in courts, it declared, the plaintiffs would be without an avenue for relief. It contended Congress could not have intended that result when it passed the Taft-Hartley Act. The proposal takes care of that concern by permitting plaintiffs, in DFR cases only, to take their cases to the Board if the general counsel dismisses. Title VII of the Civil Rights Act of 1964 is a model for this approach.

I wish to suggest, however, that the Supreme Court's anti-preemption rationale in *Vaca* is otherwise seriously flawed. In 1959 when Congress last looked at the National Labor Relations Act in any detail, it had no idea that the *Humphrey* v. *Moore–Vaca* expansion of the duty of fair representation would occur or that the NLRB would assert unfair labor practice jurisdiction over DFR cases. The duty of fair representation was, primarily, a race discrimination vehicle, and not a very effective one, at the time when there were no others to speak of in employment. It was also a modest check on nonrace, invidious discrimination. Since 1944, however, all the evils toward which the DFR judicial creation were directed have been specifically addressed by the Congress.

As the Supreme Court has belatedly recognized, most union DFR breaches these days will be unfair labor practices, and some may also result in unfair labor practice charges against employers.[137] There seem, therefore, no good reasons to continue DFR outside the primary jurisdiction of the National Labor Relations Board. The clear benefits of inclusion are uniformity and certainty in labor law, which should be welcomed by unions and management alike; a reduction in the multiplicity of tribunals before which collective bargaining parties must appear on the same facts, less strain on the judicial system, and less drain of the financial resources of employees. Even the lawyers would benefit for the DFR traffic would be labor law practice before the NLRB, and clarity in standards

---

137. *See*, DelCostello v. Teamsters, *supra* note 17.

would more rapidly emerge permitting them to serve their clients with greater competence.

The scholars might lose, for in a relatively short period of time the duty of fair representation as a subject would join national emergency disputes as an issue of interest only to historians.

Appendix A: DFR Cases in U.S. Courts, 1965–83

	U.S. Supreme Court	U.S. Courts of Appeals	U.S. District Courts	All Highest Courts, All States	All Reported Courts, All States*	Total (columns 1–3, 5)**
1965	0	5	9	4	7	21
1966	0	6	10	2	3	19
1967	2	12	19	7	10	43
1968	0	7	14	1	3	24
1969	2	8	25	1	4	39
1970	2	17	28	0	7	54
1971	2	21	32	7	12	67
1972	0	28	40	1	3	71
1973	0	24	64	4	8	96
1974	1	26	67	3	8	102
1975	2	41	60	6	17	120
1976	1	24	87	6	15	127
1977	2	29	85	6	18	134
1978	0	43	108	5	16	167
1979	2	41	85	9	20	148
1980	2	63	133	5	18	216
1981	3	59	146	4	23	231
1982	0	60	161	6	24	245
1983	3	39	46	2	4	92

Source: LEXIS search of August 1, 1983, using the search request "FAIR! w/5 REPRESENT! w/6 DUTY and UNION and DATE IS (year)." The LEXIS materials were prepared by Nancy Paul, University of Wisconsin-Madison Law Library.

Notes: * Total cases 2,016. This total does not include NLRB cases.

** The totals in column five include the totals in column four.

Appendix B: DFR Litigation Activity

We have in process another DFR project that uses 1,285 BNA/CCH reported decisions for the years 1965 to 1982. [preliminary report by Denise O'Fria (J.D., Wisconsin Law School, May 1983) on file at the law school.] The following is an excerpt from our research, which I include with the caveat that we do not purport to report these as anything more than rough statistics—but we believe them to be useful in examining the DFR problem. We hope to refine this project and publish it elsewhere.

The DFR decisions are categorized according to the nature of the decision—as preliminary, no BDFR (decisions on the merits where the court found that the union did *not* breach its duty of fair representation), BDFR (decisions on the merits where a breach of the union's duty was found), and other. Preliminary decisions are those that do not address the merits of the issues raised and that arise before a decision on the merits. Decisions regarding jurisdiction, statute of limitations, and exhaustion of contractual or intraunion remedies are included in this category. Also included in the preliminary category are those decisions that denied motions for summary judgment or dismissal. Decisions by an appeals court (state supreme courts, federal courts of appeals, or U.S. Supreme Court) are categorized as No BDFR or BDFR if they affirmed lower court findings or if they reversed the lower court and if they addressed the DFR issue directly. If the ap-

Findings in DFR Cases, by Period: 1965–82

(percentages in parentheses)

	BDFR	No BDFR	Total
1965–70			
NLRB	8 (50)	8 (50)	16 (100)
Courts	17 (16)	92 (84)	109 (100)
All decisions	25 (20)	100 (80)	125 (100)
1971–75			
NLRB	24 (48)	26 (52)	50 (100)
Courts	19 (10)	174 (90)	193 (100)
All decisions	43 (18)	200 (82)	243 (100)
1976–80			
NLRB	61 (60)	41 (40)	102 (100)
Courts	33 (15)	193 (85)	226 (100)
All decisions	94 (29)	234 (71)	328 (100)
1981–82			
NLRB	5 (45)	6 (55)	11 (100)
Courts	9 (11)	73 (89)	82 (100)
All decisions	14 (15)	79 (85)	93 (100)
1965–82			
NLRB	88 (52)	81 (48)	169 (100)
Courts	88 (14)	532 (86)	620 (100)
All decisions	176 (22)	613 (78)	789 (100)

Findings in DFR Cases, by Forum: 1965–82

Forum	Preliminary Issue	No BDFR	BDFR	Other	Total
U.S. Supreme Court	4	1	1	1	7
Circuit Court of Appeals	116	132	48	22	318
Federal District Court	267	351	28	26	672
NLRB	1	81	88	12	182
State Court or Administration Agency	44	48	11	3	106
Totals	432	613	176	64	1285

peals court did not affirm or reverse the lower court decision on the merits, but rather reversed with respect to a procedural issue and remanded for a new decision on the merits, the decision was counted as a preliminary decision. Finally, the "other" category includes decisions in which the DFR issue was merely ancillary. For example, decisions regarding appropriate remedies for a BDFR (breach of the duty of fair representation) or decisions addressing an employer's right to raise the DFR issue as a defense to a section 301 action or NLRB charges.

Of the 1,285 DFR decisions included in this study, 432 (33 percent) were preliminary decisions, 613 (48 percent) found no BDFR, 176 (14 percent) found a BDFR, and 64 (5 percent) were in the other category. Of the 789 decisions that addressed the merits of the DFR issue, 22 percent found a breach of the duty and 78 percent found no breach of the duty. These percentages change significantly when the NLRB and court decisions are segregated: 169 NLRB decisions addressed the merits of the DFR issue; 52 percent found a breach of the duty; 48 percent found no breach of the duty. In the federal and state courts, 620 decisions addressed the merits of the DFR issue. Fourteen percent of the court decisions found a breach of the duty, 86 percent found no breach of the duty. The fact that the NLRB screens its complaints before a hearing probably accounts for the higher percentage of BDFR findings by the NLRB. Although the number of DFR decisions rose steadily over the period 1965–82, the relative level of BDFR findings, expressed as a percentage of the total remained relatively stable for both the NLRB and the courts. This is demonstrated by the table that groups the decisions into four periods.

Appendix C: Proposed Draft Amendment to the NLRA

The National Labor Relations Act, as amended, shall be amended as follows:

(A) Section 3(d) is amended by inserting before the last sentence of said subsection the following:

"*Provided that*, whenever a charge is filed alleging a violation of a union's duty of fair representation and breach of the collective bargaining agreement by the employer, the charging party shall have the right to prosecute such charge before the Board despite a refusal by the General Counsel to issue a complaint."

(B) Section 8(a) is amended by adding at the end of subsection (5) the following:

"(6) To discharge or otherwise discriminate against an employee in breach of the provisions of the collective bargaining agreement governing the wages, hours, or other conditions of employment of any such employee."

(C) Section 8(b) is amended by adding at the end of subsection (7) the following:

"(8) To engage in any activities which discriminate against, or otherwise adversely affect the wages, hours, or other conditions of employment, of any employee by failing, or refusing to represent any such employee fairly, honestly, or in good faith, or by acting in reckless or callous disregard of the rights of any such employee. *Provided* that it shall not be an unfair labor practice for a labor organization to fail or refuse to represent any such employee where in its good faith judgment it has determined, pursuant to the applicable procedures of its constitution and bylaws, that the employee's claim has insufficient merit to warrant further action, or where its failure to act is the result of ordinary negligence.

Provided further that, not withstanding any other laws, violation of any other provision of this title shall not be construed to be a breach of the union's duty of fair representation."

(D) Section 301 is amended by adding thereto the following:

"(f) Nothing in this section shall be construed to authorize suits to enforce the provisions of sections 8(a)(6) and 8(b)(8) of this Act. The enforcement of such subsections shall be subject to the exclusive primary jurisdiction of the Board, and subject to judicial review as provided in Section 10 of this Act."

Acknowledgments

The editor is grateful for the invaluable assistance of her colleagues in planning and administering the 1983 conference. Both Associate Dean Lois S. Gray and Alice B. Grant, Rochester district director of the Extension Division, offered many helpful suggestions for the content and format of the program. Carol Wittenberg, the director of the metropolitan district, was responsible for efficiently handling the entire administration of the conference. I also wish to take this opportunity to thank the faculty members who chaired the individual sessions of the program: Charles M. Rehmus, James A. Gross, Matthew A. Kelly, and Homer LaRue.

For invaluable aid in preparing the manuscript for publication, the professional talents of Frances Benson, director, and Holly Bailey, editor, of the ILR Press deserve special recognition. Finally, I am most appreciative of the willingness of Margaret S. Leibowitz, Esq., to undertake the tedious but indispensable chore of serving as legal editor of this volume, with the assistance of Loren Krause, Esq.

Cases Cited: Master Index

Cases Cited: Index by Jurisdiction

Decisions of the Federal Circuit Courts of Appeals

Decisions of the Federal District Courts

General Index

293

Contributors

Benjamin Aaron is professor of law, University of California, Los Angeles, School of Law, and researcher, UCLA Institute of Industrial Relations. A past president of the National Academy of Arbitrators and of the Industrial Relations Research Association, he is currently regional vice president (North America) of the International Society for Labor Law and Social Security and a member of the United Auto Workers Public Review Board. He is the author and editor of various books and articles on labor law and industrial relations.

Andrea S. Christensen is a partner in Kay, Scholer, Fierman, Hays, and Handler in New York City. She serves on the American Bar Association's Committee on Developing Law under the NLRA. An adjunct professor at the New York University School of Law, she is the author of many law review articles on labor relations subjects and the editor of *Labor and Employment Law Newsletter*.

Harry T. Edwards is Circuit Judge, United States Court of Appeals for the District of Columbia. He has taught in the law schools at the University of Michigan and at Harvard University, where he also taught at the Institute for Educational Management. He has been a member of the board of directors of the National Academy of Arbitrators and a presidential appointee to the International Women's Year Commission. Among his previous works are *The Lawyer as a Negotiator*, *Collective Bargaining and Labor Arbitration*, *Labor Relations Law in the Public Sector*, and *Higher Education and the Law*.

James E. Jones, Jr., is John Bascom Professor of Law, University of Wisconsin Law School. Before turning to teaching, he held a number of positions in the U.S. Department of Labor and from 1967 to 1969 served as associate solicitor of labor. He is a coauthor of *Employment Discrimination*, and *Foundations of Equal Opportunity*, as well as a contributor to *The Duty of Fair Representation*.

296

David Y. Klein is executive director of the Public Review Board of the United Auto Workers. A former attorney for the National Labor Relations Board, he now engages in private practice representing trade unions, section 302 trusts, and individuals.

Richard Lipsitz is a senior member of the firm of Lipsitz, Green, Fahringer, Roll, Schuller and James in Buffalo, New York, and has practiced labor law representing unions since 1949. A speaker at numerous conferences on the duty of fair representation and other subjects in labor relations law, he was a visiting senior lecturer at the New York State School of Industrial and Labor Relations and a contributor to *The Duty of Fair Representation*.

Jean T. McKelvey is professor at the New York State School of Industrial and Labor Relations, Cornell University, where she teaches collective bargaining, labor law, and arbitration. She is a mediator and arbitrator who has been appointed to the Federal Service Impasses Panel and the Public Review Board of the United Auto Workers. She is the author of many works on industrial relations and the editor of *The Duty of Fair Representation*.

Harold R. Newman is chairman of the New York State Public Employment Relations Board. In addition, he has been the director of the board's counciliation office for more than nine years. Newman has lectured widely and published numerous articles on labor relations theory and practice. He is a member of the Labor and Community Disputes Panels of the American Arbitration Association and president-elect of the Association of Labor Relations Agencies.

Robert J. Rabin is professor of law at Syracuse University College of Law. He is coauthor of a casebook on labor law and of the handbook *The Rights of Union Members*. An active labor mediator and arbitrator, Rabin is the editor of *The Labor Lawyer*, a journal of labor law published by the American Bar Association.

Clyde W. Summers is Fordham Professor of Law at the University of Pennsylvania School of Law. He taught previously at the Yale University School of Law. He was secretary of the section on labor relations law, American Bar Association, an alternate member of the Connecticut State Labor Relations Board and of the Connecticut State Mediation Board, and a hearing officer for the Connecticut Human Rights Commission. The author of *Rights for Union Members* and a number of labor law casebooks, he was a contributor to *The Duty of Fair Representation* and *Arbitration in Practice*.

Paul H. Tobias of Tobias and Kraus, Cincinnati, Ohio, has specialized in labor law for more than twenty-five years, representing companies, unions, and more recently, individual employees. He has represented many plaintiffs in section 301–DFR suits in jury trials and on appeal. He is the author of law review articles on the duty of fair representation and, as a speaker at bar association seminars, an advocate for the plaintiff's position.

John C. Truesdale is executive secretary of the National Labor Relations Board. A former field examiner in the regional offices of the Board, he worked from 1957 to 1963 for the National Academy of Sciences before returning to the Washington offices of the Board. From 1977 to 1981 he was a member of the Board.

Seymour M. Waldman is an attorney with Vladeck, Waldman, Elias and Engelhard who has represented international, district, and local labor organizations throughout his professional career. He has written for various labor publications, including the New York University Conference on Labor. A member of the labor law committees of the New York State Bar Association and the Association of the Bar of the City of New York, he serves as cochairman of the Committee on Antitrust and Labor Relations Law of the American Bar Association's Section of Labor and Employment Law.